TURNSTILE JUSTICE
Issues in American Corrections

Edited by

TED ALLEMAN
Late, The Pennsylvania State University

ROSEMARY L. GIDO
Indiana University of Pennsylvania

Prentice Hall, Upper Saddle River, New Jersey 07458

Library of Congress Cataloging-in-Publication Data

Turnstile justice : issues in American corrections / [edited by] Ted
 Alleman, Rosemary Gido.
   p. cm.
  Includes bibliographical references.
  ISBN 0-13-301227-1
  1. Corrections—United States. I. Alleman, Ted. II. Gido,
Rosemary L.
HV9471.T87 1998   97-30516
365'.973—dc21   CIP

Acquisition Editor: Neil Marquardt
Editorial Assistant: Jean Auman
Managing Editor: Mary Carnis
Project Manager: Linda B. Pawelchak
Production Coordinator: Ed O'Dougherty
Cover Director: Jayne Conte
Cover Design: Joe Sengotta
Cover Art: Courtesy of David Rooney
Electronic Page Layout: Clarinda Company
Electronic Art Creation: Asterisk Group
Marketing Manager: Frank Mortimer Jr.
Printing/Binding: RR Donnelley & Sons

 © 1998 by Prentice-Hall, Inc.
Simon & Schuster / A Viacom Company
Upper Saddle River, New Jersey 07458

Printed in the United States of America
10 9 8 7 6 5 4 3 2 1

ISBN 0-13-301227-1

Prentice-Hall International (UK) Limited, *London*
Prentice-Hall of Australia Pty. Limited, *Sydney*
Prentice-Hall Canada Inc., *Toronto*
Prentice-Hall Hispanoamericana, S.A., *Mexico*
Prentice-Hall of India Private Limited, *New Delhi*
Prentice-Hall of Japan, Inc., *Tokyo*
Simon & Schuster Asia Pte. Ltd., *Singapore*
Editora Prentice-Hall do Brasil, Ltda., *Rio de Janeiro*

This book was conceptualized by Ted Alleman as part of his continuing mission to put forward quality educational materials for students of criminal justice. I was privileged to join Ted in bringing together the contributors for this book. We had no idea that Ted's life would be so tragically shortened, as he left us on May 16, 1996. Ted's spirit and concern for the incarcerated come through the pages of his writings. May this book challenge those who read it to think critically about "turnstile justice" and the implications of imprisonment as we enter the twenty-first century.

Rosemary L. Gido

CONTENTS

TEN

Health Care for Women Offenders:
Challenge for the New Century   176

Phyllis Harrison Ross, M.D.
New York Medical College at Metropolitan Hospital

James E. Lawrence
New York State Commission of Correction

ELEVEN

Problems Facing Immigration
and Naturalization Service Detention Centers:
Policies, Procedures, and Allegations   192

Michael Welch
Rutgers University

TWELVE

Boot Camps in Prisons, Jails,
and Juvenile Detention Centers   205

Melissa I. Bamba
CSR, Inc., Washington, D.C.

Doris Layton MacKenzie
University of Maryland

PREFACE

Turnstile Justice: Issues in American Corrections provides students and practitioners in the field of corrections with a set of thoughtful and critical readings on contemporary correctional issues. Designed as a freestanding text or supplement to course materials across the criminal justice/corrections spectrum, the book offers a sociology of corrections—a perspective for analyzing the social context within which current American punishment philosophy and practice take place. The author of each chapter provides factual information and data on an issue or topic and then invites the reader to step back and critically examine the impact of the correctional problem on the system or society.

The first three chapters set the tone for the entire book by outlining a context for studying American corrections. In Chapter 1, Ted Alleman asks us to look beyond the current ideology and rhetoric of corrections and evaluate the impact of U.S. correctional practices. These questions are a focus for the issues covered in the remaining chapters.

> What types of people are subject to correctional control? Who is being imprisoned, why, for how long, and under what conditions? Is there any evidence that citizens are being imprisoned to further political ends? Is there any evidence of biased or discriminatory treatment on the part of the correctional system?

> Does the punishment fit the crime? Is the cost of punishment in line with the cost of crime? Is there any evidence that fear and emotion, rather than fairness and justice, are driving correctional policy making? Are there segments of the correctional population that are subject to levels of control beyond those required?

> How effective is the criminal justice system? Are correctional agencies able to deliver on promises of less crime in exchange for more resources? Which correctional practices result in lowered rates of recidivism and which do not? In terms of doing justice and protecting society, which offender types must be imprisoned and which need not be?

> What are the conditions of confinement? Are they humane and fair? Are correctional environments safe and secure, or violent and dehumanizing? What effect does correctional practice have on those released from the system as well as those who find themselves working with or living next to ex-offenders?

Are correctional practices the outcome of informed and reasoned debate, or are they simply reflective of unfounded fear and ignorance? On what basis is new criminal legislation proposed—is it advanced on the basis of slick political slogans and references to single-instance horror stories (such as the Willie Horton case), or is it an outcome of an informed public debate that combines established facts with clear policy alternatives?

What is the proper role of corrections in a democratic society? Is there evidence that the criminal justice system is treating as criminals citizens who are generally nonviolent and law-abiding? Are there victimless acts that are being defined as crimes? Are classes of innocent people being confined for political or economic reasons? To what extent are expenditures on crime and crime control diverting funds from other legitimate and needed social services? To what extent are we, as citizens, willing to trade personal liberties and freedoms for an increased police presence in our lives?

Alleman (Chapter 2) next provides a unique, comprehensive analysis of the implications of the three predominant American correctional philosophies—utilitarian, justice, and rehabilitation—on the treatment of offenders. A practical typology matrix (page 30) summarizes features of each punishment approach. Chapter 3 rounds out this first part with a case study of the "lived reality" of a prisoner named Nathan McCall. Alleman draws out the lessons of the possibility of change and rehabilitation from McCall's true life story as a challenge to contemporary correctional systems to identify, encourage, and support incarcerated individuals who wish to break with their criminal pasts.

The second part focuses on two key correctional issues of our time—the politics of crime and punishment (Chapters 4 and 5) and prison and jail overcrowding (Chapters 6 and 7). In Chapter 4, Joseph Lehman and Lee Ann Labecki offer an insightful analysis of the role of the media, the public, and politicians in shaping crime policy and sentencing practices over the last twenty years. The increasing reliance on incarceration and "get tough" legislation has forced correctional administrators to become "reactors" to prison overcrowding, resource shortages, and shifting inmate profiles. Lehman and Labecki call for a more proactive correctional administrator role to shape sentencing policy and the media/political dialogue on corrections. Similarly, Samuel Richards reflects on the effects of the politicized war on drugs on U.S. prison overcrowding in Chapter 5. Arguing for a reexamination of the legalization of marijuana, Richards documents the costs of criminalizing marijuana, particularly in the utilization of prison space for drug offenders versus violent felons at the federal and state levels. Chapters 6 and 7 shift the emphasis to prison and jail crowding and its management. Stojkovic and Klofas (Chapter 6) explain the historical shift to defining crowding as a managerial problem rather than an empirical or moral one. They focus on jail crowding and the unique problems of jail management—high turnover and admissions, overflow of inmates from other systems, and slow court case processing. "Front door" and "back door" strategies to reduce crowded prisons are discussed, along with the "politicized" issue of jail and prison construction. In Chapter 7, James Houston reviews the history and application of unit management as the model tool that has emerged for managing correctional institutions in the last twenty-five years. Beginning with its application in the U.S. Bureau of Prisons, Houston shows the advantages of unit management in improved staff-inmate relations, increased staff job satisfaction, decrease in inmate assaults, and overall improved safety and security.

The remaining chapters (8 to 12) offer a comprehensive evaluation of four emerging correctional issues—educational services for inmates, treatment needs of women offenders, noncitizens in U.S. federal detention centers, and boot camps as alternatives for incarcerating adults and juveniles. In Chapter 8, Taylor and Tewksbury examine the history and political debates around the issue of postsecondary correctional education. Given current reductions in Pell Grants to finance inmate college degrees, the chapter offers an in-depth review of the impact of educational programming. Barbara Zaitzow in Chapter 9 and Phyllis Harrison Ross and James Lawrence in Chapter 10 challenge the traditional treatment regimes of women's prisons in the United States. Zaitzow offers critiques of all types of female programs—educational, vocational, and mental health—and makes recommendations for improvements across the system. Harrison Ross and Lawrence document the increase of poor and minority women in U.S. prisons and the impact on correctional systems of increased and intensified demand for specialized health care services. Michael Welch assesses allegations of human rights violations in Immigration and Naturalization Service (INS) detention centers and outlines the problems inherent in INS detention practices in Chapter 11. Melissa Bamba and Doris MacKenzie complete this last part with a unique, in-depth evaluation of boot camps in a variety of settings—prisons, jails, and juvenile detention centers.

Rosemary L. Gido

ABOUT THE CONTRIBUTORS

Ted Alleman was an instructor of sociology and criminal justice at two Pennsylvania State University campuses for twenty years. Drawing on his experience as a systems analyst, he designed a computerized jail management system used in Pennsylvania and New Jersey and authored the text *Introduction to Computing in Criminal Justice* (1996). Mr. Alleman also taught in several Pennsylvania correctional institutions. He was the co-author of *It's a Crime: Women and Justice* (1993).

Melissa I. Bamba is a research associate with CSR, Inc., in Washington, D.C. She is currently pursuing a Ph.D. in criminology from the University of Maryland. Her research interests include the role of religious fundamentalism in the development of militia organizations in the United States and comparative historical analyses of policing in the United States, South Africa, and Northern Ireland.

Rosemary L. Gido is assistant professor in the Department of Criminology, Indiana University of Pennsylvania. The former director of research, Office of Program and Policy Analysis, New York State Commission of Correction, she directed the first national prison-based study of HIV/AIDS in the New York State prison system. A teacher at the college or university level for twenty-five years, her current research interests are intermediate punishment evaluation and alternatives to incarceration for women.

James Houston is associate professor of criminal justice at Appalachian State University. After twenty years in the field of corrections, Dr. Houston returned to teaching. He is the author of *Correctional Management* (1995) and the co-author of a second book on criminal justice policy.

John Klofas is professor and chairperson in the Department of Criminal Justice, Rochester Institute of Technology. His research has been in the area of prisons and jails, and he is the co-author of *Criminal Justice Organizations: Administration and Management*. Most recently, he has been focusing on issues of metropolitan development and criminal justice.

Lee Ann S. Labecki is the director of Management Information Services for the Pennsylvania Department of Corrections. Since 1992, she has served as a consultant on riot/disturbance management issues to the National Institute of Corrections Training Academy. She is a member of numerous national criminal justice research associations.

James E. Lawrence is director of operations for the New York State Commission of Correction. His twenty years' experience in the fields of prisoner mortality and correctional health care include work as a forensic medical investigator and director of the New York State Correction Medical Review Board. He has taught various topics in correctional health care at New York Medical College School of Public Health and authored several articles on correctional health care.

Joseph D. Lehman is the secretary of corrections for the Washington Department of Corrections in Olympia, Washington. He previously served as commissioner of corrections in the states of Maine (1995–1997) and Pennsylvania (1990–1995). He is active in a number of national criminal justice associations and is an officer for the Association of State Corrections Administrators.

Doris Layton MacKenzie is director of the Evaluation Research Group and associate professor in the Department of Criminology and Criminal Justice at the University of Maryland. She directed the National Institute of Justice *Multi-Site Study of Boot Camp Prisons*. Dr. MacKenzie has edited four books and published more than thirty articles on corrections and inmate adjustment and behavior.

Samuel M. Richards is an instructor in the Sociology Department, The Pennsylvania State University. He has conducted research on socioeconomic change in Latin America. His current interests are race and ethnic inequality and drug policy in the United States.

Phyllis Harrison Ross, M.D., is a nationally recognized expert in forensic psychiatry and correctional medicine. Currently professor of clinical psychiatry at New York Medical College at Metropolitan Hospital, Dr. Harrison Ross is president of the Medical Board, staff associate medical director, and director of the Department of Psychiatry and Community Mental Health Center at Metropolitan Hospital Center in New York, New York.

Stan Stojkovic is associate professor of criminal justice and coordinator of the criminal justice programs at the University of Wisconsin–Milwaukee. He is co-editor of *Crime and Justice in the Year 2010* (1995) and co-author of *Corrections: An Introduction* (2nd edition, 1997). Dr. Stojkovic is completing the second edition of his co-authored book *Criminal Justice Organizations: Administration and Management*.

Jon Marc Taylor is an inmate at the Jefferson City, Missouri, Correctional Center. He holds B.A. and M.A. degrees from Ball State University. The winner of both the Nation/I.F. Stone and Robert F. Kennedy Awards for student journalism, Mr. Taylor has authored scholarly articles that have appeared in the *Journal of Contemporary Criminal Justice, Journal of Correctional Education,* and *The Criminologist.*

Richard Tewksbury is associate professor in the Department of Justice Administration at the University of Louisville. Dr. Tewksbury's research interests include correctional education program evaluation, criminal victimization predictors, men's sexual behavior, and public health program evaluation. He is the author of *Introduction to Corrections* (1997) and the editor of the *American Journal of Criminal Justice.*

Michael Welch is associate professor in the Administration of Justice Program, Rutgers University. In addition to correctional experience at the federal, state, and local levels, he has published widely in corrections and social control. He is the author of *Corrections: A Critical Approach* (1996) and is writing a book on the detention of undocumented immigrants.

Barbara H. Zaitzow is assistant professor in the Department of Political Science and Criminal Justice, Appalachian State University. A member of several national and regional sociological and criminal justice organizations, her primary research interests include female criminality, corrections, and alternatives to incarceration.

ONE

Introduction to the Study of Correctional Issues
A Sociology of Corrections

TED ALLEMAN
The Pennsylvania State University

INTRODUCTION

This introduction to the study of correctional issues invites the reader to adopt the perspective of the *sociology of corrections.* By taking into account the context within which U.S. punishment philosophies and practices take place, one can engage in an informed debate and avoid the overstated and simplistic arguments that often characterize public discussions of corrections. This stance requires an objective assessment of how you are treated should you become involved in the corrections system. Similarly, the role of power needs to be examined in understanding the "politics of crime and punishment" and how this plays out in the definition and application of law, law enforcement, social control, and punishment. A key question emerging from this discussion is "What is the proper role of corrections in American society?"

Corrections, as the term is commonly used, refers to the ways in which those persons arrested or convicted of crimes are handled by agents of the criminal justice system. For those who work with or in the criminal

1

justice field, *corrections* commonly refers to jails, prisons, community-based treatment programs such as half-way houses, and programs for probation and parole (Schmalleger, 1995). In comparison, a *sociology of corrections* is a much broader perspective that takes into consideration the societal context within which predominant punishment philosophies and practices take place.

If defined too narrowly, the study of corrections becomes merely an exercise in how to manage and control offender populations. For those who define criminals as "bad people" and assume that the criminal justice system is just and fair in its operation, correctional issues become merely management issues. From this narrow perspective, the justice system itself is seldom questioned and, since criminal offenders are seen as deserving of their fate, correctional treatment is simply viewed as something that correctional agencies do. When examined from the system's point of view, practices may be more or less efficient, cost effective, or appropriate, but the nature of the practices themselves is seldom questioned. Uncritically accepting the system and its operation considerably diminishes an analysis of the broader social concerns and issues associated with punishment practices.

On a more personal level, the actions of agents of the criminal justice system can impact people's lives considerably. In the course of the administration of justice, criminal justice agents (including police, magistrates, judges and attorneys, probation and parole agents, and jailers) variously have the power to charge, shoot, detain, prosecute, convict, imprison, and sanction. As citizens, we are all subject to the rule of law. Each of us is potentially subject to arrest and subsequent punishment. We can end up in jail as the result of driving after drinking, arguing and fighting, being falsely accused, acting to obstruct behaviors that we find objectionable or immoral (such as restricting access to an abortion clinic or blocking workers from entering a nuclear construction site), or simply pulling our pants down in public. As rates of arrest and incarceration escalate, more and more people are being drawn into the system. In addition to seeing the criminal justice system as those agencies that deal primarily with violent and dangerous criminals, it is increasingly important that we consider the impact of criminal justice practices on people like ourselves.

This country's punishment practices have become institutionalized. Like religion, education, and politics, corrections maintains characteristic sets of practices and beliefs that affect the way many people live and work. Nationwide, corrections employs hundreds of thousands of people; maintains a huge inventory of plants and equipment; operates tens of thousands of facilities including offices, detention centers, treatment facilities, jails, and prisons; and officially documents and/or processes millions of citizens annually. In addition to being a large and expanding enterprise, corrections, too, serves as an important agent of socialization. Punishment practices mold as well as reflect public opinion concerning deviance and its control. As social institutions, correctional agencies make demands of as well as serve the needs of citizens.

Why study corrections? From the perspective presented here, it is clear that corrections is much more than simply the actions of those agencies that officially process and punish hardened criminals. Correctional practice has become a factor in the lives of many. The impact of corrections is multidimensional. Correctional issues that generate the most emotion and controversy are those that go beyond the mere treatment of convicted felons. The following considerations point to the importance of taking into account the broader social impact associated with punishment practices.

FIRST CONSIDERATIONS

Various levels of debate exist. Advocated here is an informed debate in which you are able to envision a full range of correctional issues and how they affect you personally, those persons handled by the system, as well as the society in which you live. Remember that correctional practices directly impact human lives, potentially yours and certainly those who are charged and sentenced. The denial of personal rights and liberties, the conditions of confinement, and, in the case of capital punishment, whether one lives or dies are all significant outcomes of correctional policies and practices. This chapter introduces a number of perspectives that serve to generate questions and debate concerning contemporary punishment practices in society.

Who You Are

Who you are as a person makes a considerable difference in how often and in what way you will personally come into contact with the criminal justice system during your lifetime. If you happen to be black, poor, and male, for example, your chances of going to jail are significant; whereas, if you are white, wealthy, and female it is improbable that you will ever experience incarceration. Gender, age, race, income, and level of education are all significant indicators of frequency of arrest, sentencing, and imprisonment. To the extent that the system engenders some form of discrimination (the differential treatment of minorities, women, the handicapped, the indigent, the mentally ill, or the homeless), this serves as a personal inducement for many to see that the criminal justice system operates fairly and equitably. Who comes to be defined as criminal and how various categories of people are affected by actual policies and practices are important considerations in the study of correctional issues.

In addition to the possibility of getting caught up in the criminal justice system, who you are is also an important determinant of your own attitudes and opinions concerning correctional policies and practices. Correctional issues can be personally involving; they have the power to generate emotion and get you angry and upset. If you are a victim of a crime, if you are personally fearful of crime, or if you know someone who has been victimized by crime, correctional issues can become personal issues. Taking sides on correctional issues can be a way of fighting back, of getting even.

Taking sides on correctional issues is good to the extent that it reflects a sense of caring or personal involvement, but, in addition to serving as a motivating force, emotion can also bias and distort human judgment. Because people tend to become emotionally charged when they consider what should be done with those who break the law (those who they envision as harming, violating, or attacking people like themselves), proposed treatments can be extreme. And perhaps for situations in which innocent people have clearly been brutalized by a criminal act, this is as it should be. But, remember too that emotion can lead to argument, not debate; blindness, not enlightenment.

People who become overly emotional about correctional issues are generally less able to deal with the subject rationally and objectively. Positions that are unrealistically based on emotional appeal tend to be one-sided, extreme, and harsh in their consequences. Accordingly, offenders tend to be stereotyped as being all the same (violent and dangerous, for example), and similar treatment strategies are promoted as being appropriate for everyone in the system ("lock them up and throw away the key"). As such, emotionally charged arguments tend to be overstated and simplistic. It is important to recognize that correctional issues, especially as they are framed by persons who have a personal stake in their resolution or outcome, can become very biased and, in some cases, quite distorted in their depictions of reality.

Consider too that not everyone experiences crime directly. For some people, crime is something they see in the movies or read about in the newspaper. But even here, there are personal predilections for developing a strong stance on correctional issues. No one enjoys seeing innocent people harmed or injured. Getting even with criminals, especially as they are portrayed in crime stories or on the nightly news, gives people a chance to express their personal sense of justice. Numerous studies substantiate the impact of the media on public conceptions of crime and criminals (Surette, 1992). Fictitious, imagined, or media-produced scenarios, therefore, should also be recognized as capable of driving correctional debate.

The social characteristics of people, the personal experiences people have with crime, as well as the degree to which people are influenced by stories or media depictions of crime are all influential variables that determine in part who and to what degree people are interested in correctional issues. Human factors are exceedingly important in the study of correctional issues. Correctional issues, after all, are to a great extent what people define them to be.

The Politics of Crime and Punishment

Imprisoning people against their will always includes the element of power. Law enforcers are agents of the state. Correctional practices are therefore inherently political. The ultimate in power politics, of course, lies with the ability to execute or imprison rival political leaders. But, using as an example the case of the thousands of Japanese Americans who were imprisoned in this country during World War II simply because they were of Japanese descent, it is also clear that political power can be used to control whole classes of innocent people. It remains a fact of life in any country that those who control who goes to prison ultimately control the power of the state.

Several aspects of correctional practice leave it open to potential abuse and corruption. Imprisonment effectively removes people from society. Shutting people away in prison can be a method of forcibly taking them out of the public arena, removing them from their sphere of influence, and publicly gagging them. Imprisonment therefore can be used as a means of silencing political opposition. Correctional practices also take place behind locked doors and are outside of the public's sight and scrutiny. People can be sent to prison and never heard from again. On a broader philosophical level, public trials can function as forums from which dissident ideas, behaviors, or practices are condemned. In this way, through the imposition of state-mandated punishment, and the tacit approval of the public to legal proceedings, structures of power in society are affirmed and continue on in their present form.

Ostensibly, criminal justice agencies deal with convicted felons. Jails, prisons, and detention facilities put criminals behind bars and see that they remain there. Additionally, probation, parole, and a variety of treatment agencies are empowered to sanction, monitor, and control the behavior of offenders while in the community. Add to this law enforcement's power to investigate, charge, and arrest, and you have an extensive legal apparatus that can be used for political as well as criminal justice purposes.

The FBI's efforts in the 1960s to discredit Dr. Martin Luther King provide a prominent historical account of the extent to which criminal justice can be used for political purposes. It must be remembered that much fire and fury was associated with the drive for racial justice in this country. People went to the streets and were openly defiant of the system. Reverend King had been jailed on many occasions for engaging in peaceful marches and sit-ins. As an activist, King was a preacher of nonviolence. But, to some powerful political leaders, portraying King as a revolutionary and a communist was more in line with their attempts to quell the civil rights movement:

In December 1963—four months after the famous civil rights march on Washington and King's "I Have a Dream" speech—a nine hour meeting was convened at FBI headquarters to discuss various "avenues of approach aimed at neutralizing King as an effective Negro leader" (Church Committee, 1976:220). Agents throughout the country were instructed to continue gathering information on King's personal life "in order that we may consider using this information at an opportune time in a counterintelligence move to discredit him" (ibid.). According to David Garrow (1981:115), the FBI went through the Southern Christian Leadership Conference's trash in hope of finding incriminating evidence against that organization and King. The FBI investigated Dr. King's bank and charge accounts, instituted electronic surveillance of King's apartment and his office, . . . The "neutralization" program actually continued until King's death. As late as March 1968, FBI agents were instructed to neutralize King because he might, according to the Bureau, become a "messiah" who could "unify and electrify the militant black nationalist movement."

When law enforcers break the law, they themselves become criminals. Political ambition can be as corrupting an influence as greed or drunkenness. And, when successfully used as a weapon in partisan politics, the political use of the criminal justice system has the potential for transforming a democracy into a police state. But, even though it is important to monitor and prevent such abuses of power, the influence of politics in criminal justice is not always this blatant or obvious. Political influence, in fact, can be found to exist in the everyday, taken-for-granted activities of the criminal justice system.

To appreciate the extent to which correctional practices reflect the exercise of power in society, it is necessary to learn to see as arbitrary that which many accept without question. More specifically, it becomes necessary to examine ordinary events to see how the criminal justice system asserts its authority over citizens. See if you recognize the elements of power that come into play in the following incident. The headline from an inside page of a local newspaper read, "Lawyers squabble over drug suspect's car."

The Blair County District Attorney's Office wants to confiscate the automobile a Bedford County man was riding in last November when he was arrested for possession of 43 grams of marijuana.

But defense attorney John Woodcock argued Monday that taking the car of disabled veteran George Mason Jr. of Clearville RD1—who pleaded guilty—would be unfair because Mason is not a drug pusher.

Instead Mason bought the 43 grams, or 1½ ounces, of marijuana in an Altoona bar to use as medicine to curb the pain he experiences from overexposure to radiation while serving with the armed forces in Germany after World War II, Woodcock said.

The law, Woodcock said, states that 30 grams is the limit between a "small" and "large" amount of marijuana, and the District Attorney's

Office cannot take a car from a presumed drug dealer if the amount of marijuana is under 30 grams.

While the amount of marijuana in the Mason case may be only slightly more than 30 grams, it is still more, said Assistant District Attorney Amy Webster, who heads the county's new program aimed at confiscating cars and houses of drug dealers.

But Woodcock said fairness should be considered by the judge when ruling on petitions to confiscate a person's mode of transportation or his home.

Mason could not be reached for comment this morning, but Woodcock said the defendant was smoking marijuana to relieve "shooting pains" through his left shoulder and up the back of his head.

"That's not abnormal," Woodcock said.

During his service in Germany after World War II, Mason was exposed to radiation from the machinery with which he worked, Woodcock said. He couldn't get marijuana through a prescription, Woodcock said, so Mason was smoking it illegally.

. . . The county late last year hired Ms. Webster to begin an intense program aimed at drug dealers.

Ms. Webster said Monday the county has already taken a house and five or six cars. But the hearings Monday represented the first challenges to the county's new practice.

. . . The county sells the vehicles and homes it seizes through a sealed-bid process. Ms. Webster said that individuals can bid on seized cars and homes by submitting proposals that will be opened publicly. *(Altoona Mirror,* 1991:B1*)*

On the surface, the circumstances surrounding the arrest are relatively routine. A man buys drugs from an undercover officer in a bar. The buyer leaves in his pick-up truck. The undercover agent alerts patrol officers to stop the vehicle and make the arrest. The arrest is made without incident. Another skirmish in the war against drugs has been won. Or has it?

The details of this incident reveal several elements of the power of the state. First is the power to define marijuana as a drug. (In this case, the person who was arrested was using marijuana as a medicine.) Second, the state has the power to define who is a drug pusher. (It is clear in this situation that the buyer was purchasing marijuana as a user, not a seller.) Third, the state has the power to impose sanctions in excess of the actual harm that may result from particular criminal acts. (Here the state confiscates a vehicle as a result of an incident that does not even have a victim.) Fourth, the state has the power to take, by force if necessary, the property of citizens (their cars, homes, and cash) and convert this property to its own use. And finally, as a fifth element of power, the state has the power to carry out its actions in a way that citizens accept as legitimate. (The announcement that citizens can personally benefit by helping the state convert the confiscated property of other citizens to cash reveals the extent to which the state's actions are viewed as acceptable.)

The details of this particular case raise a number of significant issues. First is the conflict of interest that is created when criminal justice agencies get to keep the property of those they arrest. Since the economic "kickback" from criminal prosecutions can be substantial (especially in drug cases), law enforcement agents are able to enrich their departments by targeting certain kinds of offenders. In such situations, one must wonder whether the police are after people for their criminality or for their property. On a broader societal level, is the proper role of the police in a democratic society to "serve and protect" or to "arrest and seize"? Fundamental problems can arise when criminal justice agencies are able to redirect their enormous coercive power over the citizenry from matters of public interest to those of self-interest.

Another circumstance at issue here is the harshness of the law itself. Regardless of your personal stance on drug use in general, the effect of marijuana on most people is nothing more than a mild euphoria (a pleasant, relaxing sense of well-being). Unlike nicotine, marijuana is not physically addicting. And, unlike alcohol, the use of marijuana is not normally associated with violent or destructive behavior. Yet, in spite of the victimless nature of marijuana use, tens of thousands of Americans, many of them young, are serving long sentences in high security penal institutions nationwide for violating marijuana laws. Why?

The term *draconian* is used to describe laws that punish offenders far in excess of any harm that may have resulted from their criminal acts. Since it is difficult to point to any substantial public harm or personal injury resulting from marijuana use, questions must be raised as to why the considerable power of the state is being used to draw such large numbers of otherwise law-abiding citizens into the criminal justice system. Why are the penalties associated with marijuana use so harsh? Who benefits? Once again, in instances such as these, correctional issues shift from topics of crime and criminals to the operation of the criminal justice system itself.

From a political perspective, it is important to recognize that police and incarcerative power go hand in hand. They are interactive; the one depends on and serves to enhance the other. In a sense, the police are the front end of the correctional system—they provide the people who are to be controlled by correctional agencies. In turn, correctional agencies take over control of those who have been arrested, thus freeing the police to concentrate on arresting still others. The power and authority of the state manifests itself in every phase of the criminal justice process. Laws as written include specifications for enforcement as well as punishment. Correctional issues therefore are inherently associated with enforcement issues.

It should be clear that the authority to arrest, convict, sanction, imprison, and/or oversee citizens are all extensions of the power of the state.

Correctional issues raise questions about why people are entering the system as well as what is to be done with them. Often, the actions of politicians, judges, prosecuting attorneys, police, and even citizens themselves fall well within the purview of correctional debates. It is important to recognize that making sense of correctional issues requires us to extend our inquiry well beyond the physical confines of the penitentiary.

Corrections as an Agent of Crime Control

Many would argue that the considerable power and authority granted to correctional agencies is essential for combatting crime and ensuring a safe and secure society. Yes, prisons are expensive, and sure there are some abuses of power, but, as the argument goes, there really are no alternatives—swift and certain punishment is necessary to prevent crime. Popular conceptions regarding the control of crime imply fairness but demand toughness. An important consideration in this regard is that most public debates about crime and punishment begin with the unquestioned, yet erroneous, notion that correctional practices are important weapons for combatting crime.

Many crimes (in particular, crimes of passion and anger) happen quite spontaneously and with little warning. Typically the police do not learn that a crime has taken place until it is reported to them. This points to the fact that the police, in the majority of cases, do not become involved with crime until after it has already happened. It is far more accurate, therefore, to say that the police spend most of their time responding to crime rather than actually preventing or controlling it. If the police are unable to prevent crime, then the validity of arguments that assume that more prisons are essential for a safer society becomes particularly open to question. When examined from this perspective, it is clear that correctional institutions control only those criminals who have been caught and prosecuted; they do not directly control crime.

According to Joan Petersilia (1992), a researcher with the RAND Corporation, there were approximately 34 million serious felonies in 1990. Yet, 31 million never entered the criminal justice system. They were either unreported or unsolved, resulting in 90 percent of serious crime remaining outside this system. Other criminologists agree: "When so much crime never comes to the attention of police, we have to begin putting police power and the criminal justice system as a whole into a smaller perspective" (Felson, 1994:8). The limited extent to which the police, the courts, and correctional institutions are, in actuality, able to control crime raises some fundamental issues concerning national crime control policies.

Since 1970, rates of incarceration have soared. Politicians, liberal as well as conservative, have made putting criminals behind bars a central election theme. One-line slogans, such as "three strikes and you're out," have reduced the complex relationship between crime and state-imposed punishment to the simplistic idea that crime rates go down as increasing numbers of people are incarcerated. This is simply not the case.

The sale and distribution of drugs, for example, is driven by the substantial demands of illegal drug markets that are not affected by arrests—as quickly as dealers are rounded up and sent off to prison others who are likewise motivated quickly take their places. Violent crimes such as assault and homicide, too, are often the result of arguments and fights that do not, in the heat of the moment, appear to be deterred by thoughts of incarceration. Another relevant factor is that, according to *Uniform Crime Reports* (UCR) statistics, most criminals are not even caught—the clearance rate (the proportion of crimes that are solved by arrest) in 1990 for robbery was 25 percent; larceny, 20 percent; motor vehicle theft and arson, 15 percent; and burglary, 14 percent (Schmalleger, 1993). And, besides lacking the capacity to impact directly on the commission of many types of crimes, the added possibility exists that imprisonment may even aggravate rates of crime.

According to a RAND study, a "matched sample" of California offenders convicted of similar crimes and with similar criminal records were followed over a three-year period. The sample was divided into two groups—those who were sentenced to prison and those who were granted probation. Those who were incarcerated were found to consistently have higher re-arrest rates (a positive 3 percent for violent offenders, 11 percent for drug offenders, and 17 percent for property offenders) (Petersilia, 1992). For anyone who is familiar with the deleterious nature of life in prison, these findings are not surprising.

Does this mean that correctional practices have no role to play in the control of crime? Of course not. There is little question that violent and dangerous persons need to be locked up. It is also clear that habitual offenders (those who repetitively commit numerous crimes) are effectively controlled by incarceration (while in prison they are prevented from committing additional crimes). But, again, as these examples help to reemphasize, correctional practices control individual offenders; they do not, and cannot, significantly affect the crime rate.

Having a realistic understanding of the role of corrections in the administration of justice is essential for using correctional resources wisely and effectively. Because of mistaken notions concerning the ability of the correctional system to control crime, the system is currently jammed with nonviolent property and drug offenders. It is also clear that incarceration, the most expensive form of control, should be reserved for dangerous and habitual offenders. And, most fundamental of all, correctional issues should not be driven by political demagogy. To the extent that corrections continues to be "sold" as a solution to crime, the correctional system will continue to expand at the expense of education, medical care, and other vital social services. A central correctional issue, therefore, is not how correctional practices can be expanded, but, rather, how correctional practices themselves can be limited, controlled, and applied more effectively.

Corrections and Social Issues

Ironically, although Americans like to tout themselves as forming the most free and democratic society on earth, the United States has the highest rate of incarceration of any country in the world. In 1990, approximately 4.3 million citizens were being supervised by correctional agencies (Shover and Inveraity, 1995). As many of the nation's prisons have filled to beyond 200 percent of capacity, newer forms of correctional control such as boot camps and electronic home and workplace monitoring have arisen to subject increasing numbers of citizens to state-imposed sanctions. As correctional practices have reached staggering numeric and economic proportions, it is time to reassess the proper role of corrections in American society.

When correctional issues are considered within a societal context, a number of fundamental questions arise:

1. What types of people are subject to correctional control? Who is being imprisoned, why, for how long, and under what conditions? Is there any evidence that citizens are being imprisoned to further political ends? Is there any evidence of biased or discriminatory treatment on the part of the correctional system?

2. Does the punishment fit the crime? Is the cost of punishment in line with the cost of crime? Is there any evidence that fear and emotion, rather than fairness and justice, are driving correctional policy making? Are segments of the correctional population subject to levels of control beyond what is required?

3. How effective is the criminal justice system? Are correctional agencies able to deliver on promises of less crime in exchange for more resources? Which correctional practices result in lowered rates of recidivism and which do not? In terms of doing justice and protecting society, which offender types must be imprisoned and which need not be?

4. What are the conditions of confinement? Are they humane and fair? Are correctional environments safe and secure, or violent and dehumanizing? What effect does correctional practice have on those released from the system as well as those who find themselves working with or living next to ex-offenders?

5. Are correctional practices the outcome of informed and reasoned debate, or do they simply reflect unfounded fear and ignorance? On what basis is new criminal legislation proposed? Is it advanced on the

basis of slick political slogans and references to single-instance horror stories (such as the Willie Horton case), or is it an outcome of an informed public debate that combines established facts with clear policy alternatives?

6. What is the proper role of corrections in a democratic society? Is there evidence that the criminal justice system is treating as criminal citizens who are generally nonviolent and law-abiding? Are there victimless acts that are being defined as crimes? Are classes of innocent people being confined for political or economic reasons? To what extent are expenditures on crime and crime control diverting funds from other legitimate and needed social services? To what extent are we, as citizens, willing to trade personal liberties and freedoms for an increased police presence in our lives?

A sociology of corrections teaches us to look beyond ideology and rhetoric to evaluate the impact of correctional practices on ourselves and the society in which we live. As seen, correctional issues have the potential to affect all of our lives considerably. Since contemporary concerns about building more prisons or coming up with new, yet affordable, means for dealing with crime and criminals stem from false notions concerning correction's crime control capabilities, it is imperative that, if true progress is to take place, we put aside these kinds of operational concerns and begin to question the correctional process itself. In light of the recent rise of corrections as a major social institution, we must make wise and informed decisions concerning how much and in what way we want crime control policies to rule our lives.

REFERENCES

Felson, M. (1994). *Crime and Everyday Life: Insights and Implications for Society*. Thousand Oaks, CA: Pine Forge Press.

"Lawyers Squabble Over Drug Suspect's Car." *Altoona Mirror,* July 23, 1991:B-1.

Petersilia, J. (1992). "An Evaluation of Intensive Probation in California." *Journal of Criminal Law and Criminology* 82:610–658.

Schmalleger, F. (1995). *Criminal Justice Today*. Upper Saddle River, NJ: Prentice Hall.

Surette, R. (1992). *Media, Crime and Criminal Justice: Images and Realities*. Pacific Grove, CA: Brooks/Cole.

TWO

Correctional Philosophies
Varying Ideologies of Punishment

TED ALLEMAN
The Pennsylvania State University

INTRODUCTION

This chapter discusses the implications of the rehabilitation, justice, and utilitarian punishment approaches to the treatment of offenders. As will be apparent, each philosophy has a different focus. Rehabilitation is most concerned with reforming the criminal, justice emphasizes fairness and restitution, while utilitarian punishment seeks swift and certain retaliation. Each of these philosophies holds a different view as to who criminals are and how they should be treated. Each philosophy, through its implementation, has a direct impact on the focus and actions of the criminal justice system.

Crime and punishment go hand in hand. Defending oneself by striking back is a predictable human response. From this perspective, punishment serves the purpose of stopping or thwarting an attack. Who among us would not raise a hand to defend ourselves or our loved ones from injury or harm? Taking an "eye for an eye" is an age-old dictum. Getting even is basic to what many mean when they use the terms *fairness* and *justice*. In a fundamental way, correctional philosophies are grounded in personal experience.

Correctional philosophies are broad-based and relatively cohesive sets of ideas that serve to guide and justify the treatment of offenders. The kinds and levels of sanctions imposed on criminal defendants are reflective of the general values and beliefs that are held concerning what kinds of people commit crimes and what should be done with them. Different philosophies imply different approaches to crime control. In American criminal justice, the philosophies of rehabilitation, justice, and utilitarian punishment represent three varying perspectives as to the proper treatment of criminal offenders.

To a significant degree, many public issues and debates hinge on which of these three philosophies is assumed to be the best strategy for dealing with crime. In addition to understanding the basis of many public debates concerning crime and punishment, a knowledge of the varying correctional philosophies that are predominant today is important for understanding how specific criminal justice programs and practices come to be adopted. Rather than taking sides as to which philosophy is personally most appealing, the following discussion encourages an objective analysis of the pros and cons associated with each of these varying approaches to corrections.

THE PHILOSOPHY OF UTILITARIAN PUNISHMENT

The utilitarian punishment model is not difficult to understand. Utilitarian punishment is based on the premise that those who commit criminal acts do so with full knowledge of what they are doing and that when they are caught and prosecuted they deserve levels of punishment commensurate with the harm or damage they have done. In addition to being "just deserts" for criminal offenders, the imposition of punishment is believed to deter others from committing offenses and, by keeping habitual offenders in prison, to incapacitate offenders from committing further criminal acts. Retribution, deterrence, and incapacitation are three of the principal rationales behind the utilitarian punishment approach.

Applying the utilitarian punishment philosophy to criminal justice is akin to "being tough on crime." Because of the fear associated with crime, the general public is responsive to the language of utilitarian punishment. Commonsense notions stemming from child rearing support the argument that problem behaviors can result when parents fail to provide and enforce clear definitions of right and wrong. When applied to criminal justice, popular conceptions of criminal offenders think them to be deceptive, malicious, and/or dangerous persons who need to have a sense of responsibility and respect for authority instilled in them. A conservative philosophy of child rearing is compatible with the "grab them by the neck and show them who is boss" orientation of utilitarian punishment. Additionally, politicians, judges, and criminal prosecutors have found that spouting the rhetoric of utilitarian punishment can be an effective political strategy for getting elected to public office. Elements of traditional Christian dogma that teach "an eye for an eye, and a tooth for a tooth" as a proper response to social transgression further add to the general appeal of the utilitarian punishment approach to criminal justice.

Utilitarian punishment is the oldest and most commonly accepted approach to criminal justice. The history of criminal justice is to a great extent a history of the imposition of different forms of punishment. It is clear that utilitarian punishment is and will continue to be a primary rationale for dealing with crime. An objective of correctional research is to clarify the true effects of utilitarian punishment and to identify when and under what conditions punishment serves as an appropriate response and an effective deterrent to crime.

History of Utilitarian Punishment

As a response to nonconformity and social transgression, punishment is as old as human history. The notion that punishment serves a general utilitarian purpose in society is of a more recent origin and can be dated from the writings of Cesare Beccaria and Jeremy Bentham in the eighteenth century.

Adding a utilitarian component to the punishment model implies that punishment results in a general social good. The social good associated with the imposition of punishment stems from the belief that penalties that have been preassigned to unlawful behavior provide a clear definition of right and wrong as well as a warning to those who might contemplate the commission of a criminal act of the consequences they will suffer as the result of their actions. Arguments that support utilitarian punishment as a general approach to crime control, therefore, assert that utilitarian punishment prevents as well as punishes criminal acts. When confronted by critics who view utilitarian punishment as simply a vengeful, vindictive, barbaric, and repressive response to the crime problem, proponents of utilitarian punishment point to the social good that punishment serves for the prevention of crime.

Cesare Beccaria, an influential social critic of his time, is commonly identified as the founder of the modern utilitarian punishment philosophy. This is ironic since Beccaria's classic work, *On Crimes and Punishment* (1764), was primarily reformist in nature and was intended to provide a social remedy to the rampant use of harsh and brutal punishments by the criminal justice system of his day. Another social philosopher, Jeremy Bentham, who was influenced by Beccaria, further refined the utilitarian punishment perspective by emphasizing his belief that people, in general, pursue that which is pleasurable and avoid that which is painful. In his book, *A Fragment on Government and an Introduction to the Principles of Morals and Legislation* (1789), Bentham expanded on Beccaria's idea that crime could be prevented through law and stressed that the imposition of sure and immediate penalties was central to the control of criminal behavior. Thus, the works of both Beccaria and Bentham established the idea that the law (and the penalties to be imposed when the law was violated) was just in terms of punishing criminals as well as effective in keeping others who might contemplate committing criminal acts from doing so.

The term *calculus* is commonly applied to the mental weighing of the pros and cons of committing a criminal act that supposedly goes through a person's mind prior to the commission of a crime. According to the classical school of criminology established by Beccaria, punishment should fit the crime and should be severe enough to outweigh any advantage or gain that might result from the commission of the criminal act. In this way, punishment (the imposition of specific sanctions on those who commit specific unlawful acts) performs a social good by acting as a deterrent to the commission of crime. Whether or not criminal sanctions have such a deterrent effect, of course, depends on the knowledge that persons have of the law and to what extent they believe that they will be caught and punished for their actions.

Utilitarian Punishment in Practice

A number of current policies and practices that stem from the application of utilitarian punishment can be identified. In summary form, the utilitarian punishment philosophy supports

> *A hard-line policy toward serious juvenile offenders.* Juvenile offenders are perceived to be dangerous and a by-product of a permissive society. Juvenile offenders must be taught that "crime does not pay." Serious juvenile offenders, especially violent offenders, should be sent to reform schools and, when appropriate, subjected to adult court proceedings.
>
> *Greater use of determinate and mandatory sentences.* Crime prevention requires stiff and sure penalties. Discretion should be taken out of the hands of judges and parole boards. Imprisonment is relied on as the primary response to serious crime.
>
> *Development of a more effective court system.* To impose sure and certain penalties, criminal prosecution should not be delayed. Upon conviction, court-mandated punishments (including application of the death penalty) should be administered as soon as possible. For criminal justice to serve as an effective deterrent to crime, criminals must face a swift and decisive sanctioning process. The courts should be more concerned with imposing justice than catering to the presumed rights of criminal defendants.
>
> *Get tough policy with drug offenders.* Advocates of utilitarian punishment see drug use as pervasive and representing a clear and present danger to the moral fiber of the nation. Drugs are seen as undermining the motivation and morals of American citizens and must be dealt with in a stern and uncompromising fashion. Maximum penalties for drug pushers and the death penalty for drug "kingpins" are advocated. Drug

use is not viewed as an excuse for crime nor is it looked on as a disease or an illness.

Expanded use of boot camps. Military style boot camps are seen as the ideal setting for resocializing misguided youths who think they are able to break the law and get away with it. A primary benefit of the boot-camp approach is the opportunity to instill respect for authority while giving new offenders one last chance to avoid imprisonment.

Use of the death penalty. The death penalty is the ultimate punishment for those offenders who have taken a life or have engaged in egregious behavior that does substantial social harm (such as distributing dangerous drugs). For those who believe in the efficacy of utilitarian punishment, capital punishment is necessary to demonstrate to incorrigible felons that serious crime will not be tolerated.

In general, the utilitarian punishment philosophy relies on imprisonment as the primary means for dealing with crime. Utilitarian punishment advocates the need to protect society by removing serious juvenile and adult offenders from the community. Utilitarian punishment also advocates a clear definition of the law and the punishment that will be imposed on those who choose to break the law. Any competing philosophy or practice that impedes or lessens the impact of the efficient delivery of punishment to convicted felons is viewed as undermining the function as well as the effectiveness of the criminal justice system.

Advantages of Utilitarian Punishment

Advocates of utilitarian punishment justify this approach in terms of retribution, deterrence, and incapacitation. Therefore, to judge its efficacy we must look at each of these functions of the utilitarian punishment approach to crime control.

Retribution. Retribution means getting even. The retributive function of criminal justice implies inflicting at least as much pain on the offender as the offender has inflicted on his or her victim. Fines, the imposition of a negative social stigma, the maintenance of criminal records, restriction of certain kinds of employment, withholding the right to hold public office, denying the right to vote in public elections, the loss of liberty through incarceration, or the loss of life through execution are examples of criminal sanctions. There is little doubt that criminal sanctions serve a retributive function. There is some argument that sanctions can always "even the score," especially when long-term trauma, physical maladies, or loss of life results from criminal acts.

Deterrence. Deterrence can be divided into two types: (1) general deterrence and (2) specific deterrence. General deterrence takes the form of laws that define the penalties that will be imposed upon violation of the law. Specific deterrence refers to the imposition of penalties on a particular person who has broken the law and is made aware of "specific" penalties that will result if subsequent violations of the law, or of conditions of probation or parole, occur. Strict penalties, whether in the form of tough laws or strict rules governing the behavior of convicted felons, are seen as essential if deterrence (prevention) of crime is to take place.

It is not clear how effective general deterrence is in terms of dissuading criminal activity. What is evident is that many people who commit crimes are aware that their behavior is illegal, but they may not know the exact nature of the penalties associated with particular crimes. When evaluating the deterrent effect of criminal sanctions, it is also important to take into consideration the fact that punishment has a subjective dimension, in that people vary as to whether or not they consider treatment by the criminal justice system as punishment. In some social circles, for example, being picked up and charged by the police may actually enhance status. In general, laws most affect those who are law-abiding. In other words, it is those people who have the greatest stake in society who have the most to lose from the imposition of criminal sanctions. Therefore, the threat of punishment often serves to keep those who are generally law-abiding anyway from committing criminal offenses.

Incapacitation. Incapacitation means that during the period of time in which an offender is institutionalized, the offender is unable to commit further criminal acts. There is no question that this dimension of utilitarian punishment works. To the extent that the criminal justice system is able to identify and incarcerate habitual offenders, the goal of preventing particular offenders from committing crimes is achieved. The problem with this approach is that it is very difficult to identify which offenders would be committing additional crimes if on the street. This approach also has many legal ramifications, since sanctions cannot be imposed for behavior that has not yet taken place.

Disadvantages of Utilitarian Punishment

In many ways utilitarian punishment is an oversimplified solution to a complex problem. There is little argument that prison is an important and necessary component of the criminal justice system. The problem associated with the utilitarian punishment approach is that prison is relied on almost exclusively as a method of crime control. Incarcerating a person for a number of years is a very expensive proposition. It is also clear that prison makes people worse, not better. Today's prisons are filled with nonviolent offenders who might be more effectively treated by alternative methods. To improve the effectiveness of the criminal justice system, we need to see prison as only one of many treatment alternatives.

It is also important to take into consideration the full effect of punishment-based policies and programs. Punishment, as a form of social control, has many drawbacks. The imposition of punishment promotes avoidance behavior. For those persons who have frequent contact with the criminal justice system, authority figures can come to be viewed as the enemy. Punishment can result in alienating youthful offenders even further from the mainstream of society. Criminal subcultures to some extent owe their existence to a commonly held antagonism toward legitimate authority. Punishment, therefore, can have unanticipated social consequences.

Punishment can also create aggression in those who are punished. When we put people in prison we run the risk of making them more angry, frustrated, or hateful than before (Jeffery, 1990). Punishment can cause people to strike out in an increasingly destructive fashion. Of course, offenders must be punished for their criminal acts, but, in order to serve as an effective deterrent, punishment must be used wisely and judiciously. The indiscriminate use of punishment can have a criminogenic effect. We must be sure that punishment does not serve to increase rates of crime among those who are processed by the criminal justice system.

To be effective, punishment must be applied as quickly and decisively as possible. But this is not how the criminal justice system works. In many cases, months and sometimes even years pass before formal sanctions are imposed by the courts. If the association between the criminal act and punishment is not clear, punishment can be essentially ineffective as an agent of change. And, if punishment is perceived to be undeserved or unwarranted, punishment can again serve to escalate destructive and antisocial patterns of behavior.

Punishment is most effective when it is only part of a correctional strategy. Punishment does get people's attention and does serve to inhibit behavior when it is applied at the right time and under appropriate conditions. But, unless revenge or hate are primary intentions, punishment by itself is generally ineffective as a correctional strategy. To make punishment effective, the offender must be provided with alternative means for reinforcement. This implies that correctional strategies must combine programs that serve to block illegal opportunities while at the same time providing behavioral programs that create legitimate opportunities (Jeffery, 1990). Punishment, therefore, proves most effective when it is used wisely and judicially as only one element in a coordinated program for change.

As a response to crime, punishment holds much personal appeal. Striking out at those who have done harm or damage is a perfectly natural reaction. It makes us feel better. But, as a correctional strategy, the limitations of relying solely on punishment must be acknowledged. If used indiscriminately and without purpose, repressive measures can clearly lay the groundwork for continued and increasingly destructive criminal behavior among inmate populations who are released from prison even more bitter and alienated than when they first entered the system.

THE REHABILITATIVE PHILOSOPHY

When someone says that rehabilitation cannot work, they are really saying that people cannot change. We all know that people do change. Some people, in fact, go through dramatic, life-altering changes. In this regard, rehabilitation can be defined as the systematic attempt to change criminal offenders so that deviant propensities, especially those that are damaging or destructive to others, are reduced or eliminated from their lives.

In terms of rehabilitative change, there are three major areas of focus. For some classes of offenders, an objective is to change the way in which they respond to cues in their environment. Another is to change the motivations of criminal offenders. And, as a third objective, it is necessary to strive to alter or reduce problem behaviors and/or change deviant lifestyles. Each of these objectives involves the creation of programs through which significant and lasting personal change takes place.

The first objective aims to change the ways in which offenders habitually perceive, interpret, and/or react to the world around them. Eliminating the tendency to see their world in a threatening, fearful, domineering, acquisitive, or egocentric manner is therefore a major rehabilitative goal. The goal of changing criminal motivations involves eliminating the desire, pleasure, excitement, or reward associated with criminal activity. The last objective, changing an offender's habitual patterns of behavior or lifestyle, is most difficult because these patterns often reflect a person's self-concept. Creating programs in which such fundamental kinds of personal change take place is not an easy task.

Methods of Rehabilitative Change

In the case of the vast majority of offenders, criminal behavior is learned. Criminality, especially in terms of offenders who demonstrate regularity and progression in their criminal careers, often involves an extended period of socialization in which criminal motivations, techniques, attitudes, and lifestyles are learned. Teaching offenders to disassociate themselves from these aspects of socialization is a difficult but not impossible task.

Socializing offenders into alternative, noncriminal social roles is a general rehabilitative strategy. In one way or another, the rewards of noncriminal social roles must come to outweigh the rewards of criminal roles. And, concurrently, the social costs of criminal pursuits must become greater than their inherent or perceived rewards. Although difficult to engineer, treatment programs must somehow guide offenders away from behavior or pursuits that are likely to result in arrest. Everyday incentives and inducements for ex-offenders must be weighted in the direction of legitimate, non-criminal careers and lifestyles. More to the point, criminal offenders, if they are to extricate themselves from further processing by the criminal justice system, must prove successful in gaining a personal overriding stake in conventional society.

The specific methods used for instituting rehabilitative change in offenders vary from one general class of offender to another. An essential element of rehabilitative strategy is the application of the most effective treatment alternatives to those classes of offenders who demonstrate rehabilitative success through reduced rates of recidivism. Identifying which strategies are most successful with which classes of offenders is a major objective of correctional research.

History of Rehabilitative Methods

Implicitly, theories of rehabilitation view criminals as people who need to be fixed. Rehabilitation starts with the premise that offenders have something wrong with them.

When put into practice, rehabilitation tends toward a model that puts offenders into some form of dependency relationship. This occurs because prisoners are seen as people who are lacking in one way or another. Correctional educators provide the schooling they are lacking, counselors provide the emotional stability they are lacking, and pastors provide the moral standards they are lacking, all with the belief that their instruction will in some way "cure" or "transform" the offender. A good part of the history of rehabilitation can be summarized by identifying the roles into which rehabilitative approaches have placed prisoners. Historically, depending on whether a religious, medical, or counseling approach to rehabilitation was taken, prisoners have been treated as sinners, patients, and/or clients.

To some extent, rehabilitative methods require the cooperation of prisoners. Programs are most successful when prisoners themselves actively seek help or assistance and are willing participants in their own resocialization. As students, they must want to learn; as sinners, they must want to be saved; and as clients or patients, they must want to be remedied or cured. Unlike justice or utilitarian punishment approaches, which do something *to* prisoners, rehabilitative methods seek to work *with* prisoners. As such, rehabilitation programs often include incentives for participation and sanctions for noninvolvement. Rehabilitation is essentially a "carrot and stick" approach to correctional treatment.

An underlying premise of rehabilitative programming is the elimination of the causes (pushes, forces, conditions, etc.) that have resulted in the commission of criminal acts. The logic of rehabilitation includes the assumption that people will not commit criminal acts if the source of their discontent, frustration, or adverse conditioning is reduced or eliminated from their lives. The true proof of rehabilitative success, therefore, lies in lowered rates of recidivism.

A General Approach to Rehabilitation

In very general terms, contemporary rehabilitative methods include the following steps:

1. Identify the conditions and/or circumstances that led or contributed to the commission of the criminal act.
2. Solicit the cooperation of the client and discuss the nature of the problem and a program for change.
3. Identify the specific behavioral goals of the program and how the program will be carried out.
4. Provide a conditioning environment conducive and supportive of the actualization of program goals.
5. Provide frequent, accurate feedback to the participant that includes a personally meaningful system of positive reinforcement.
6. Perform follow-up evaluations and reinforcement sessions after specific programs have been completed.
7. Have one program flow into another in terms of arranging a long-term rehabilitative strategy designed to address all aspects of the participant's individualized needs.

Rehabilitation is a scientific approach to changing offenders. Criminality, like all other forms of social behavior, is seen as a byproduct of social and/or personal factors and conditioning. To a great extent, criminals are viewed as social actors who have been unduly exposed to and influenced by adverse social conditions. Remove or eliminate the cause, so say rehabilitative practitioners, and the consequences (criminal behavior) will be eliminated. The rehabilitative philosophy adds an aura of exactness and definitiveness to the dynamic, bizarre, and many times unpredictable world of criminality.

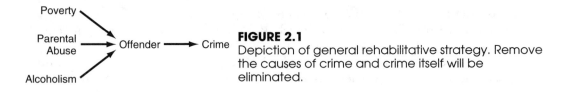

FIGURE 2.1
Depiction of general rehabilitative strategy. Remove the causes of crime and crime itself will be eliminated.

By viewing criminality in terms of cause and effect, rehabilitation programs process offenders according to plan and design. Rehabilitative strategies place a great emphasis on technique and method. Because of the scientific nature of rehabilitative approaches to corrections, the mistaken assumption can be engendered that programs work simply because they are well designed or properly administered. The truth is that defining and "programming out" undesirable personal traits or behaviors is a difficult, complicated, and less than certain process. The success of instituting programmed change in a prison environment is subject to the following factors and considerations.

Realities of Instituting Prison-Based Rehabilitative Programs

- All prisoners are not responsive to rehabilitative programs. Some prisoners do consciously choose criminality as a life course.
- If effective treatment programs are not offered, prisoners generally come out of prison worse off than when they went in.
- Many programs instituted in prison are ineffective. They do not address individual needs and are simply "window dressing" that allows the administration to claim that programs are being offered.
- Many offenders fail to face up to the actual harm that has resulted from their criminal actions. Directly confronting prisoners on this issue generally does not work. Although difficult, rehabilitative programming should include subtle, indirect, but effective means of overcoming prisoner's attempts to deny and avoid responsibility for their actions. Offenders who do not come to have a degree of empathy for their victims will have difficulty consciously altering their behavior upon release.
- Incarceration in maximum security warehoused institutions is expensive and generally ineffective as a rehabilitative strategy for the majority of offenders. Valuable prison space, especially in maximum security institutions, should be reserved for the most violent and habitual types of offenders.
- Rehabilitation and treatment philosophies have come and gone, but the realities of prisons, along with their primary orientation toward the security, custody, and control of prisoners, have changed little over their two-hundred-year history. Prisons have a built-in resistance to programs and policies that treat prisoners as positive, potentially productive human beings.
- Effective treatment options exist but they will not be used extensively (system wide) unless they seem to fit in with an overriding political or economic rationale.
- Prisoners, as a group or class of people, are politically impotent. Unfortunately, the only avenue by which the majority of prisoners can

bring attention to unfair or inhumane prison conditions is through some form of collective violence or protest.

- The history of enlightened wardens and superintendents is a history of their objectives and programs being undermined by incompetent bureaucrats and lower-echelon staff. Rehabilitative programs that are not understood, supported, and participated in by all levels of the prison bureaucracy will eventually fail.

- Out of all the criminal justice agencies, prisons represent a significant opportunity for the change and reform of prisoners. It is only when felons are incarcerated that the system potentially has complete control over their behavior and social environment. Ways in which incentives and programs for change can be effectively implemented in prison environments are often overlooked by administrative staff who are simply interested in maintaining custody and control over the prison population.

- The rehabilitative, justice, and punishment models are not necessarily competing treatment alternatives. Offenders vary significantly from one another and respond differently to the way in which they are treated by the system. To be successful at reducing crime, the criminal justice system must become more sophisticated and diverse in terms of its treatment options.

Advantages of Rehabilitation

Prisoners, like all people, are capable of changing for the better. Therefore, the continual development and identification of successful programs is a worthy objective of corrections. It is true that some rehabilitative programs have failed. But this does not mean that rehabilitation as a general correctional strategy is a failure. Many individual rehabilitative programs have failed because

1. Offender types have not been appropriately matched with specific programs.
2. Custodial staff typically are not educated or included in rehabilitative programming; therefore, they often work to undermine methods with which they do not agree or do not understand.
3. Most treatment programs have not been designed to carry over into the community.
4. Follow-up and objective evaluation generally have not been used to identify good programs and eliminate poor ones.

Rehabilitation is a positive, constructive way of dealing with criminal offenders. Our prisons and jails are filled with offenders who respond well to rehabilitative programs and would jump at the chance to work their way out of prison and out of trouble with the law. Treatment programs that are clear, objective, and not subject to manipulation, by prisoners or staff, have good histories of success. Successful programs that result in reduced rates of recidivism should be expanded and made generally available to inmate populations.

Disadvantages of Rehabilitation

Some programs can lead to abuse. Prisoners should not be forced or coerced into participation in rehabilitative programs. Prisoners who decide that they do not wish to participate in programs should not be threatened with additional years of imprisonment. Like all correctional philosophies, rehabilitation can become dogmatic and authoritarian in its application.

It is very difficult to reverse years of antisocial conditioning by administering a few programs of short duration to prisoners. Because rehabilitative programs are offered does not mean that rehabilitation is actually taking place. Programs that are improperly administered or designed can be a total waste of time, money, and effort.

It is also difficult to punish and rehabilitate at the same time. The punitive nature of prison can outweigh any potential benefits associated with rehabilitative programming. It is difficult to successfully implement rehabilitative change in punitively oriented prison environments.

It is simply not true that all prisoners commit crimes because of some personal or social defect. Like all correctional strategies, rehabilitation applies to some but not all offenders. Effective rehabilitation programs successfully recognize and meet the needs of particular types of prisoners. Otherwise, rehabilitation as an exclusive approach to corrections is inherently no better or worse than its justice or utilitarian punishment counterparts.

THE JUSTICE MODEL

The justice model, as an approach to the treatment of criminal offenders, lies conceptually somewhere between the rehabilitation and the utilitarian punishment philosophies. The justice approach to treatment contains elements of both philosophies and is currently a popular approach to corrections. The model was first elaborated by David Fogel in *We Are the Living Proof,* published in 1979. Since then, the rationale of the justice model has been used by administrators nationwide to implement a wide variety of correctional strategies. By recognizing the need for rehabilitative programs (but downplaying their importance) and by sharing with the philosophy of utilitarian punishment the desire for sure and determinate sentencing, the justice model fits the mood of the times in terms of being tough on crime in a purportedly humane and constitutional fashion.

The justice model incorporates two of the fundamental tenets of present-day corrections—those of punishment and treatment. The model, by insisting on consistent, determinant sentences, validates an emphasis on punishment. But far from being simply a "lock them up and throw away the key" type of approach, the justice model also emphasizes that an obligation of the system is to provide educational, counseling, and treatment programs to all prisoners who voluntarily request them. Pragmatically, the justice model allows jails and prisons to continue to be run with a predominant "security, custody, and control" focus while concurrently providing a role for the treatment infrastructure that is an established fixture in most correctional institutions.

Although the justice model clearly recognizes the rights of prisoners and advocates a number of measures designed to address inmate concerns, the justice model, to some extent, has been co-opted by utilitarian punishment proponents who find it expedient to justify the implementation of their custody-oriented strategies by speaking the language of justice. Because the justice model takes a passive approach to treatment, the warehousing of prisoners has evolved over the past two decades as a predominant administrative strategy. In many instances, the adoption of the justice model has resulted in an ever-increasing flow of prisoners into large, warehoused facilities. Ironically, such consequences were never envisioned nor intended by those who initially formulated the justice approach to corrections.

Elements of the Justice Approach to Corrections

The justice model is intended to be a fair and equitable approach to corrections. To its credit, the justice model takes into consideration all of those who are affected by crime: offenders (those charged with crimes and are forcibly processed as criminals), correctional personnel (those hired to see that punitive mandates are carried out), and victims (those who experience personal loss or suffering as the result of crime). Even though the implementation of the justice model has not yielded all that it promises, it is a viable approach to correctional treatment that addresses many of the problems inherent in the imposition of punishment in a democratic society.

Coming from a rehabilitation background, "revisionists" such as David Fogel have maintained a positive regard for prisoner's rights as well as a general distrust of the power of the state (Bartollas, 1985). Admittedly, the destructive prison riots of the 1970s played a role in the development of this new approach to correctional treatment (Fogel, 1982). It is clear that in prison, custody and control practices generally override concerns for prisoners' rights. As such, if pushed too far, justice practitioners are well aware that contempt and rage can breed and fester among prisoners sometimes to the point of riot. Instituting administrative controls such as establishing prisoner grievance processes and using outside ombudsmen to settle prisoner/staff disputes is seen as important for preventing prison violence. Treating prisoners as responsible persons who deserve a say in the affairs of the prison is also advocated as part of the justice approach, but, in practice, this is often successfully resisted by correctional staff who maintain traditional custody and control perspectives.

The justice model advances a number of specific revisions to the correctional system. Some have been adopted, and some have not. In outline form, the following can be identified as being central elements of the justice model:

Retribution rather than deterrence or reformation. As a primary goal of the correctional system, the justice model justifies a level of punishment proportionate to the harm resulting from criminal acts. Punishment is viewed as a legitimate goal of the justice system. Offenders deserve to be punished but only to the extent that they have inflicted harm on others. Unlike the rehabilitative philosophy, reforming the criminal is not a legitimate goal of the system. And, unlike the utilitarian punishment approach, punishment is not seen as an appropriate means of attempting to prevent crime. In simple terms, those who violate the law deserve to be punished. No additional rationale for state-imposed punishment is needed or, in terms of the justice model, justified.

Criminal offenders have full knowledge of their criminal acts and must be held responsible for their actions. Unlike a rehabilitative approach, those who break the law are not seen as acting out of need or want or ignorance. Offenders in large part are viewed as people who, after a conscious weighing of the consequences, have decided to commit a criminal act. The justice model provides no excuses for criminal behavior. Without question, criminal behavior is defined as wrong and punishable by law. The justice model, like utilitarian punishment, holds offenders personally responsible for their criminal actions.

Offenders should be required to make restitution to the victims of their crimes. An idea that clearly differentiates the justice model from both rehabilitation and utilitarian punishment is an emphasis on victim restitution. The justice model, whenever possible, advocates that offenders be made to repay the victims of their crimes. The justice model makes the victim a central element in judicial and correctional decision making. Justice practitioners attempt to restore victims to their precrime condition. The presentence investigation report, for example, is used to document the damage to persons and/or property that resulted from the defendant's actions and then applied in the form of court-mandated restitution plans (Bartollas, 1985). Sanctions such as deducting prisoner wages from direct monetary payments to victims and/or requiring some form of community service as part of an offender's sentence are examples of practices that grew out of the justice model.

Discretionary justice should be eliminated. In order to do justice, sentences should be fair and exact. Determinate sentencing is a hallmark of the justice approach. Justice practitioners want judges to follow sentencing guidelines so that the punishment fits the crime, not the defendant or the circumstance. According to the justice model, defendants who commit similar crimes should be given similar punishments. This is seen as the only fair way of dispensing justice. To make justice exact, the justice model requires convicted felons to serve the full term of their sentence. Practices such as sentencing felons to a variable term (five to seven years, for example) or releasing prisoners early to parole are eliminated from systems employing the justice model. In terms of reform, the justice model seeks to eliminate indeterminate sentencing and abolish parole altogether. According to the justice approach, convicted felons should know upon sentencing the date of their release from prison. The only exception to this is the reduction of time served by allowing prisoners to earn "good time" credits in exchange for good behavior in prison.

Advantages of the Justice Model

The justice model is a pragmatic approach to corrections. By emphasizing "justice" and "fairness" as centerpieces of its operational mandate, the justice model champions a correctional system that recognizes the rights and responsibilities of all the parties involved: victims, offenders, and correctional staff. The justice model accepts the reality of crime and, unlike rehabilitation or utilitarian punishment, it has no illusions about being able to stop or prevent crime. Given the fact that crime exists, the justice model reacts by meting out punishment proportionate to the harm that has been done, creates a system that treats felons humanely, and does all that is possible to restore victims to their precrime condition.

Disadvantages of the Justice Model

As a philosophical approach to corrections, the justice model is sound in its orientation. In practice, however, the justice model contains elements that weaken it as an overall correctional strategy.

By insisting that rehabilitative programs be totally voluntary, some prisoners with identifiable problems may never be treated. Such a passive approach to treatment demands nothing of prisoners. As a result, the primary goal of many prisoners becomes that of simply sitting back and doing their time. This means that upon release, if their crimes were in fact the consequence of personal or social problems, recidivism is likely.

Prisons that employ the justice model tend to be warehoused facilities. The warehousing of prisoners results when large numbers of compliant prisoners are herded in large groups, day in and day out, from one activity to the next. Prisoners who do their time in warehoused facilities basically eat, sleep, and recreate their way through the correctional system. A basic flaw of the justice model of corrections is that "correction" is missing from its operational definition.

In addition, over the past decade, the language of corrections has been used to justify a punitive orientation toward the treatment of offenders. Utilitarian punishment practitioners readily adopt the determinate sentencing and retribution emphasis of the justice model while forgetting justice's emphasis on prisoner rights and humane treatment. Additionally, punitive-oriented practitioners actively support the abolition of parole while ignoring justice's demands for reduced sentences and less of a reliance on prison as the primary means of crime control. To some extent, the massive overcrowding of America's prisons can be attributed to utilitarian punishment practices that have been implemented under the rubric of justice and fairness for all.

CONTEMPORARY CORRECTIONAL PHILOSOPHY— AN INTEGRATIVE PERSPECTIVE

Utilitarian punishment, justice, and rehabilitation are three competing philosophies of correctional treatment. Throughout the history of corrections, each of these philosophies has, at one time or another, come into prominence and has dominated correctional practice. Upon assessing the advantages and disadvantages of each approach, which is best? Which of these philosophies most effectively reduces crime, reforms criminals, and protects society? The correct answer is none of them.

For too long we have accepted as legitimate arguments that portray criminals as being all of one type and correctional strategies that are successful with everyone. The truth is that utilitarian punishment works with some offenders and fails with others, justice works with some offenders but fails with others, and rehabilitation works for some offenders and fails with others. Each philosophy works well with certain classes of offenders and fails miserably when used as a sole approach to correctional treatment. Successful strategies for dealing with criminal offenders, therefore, hinge on our knowledge of the full range of correctional options available to us and our willingness to match specific offender types with adequate and effective treatment strategies.

Table 2.1 provides an overview of each of the major correctional philosophies. By identifying the major elements of each philosophy, this typology can be used to compare and contrast traditional responses to crime and the treatment of convicted felons.

Major issues in contemporary corrections stem from the predominately punitive approach to crime that has been undertaken over the past twenty-five years. Associated with the use of imprisonment as the principal mode of

TABLE 2.1 Typology of Correctional Philosophies

	Utilitarian Punishment	Justice	Rehabilitation
Image of the Criminal	Deliberate, calculating, habitual, and, at times, vicious in their criminality	Citizens who happen to break the law	People who, no matter what they may have done in the past, can be changed for the better
Principle Orientation	Swift and certain retaliation	Fairness and restitution	Reformation of criminals
Sentencing	Determinate, maximum penalties	Determinate penalties commensurate with harm or damage done	Indeterminate sentences that motivate offenders to participate in their own rehabilitation
Criminal Motivation	Criminals rationally decide to take advantage of their victims	Criminals are aware of their crimes and are also aware of the consequences if caught	Criminals are not fully aware of the reasons for their actions
Purpose of Punishment	Inflict pain on criminals, prevent further victimizations, and deter those who might consider engaging in crime	In terms of fairness, punish criminals to the same degree that they have harmed their victims	Use punishment to make criminals realize the harm they have done and want to participate in their own reformation into lawabiding citizens
Primary Treatment	Incarceration in prison	A least restrictive approach that imposes punishments commensurate with crimes	A variety of settings (from prison to half-way houses) designed to resocialize offenders and, prior to release, prepare them for integration back into the community
Apt Offender Types	Hardened, habitual, violent criminals who have little regard for their victims	Citizens who commit crimes and must pay the consequences of their actions	Disadvantaged persons who would not commit crime if they had other alternatives available to them
Distinctive Characteristics	Hard-line approach that assumes prison to be a central element of crime control	Accepts crime as a fact of life, treats offenders as citizens who have debts to repay, and attempts to return victims to their precrime condition	Institutes programs that reform criminals and release from custody persons who are less likely to commit further criminal acts

correctional practice has been an escalating rate of incarceration (at the same time that the rates of many types of crimes have remained steady or have dropped), the growth of large numbers of dangerously overcrowded prisons (filled in many instances with nonviolent offenders), and skyrocketing public expenditures on correctional facilities (that now directly rival education, medical care, and other public services for funding). Although these present-day concerns are a direct outgrowth of the predominant use of utilitarian punishment and justice practices, and even though present imprisonment practices clearly cannot continue without generating enormous social and economic costs, it would be a mistake to argue now for a complete switch to rehabilitative strategies.

A large and diverse array of people make up America's prison populations. Some offenders are addicted to drugs, some are violent and dangerous, some suffer from a range of personal or social problems, many are poor and undereducated, while still others have simply made bad decisions. Choosing one approach for dealing with this diverse array of criminal offenders is as silly as trying to fit everyone into the same size suit of clothes—it just won't work.

So, what is the answer? Do solutions exist? For correctional treatment to advance, it is necessary to move beyond emotional and one-sided arguments for the strict use of one approach or another. Crime is a complex, multidimensional phenomenon reflecting the actions of diverse populations of people responding to a wide range of social, personal, and situational events. Therefore, in order to be effective, the reality of crime requires that crime control measures become equally diverse and sophisticated. By learning to incorporate the relative strengths and weaknesses of each of the major philosophical approaches to crime control, correctional practices of the future need not suffer from the narrow and often dogmatic practices of the past.

REFERENCES

Bartollas, C. (1985). *Correctional Treatment: Theory and Practice.* Englewood Cliffs, NJ: Prentice Hall.

Beccaria, C. (1764). *On Crimes and Punishment.* Reprint, Indianapolis: Bobbs Merrill, 1963.

Bentham, J. (1789). *A Fragment on Government and an Introduction to the Principles of Morals and Legislation.* W. Harrison (ed.). Oxford, England: Basil Blackwell, 1967.

Fogel, D. (1979). *We Are the Living Proof: The Justice Model for Corrections.* Cincinnati, OH: Anderson.

Jeffery, C.R. (1990). *Criminology: An Interdisciplinary Approach.* Englewood Cliffs, NJ: Prentice Hall.

THREE

Correctional Case Studies
Lived Realities
of Incarcerated Persons

TED ALLEMAN
The Pennsylvania State University

INTRODUCTION

What can we learn from exploring the "lived reality" of incarcerated persons—those levels of human experience in which perception, emotion, and thought manifest themselves into immediate action? By exploring the prison experience of Nathan McCall, this chapter draws us into a firsthand account of conquering the destructive forces of imprisonment. Through Nathan's writings, we can learn about trying to adapt and fit into a prison environment, about carving out a role in order to survive among violent peers, and about learning to gain control over one's life.

When discussing prison or prison issues, the points of view of prisoners are seldom given much, if any, consideration. The images of prisoners are determined primarily by the stigma of crime. Prisoners are seldom thought of as people who have anything constructive to offer or say.

The primary operational objectives of jails and prisons, as evidenced by their policies, practices, and procedures, are oriented toward the security, custody, and control of prisoners. Clearly, jails and prisons are penal institutions, and prisoners are incarcerated (held against their will) for the purpose of punishment. For institutional reasons, prisoners are in many ways depersonalized into objects who simply must be fed, housed, and observed twenty-four hours a day. Because of the crimes for which they have been convicted, prisoners are commonly thought of as different kinds of people who are not worthy of respect and cannot be trusted. Prisoners have to be watched, not understood. Inside the penal institution, approaching prisoners with sympathy, compassion, or friendship can be taken as an infraction of the rules or even a breach of security. Within the purview of corrections, seriously considering what prisoners have to say is objectionable to many and treasonous to some. Even for those who personally hold no particular animosity toward convicted felons, prisoners are not considered to be people who can provide good advice.

But the case can be made that we have much to learn from prisoners. After all, the true effects of correctional policies, practices, and programs become evident in the impact they have on the individual lives of prisoners. How does the experience of incarceration change a person? What are the social consequences of being publicly labeled a felon or an ex-con? Are the "pains of imprisonment" real or imagined? Does the experience of having served time increase or decrease the likelihood of future criminality? Good answers to questions such as these can be arrived at only through a knowledge of prisoners' life experiences. And in many cases, this knowledge can only come from prisoners themselves.

The case study method is used when we need to gain a firsthand account of events, persons, or processes. Data from case studies are generated from the subject's point of view. Instead of observing or measuring social consequences, case study material documents what it is like to live or experience events. Because of its introspective and subjective origins, case study data reflect the subtle, emotive, and personal side of human affairs. Case study material provides insight into what can be termed *lived realities.*

Human actions, at their most basic and impulsive level, are "happenings." In real life (the level of human experience that we refer to here as lived realities), behavior can be so spontaneous that it surprises even the person initiating it. Part of the phenomenon of living, and its mystery, comes about as we experience ourselves. The term *lived reality* refers to this most immediate, sometimes instinctive, level of human experience in which perception, emotion, and thought manifest themselves into immediate action.

Lived realities exist at that level of behavior at which personal being and social force meet. At this level, actions are spontaneous and real. Lived realities are personal events that reflect who we really are as human beings. In that moment of danger, fear, happiness, sadness, surprise, or apprehension, we reveal our true selves by what we do, how we act, and how we react. Lived realities involve as much a response to others as they do a response to ourselves. The phrases "I couldn't help myself" or "it just happened" are commonly used to express the unanticipated or unplanned aspects of our own behavior.

Exploring the realm of lived realities is important to understand people as well as the experiences that have molded and shaped them as human beings. What kind of a person would hold a pistol to a stranger's head and fire if that person didn't hand over a wallet? What kind of a person would batter and perhaps even kill a spouse? What kind of a person would sexually molest a child? What kind of a person would victimize others for personal or financial gain? The brutality, cunning, and deceptiveness of criminal behavior cannot be adequately understood without some knowledge of the lived realities of those who murder, assault, rape, or rob.

Likewise, from the criminal's perspective, how do people come to act as they do? People develop as the result of personal as well as social processes. People have personal histories that reflect an accumulation of decisions and choices they have made as well as the impact of particular events and situations they have experienced. What impact might incarceration in a juvenile facility have on a child? How does one respond to years of physical and/or sexual abuse at the hands of one's parents? What is it like to grow up afraid and unwanted? What is it like to grow up in a neighborhood where you have to fight to survive? People are products of personal as well as social processes, and to know a particular person is to know where he or she comes from and has experienced, as well as how he or she acts.

Insights into lived realities are gained through case study materials such as personal documents, participant observation records, and third-person reports. Case studies provide insight into lived realities as presented from the subject's point of view. Personal documents, life histories, intensive interviews, questionnaires, statistical records, and rating scales are methods commonly used to generate case study material (Franklin and Osborne, 1971). The case study method seeks to understand the experience as well as the rationale behind particular kinds of human events.

Human action, in terms of what people do and where and how they do it, often includes the use of physical objects or materials. Personal articles that reflect lived realities may be spontaneously or intentionally generated. Spontaneous materials appear as human behavior takes place; intentional materials generally arise after the fact. Spontaneous materials provide insight into events themselves; intentional materials reveal the nature of the event from the participant's perspective.

Prisoners who are being stalked by other prisoners, for example, may construct homemade weapons of various sorts and hide them in strategic locations throughout the prison. The weapon (perhaps a razor blade melted into a toothbrush handle) becomes a direct outgrowth of this particular kind of lived reality and serves as an example of spontaneously generated case material, whereas a letter to a friend describing the situation becomes an intentional rendering of the lived reality. The weapon itself (recognizing the bloody gashes that a weapon of this sort would produce) along with the letter (describing the fear, anxiety, and sense of desperation associated with being hunted) supplement each other in arriving at an understanding of the nature of this particular kind of lived reality.

There are many methods that can be used to generate case material. It is important to remember that the one common denominator of all case studies is that the material presented must be from the subject's perspective. Imposing outside judgments or standards on behavior violates sound case study methodology. Case studies of prisoners seek to document the perspectives of those who experience the criminal justice system in a direct and personal way. As the following case study example illustrates, many of the true effects of correctional practices can be revealed only through the personal accounts of those who experience corrections as a lived reality.

PRISON EXPERIENCES OF NATHAN MCCALL

Overview

Nathan McCall is the author of a recently published book by Random House entitled *Makes Me Wanna Holler: A Young Black Man in America.** The full account of what Nathan McCall says concerning his prison experiences requires a careful reading of his book. In this section, we draw upon only a small sample of Nathan McCall's story to illustrate the value of autobiographical material in understanding prison life.

Unlike most, Nathan McCall's account of prison life is a success story. If we are ever to pay more than lip service to the term *corrections* (implying, of course, to correct or change people for the better), we must understand how positive individual change takes place. Nathan's story is one of a young black man who was on the same institutionalized treadmill as thousands of others who spend much of their lives engaging in progressive levels of crime and incarceration. Nathan's story is unique in that he provides a firsthand account of what it takes to pull oneself free of the destructive social and institutional forces of imprisonment.

Nathan McCall's Story

Nathan's story begins with recollections of what it was like for him, a twenty-year-old black man with a twelve-year sentence for armed robbery, to enter a correctional institution knowing that he was going to be there for a long time. The sights, sounds, smells, and stares infiltrated his mind. Nothing was taken for granted, especially the stares.

> When we entered the cellblock, a few inmates glanced up at us, then went back to what they were doing. A few others watched closely in

the way that jail house veterans study newcomers. I learned over time that seasoned inmates can tell a lot about a guy just by how he acts and what he does when he first walks in. They can tell if it's his first time in jail or if he's a regular. They can sense whether he's scared to death or fearless. A new guy's demeanor determines who approaches him, when, and how. (McCall, 1995:150–151)

We should recognize the fact that prison is a different kind of world. In our daily lives we all come across people as well as situations that make us uncomfortable. Coping with unpleasant surroundings and offensive people is a common experience, with avoidance being a principal strategy. But in prison, life takes place in a closed arena: a boxlike environment that contains people who are forced to live in daily contact with one other. Part of the experience of living in prison means facing the unpleasantness of prison life with others whom one may not care for or even like. Not being able to choose, or avoid, one's associates is a principal determinant of the social dynamics of prison.

For those who enter prison without a criminal past or even criminal associates, prison life, at least initially, can be an intense experience. Feelings of fear, apprehension, depression, and loneliness are common. But it is not the same for everyone. For some, like Nathan, going to prison meant seeing old buddies and friends.

Many of the guys were long-time hustlers who knew each other from the streets and had previously done prison time together. On the day I arrived on the yard, a group of the homeboys . . . were standing around waiting eager to hear the latest word from the streets. Some of those guys had been locked up for years and had no idea how much the block had changed since they'd left. We talked for hours and caught up on each other's lives. They offered to help me adjust in any way they could: choice food stolen from the kitchen, specially pressed clothes from the laundry. "anything you need, homeboy, just let us know." I went to my cell that evening riding a cloud. (McCall, 1995:170)

Recognizing the special kinds of social relationships that develop in prison is important to understand coping mechanisms and how the prison experience changes people. As mentioned, social interaction in prison often takes place between people who do not choose to be around one another. It is as difficult to choose those with whom one associates within prison as it is to avoid the daily reminders of one's criminal status. Prisoners, as a group, are often treated as dangerous, untrustworthy, and, in some instances, despicable people. Being thought of and dealt with as a bad person often leads to bad results.

For some, adapting to prison is an alienating and enraging experience. Fighting the system, fighting each other, or fighting reality can lead to rounds of alienation, aggression, or withdrawal. Becoming a lone wolf, or, for those who are less aggressive, less strong, or less treacherous, becoming detached, withdrawn, or even psychopathic is another kind of personal adaptation to prison. Clearly, some leave prison with permanent psychological scars. As a result of their prison experiences, some become more like what they are thought to be—dangerous, antisocial, and withdrawn.

For others, especially those who find it easy to associate with other prisoners, adapting to prison means becoming one of the crowd—becoming more like other prisoners (more like those who will likely commit further crimes and make stays in jails and prisons a repetitive part of their lives). For those like Nathan McCall who desire to break the cycle, having prisoners as good personal friends can be a mixed blessing.

> More than half the guys were old-timers. Some of those cats had so much time to serve that they had no hope of getting out and no incentive to follow rules. They couldn't care less if they got into a fight and made a short-timer miss parole. The hard-nosed among them walked around posturing like they were the baaddest niggers in the world, wearing vicious scowls and repeating Southampton's macho credo: "If you ain't no killer, don't [expletive] with me." The gang scene posed a dilemma for me. Hanging with my homeboys offered guaranteed backup, which practically every inmate needs to live in peace. But it also made it harder for me to break with the past. (McCall, 1995:171)

Breaking with the past is what Nathan McCall's story is all about. Today, Nathan McCall is a reporter for the *Washington Post,* a college graduate (with honors), and a published author. Nathan McCall no longer fits the profile of a criminal. Prison may have been in Nathan McCall's past, but it most certainly is not in his future. How was this considerable turnaround accomplished? What can we learn from Nathan McCall's prison experiences about successful and positive change? The keys, as revealed through his writings, are personal as well as social.

Making a personal commitment to change your life condition is a natural first step. But how does even a desire for change come about? Part of the answer, part of what it takes to break with your past, is to begin to see problems with your present condition. And the difference between who you are and who you want to be often becomes most evident when you have the opportunity to directly compare yourself with others whom you respect or admire. Although good role models may not be plentiful in prison, Nathan McCall was able to find a few. One person who had a significant influence on Nathan was another prisoner named Mo Battle.

Mo Battle taught me how to play chess. I'd never been exposed to the game on the streets. Like him, the other guys in the cellblock who know how to play had learned on previous trips to prison. One day, I made a move to capture a pawn of his and gave Mo Battle an opening to take a valuable piece. He smiled and said, "You can tell a lot about a person by the way he plays chess. People who think small in life tend to devote a lot of energy to capturing pawns, the least valuable pieces on the board. They think they're playin' to win, but they're not. But people who think big tend to go straight for the king or queen, which wins you the game." I never forgot that. Most guys I knew, myself included, had spent their entire lives chasing pawns. The problem was, we thought we were going after kings. Mo Battle also pointed out the racial symbolism in chess. "The white pieces always move first, giving them an immediate advantage over the black pieces, just like in life," he said. The most important thing that Mo Battle taught me was that chess was a game of consequences. "Don't make a move without first weighing the potential consequences," he said, "because if you don't, you have no control over the outcome." I'd never looked at life like that. I had seldom weighed the consequences of anything until *after* I'd done it. I'd do something crazy and then brace myself for the outcome, whatever it happened to be. I had no control over the outcome and no control over my life. When I thought about it, that was a helluva stupid way to live. (McCall, 1995:153–154)

For Nathan, learning to gain control was learning that his life had to have some direction—a sense that he was going someplace where he wanted to be. Again, a positive role model, this time in literary form, was instrumental in teaching him a valuable lesson about life in general and his in particular.

I ran across a quote by Oliver Wendell Holmes—an encouragement to keep me pushing ahead: "I find the great thing in this world is not so much where we stand as in what direction we are moving. To reach the port of heaven, we must sail, sometimes with the wind and sometimes against it—but we must sail, and not drift, nor lie at anchor." It brought a kind of relief to be able to describe my pain. It was like, if I could describe it, it lost some of its power over me.

I was consciously involved in an ongoing search to understand the meaning of my existence, and the searching itself gave me a sense of purpose that I'd never known. (McCall, 1995:181–182)

Besides having a desire for change, or even a restless search for some sort of positive direction, profound individual change requires a change in character. What is personality anyway other than an habitual way of responding and presenting oneself to others? Personality not only molds the way others think of you, it molds the way you think of yourself. Again, literature helped to plant the seed for Nathan McCall's transformation.

> Beyond the short stories I'd read in high school, I hadn't done much reading. One day . . . I picked up a book featuring a black man's picture on the cover. It was titled *Native Son,* and the author was Richard Wright . . . The book's portrait of Bigger captured all those conflicting feelings—restless anger, hopelessness, a tough facade among blacks and a deep-seated fear of whites—that I'd sensed in myself but was unable to express . . . There was one passage that so closely described how I felt that it stunned me. It is a passage where a lawyer is talking to Bigger, who has given up hope and is waiting to die: "You're trying to believe in yourself. And every time you try to find a way to live, your own mind stands in the way. You know why that is? It's because others have said you were bad and they made you live in bad conditions. When a man hears that over and over and looks about him and sees that life is bad, he begins to doubt his own mind. His feelings drag him forward and his mind, full of what others say about him, tells him to go back. The job in getting people to fight and have faith is in making them believe in what life has made them feel, making them feel that their feelings are as good as those of others." After reading that, I sat up in my bunk, buried my face in my hands and wept uncontrollable. I cried so much that I felt relieved. It was like I had been carrying those feelings and holding in my pain for years, keeping it pushed into the back of my mind somewhere. (McCall, 1995:164)

Many who experience significant changes in their lives report going through a period of emotional breakdown. "Hitting bottom" often seems to be a prerequisite for "bouncing back." But reconstructing one's psyche—building a new self by criticizing the old—involves not only seeing one's self in a new light but also altering habitual ways of perceiving and behaving. Again, Nathan McCall found strength through literature.

> I was most attracted to black classics, such as Malcolm X's autobiography. Malcolm's tale helped me understand the devastating effects of self-hatred and introduced me to a universal principle: that if you change your self-perception, you can change your behavior. I concluded that if Malcolm X, who had also gone to prison, could pull his life out of the toilet, then maybe I could too. (McCall, 1995:165)

Seeing himself now in a new light, accompanied by purpose and a sense of direction, Nathan McCall began to reinterpret the world around him. One significant change involved seeing himself as being different from those with whom he had previously identified. Escaping from his past meant leaving behind those who still lived the old life—those who were still trapped by the social and emotional entanglements that made them grist for the incarceration mill.

> In those moments when they weren't profiling with their bodies, some of my tough-acting homies would stop by my perch on the yard or in my cell to ask, "What you readin?" I sensed they wanted to improve themselves but didn't want their other homies to see them, because self-improvement was not a macho thing. They held many misguided ideas about manhood. (McCall, 1995:208)

The recognition that much of the behavior of his homies was based on fear, not toughness, led him to see them differently than he had previously. Being aware that they were operating from an unstable position "helped me see my homies and the other toughs at Southampton as they were (and as I had been): streetwise, pseudo baad-asses who were really frightened boys, bluffing, trying to mask their fear of the world behind muscular frames" (McCall, 1995:208).

Equipped with a new self-image, a sense of purpose, and the knowledge that prison and all that it represented was not for him, Nathan was ready to face the parole board and then proceed with the rest of his life. Nathan's story is not unique, but, unfortunately, it is also not typical. What can be learned about positive, productive change from Nathan's story?

Nathan's story is one of self-reliance, self-fortitude, and self-knowledge. This is important to point out because clearly it was not the system that induced or even encouraged Nathan to change. The fact is that Nathan changed in spite of the system. If he had been content, like most of those sharing his social condition, to simply adapt to prison and act as he was expected to act—as a convicted felon—then he, like most who live the prison experience, probably would not have made it. Using the large numbers of prisoners who recidivate soon after release from prison as a gauge, Nathan's story is one of system failure as much as it is one of personal success.

In corrections, we often hear it said that if people are going to change, they must want to change. The implicit meaning of this phrase is that change is the primary responsibility of the individual, not the system. But isn't this really a cop out, merely a way for correctional staff to do what is easy (simply process, house, and guard) and avoid what takes some effort and caring?

Can it be that high rates of recidivism are natural by-products of an environment in which human initiative and drive are stymied? In what ways can correctional environments be reconstructed to nurture and encourage positive change? What can be done to make personal success, rather than recidivism, characteristic of correctional systems? Stories like Nathan's provide evidence that individual productive change is possible.

A challenge of corrections is to identify ways in which the system can identify, encourage, and support those who wish to break with their criminal past.

REFERENCES

Franklin, B.J. and Osborne, H.W. (eds.) (1971). *Research Methods: Issues and Insights.* Belmont, CA: Wadsworth.

McCall, N. (1995). *Makes Me Wanna Holler: A Young Black Man in America.* New York: Random House.

FOUR

Myth Versus Reality

The Politics of Crime and Punishment and Its Impact on Correctional Administration in the 1990s

JOSEPH D. LEHMAN
Washington (State) Department of Corrections

LEE ANN S. LABECKI
Pennsylvania Department of Correction

INTRODUCTION

Beginning in the 1980s and continuing in the 1990s, the policies and laws that define correctional systems, including who is incarcerated, have moved away from providing frameworks for judicial discretion to establishing mandates based on the assessment of limited criteria imposed on broad categories of crimes and offenders. This chapter examines the role of crime policy and its intended and unintended consequences on crime, punishment, and corrections. Specific issues considered include the current state of corrections; the role of the media, the public, and politicians in shaping crime policy and sentencing practices; and the impact of these policies on correctional systems. The chapter concludes with a discussion of the changing role of correctional administrators, who are expected to act as policy makers and media managers in addition to the traditional roles of facility manager and program implementor.

THE CHALLENGES OF CRIMINAL JUSTICE POLICY AND CORRECTIONAL ADMINISTRATION IN THE 1980S AND BEYOND

The nexus between policy and practice within corrections changed significantly during the 1980s. The policies and laws that define the parameters for corrections systems, including who is incarcerated, have moved away from providing frameworks for judicial discretion to establishing mandates based on the assessment of limited criteria imposed on broad categories of crimes and offenders. With this shift toward policy-based justice, consideration of the individual behavior and characteristics of the offender has been overshadowed by ideology and politics. For the most part, however, the role of policy and its intended and unintended consequences remains largely unexamined.

In terms of our correctional systems, the criminal justice policies of the 1980s resulted in unprecedented changes in our correctional populations. From 1980 to 1990, the U.S. Department of Justice reported that the number of inmates in state and federal prisons increased by 129 percent, from 329,821 in 1980 to 755,425 in 1990 (see Figure 4.1). Furthermore, the National Council on Crime and Delinquency projects that this population

FIGURE 4.1 State correctional populations in the United States—fifty year population overview, 1940 to 1990. (*Source:* U.S. Department of Justice.)

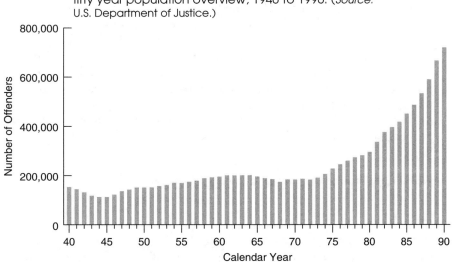

will approach 1 million by 1994—representing an increase of more than 200 percent in just fourteen years (Clark Foundation, 1992:3). Forecasters project that the offender population growth is likely to continue for the foreseeable future.

Recognizing that criminal justice policy has undertaken a dramatic transformation during the last ten to fifteen years, it is compelling to consider the catalysts for such change. This chapter provides the reader with a broad prospectus on the current state of affairs in criminal justice, examining how we have arrived at our current state of affairs. Questions addressed include, What are the factors that shaped and are shaping criminal justice policy in the 1980s and 1990s? What role do the media, public opinion, and politicians play in shaping this policy? Is this policy grounded in fact or fiction? What are the impacts of these policies on correctional administration? And finally, what lies ahead?

Correctional Paradigms

When considering the status of criminal justice policies and correctional systems today, it is useful to first revisit the four somewhat divergent goals of incarceration: retribution, deterrence, incapacitation, and rehabilitation. Whether or not they are realized by their various proponents, criminal justice policies tend to be based on one or more of these philosophies. At the one extreme of the dichotomy is the incapacitation doctrine, which asserts that prisons are of value in that they remove offenders from society. The incapacitative position is closely followed by the retributive theory, which asserts that incarceration is a just deserts policy for the commission of serious offenses. Advocates of the deterrence theory suggest that incarceration serves a larger purpose by not only discouraging the future criminality of the individual offender but also by dissuading criminal behavior of would-be offenders. Finally, at the other extreme of the dichotomy, the rehabilitative theory holds that individuals can be changed through effective programming so that they can successfully reintegrate into their communities upon release. In general, as with most social programs, the philosophies that shape public policy tend to swing like a pendulum somewhere between the philosophical extremes. These philosophies of incarceration serve as the primary basis on which we develop an individual or societal crime ideology.

PUBLIC POLICY: FROM WHENCE DOES IT COME?

An individual's opinion about crime and punishment is largely attributable to actual or vicarious experiences, real or imagined, and a distilling process that naturally takes place as a result of casual conversations among family, friends, and co-workers. Except for those who as a matter of their vocation or avocation study the phenomenon of crime, this informal formation of crime ideology—our convictions about how we should deal with criminals—tends to be the norm rather than the exception.

One important difference between the current and previous decades emerges from the quantity and quality of information that we receive about crime today—the experiences broadcasted to us on a daily basis by the media. It is not simply a matter of what is reported; rather the difference is more a matter of the rapidity and the graphic format by which we are informed about crime. Improvements in communication and information technologies ensure that we are no longer insulated from tragic events by virtue of geography and time. We learn about tragic incidents almost instantaneously. Equally important, we are told about them through a variety of communication media. As noted by Berman (1987), criminal justice programming accounted for nearly 80 percent of all television programming during the mid-1980s. In large part, the gatekeepers of these communications are the media and the politicians. The public, in turn, acts as the audience that processes the information and issues edicts for change. As such, all three parties—the media, the politicians, and the public—are integrally linked together in a symbiotic relationship that has spurred the crime policies of the 1980s and 1990s.

Crime Policy Catalysts

In reviewing the events of the last quarter of this century, it is apparent that the "get tough" crime policy frenzy emerged from the interactive influences of the media, the public, and the politicians. As has been suggested by noted criminologist Dr. Albert Blumstein of Carnegie Mellon University, it is noteworthy that the intense focus on the development of a crime strategy by these three players has occurred at a time when the threats from our external adversaries have diminished and the nation's economic outlook has improved (Blumstein, 1993). Considering the significant implications of recent crime policies on the utilization of public resources, it is important to consider the role that each catalyst plays in the formation of these public policies on crime (see Figure 4.2).

The Media.   The role of the media in influencing public opinion and public policy has long been debated. In fact, in 1671, Milton noted that "Evil news ride post, while good news baits" (Ericson, 1991:239). Today, the media continues to play a prominent role in our everyday lives. Zucker (1978:239) noted that "People today live in two worlds: a real world and a media world . . . [with] the first limited by direct experience [and] the second . . . bounded by the decisions of editors and producers." After fifty years of study, researchers have found that the sheer "repetitiveness and

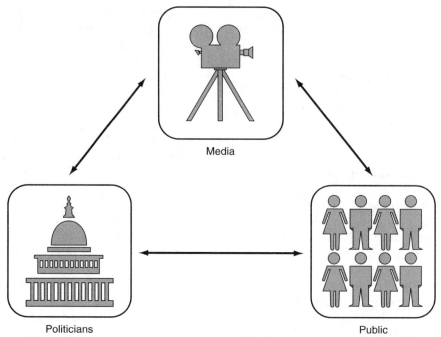

FIGURE 4.2 Setting crime policy in the 1990s.

pervasiveness" of the media's coverage of crime can shape public opinion, especially when individuals have few other information sources and a limited knowledge of the subject matter.

There is little doubt that the media, in written and electronic form, is the public's primary source of crime information: In 1982, "94 percent of U.S. residents cited the news media as their most important source of information" (Roberts, 1992:116). Reliance on media for information would be a lesser concern if the information accurately reflected the status of crime in the United States. Unfortunately, researchers have found that the media seeks to shape as much as to reflect the public's perception of crime by (1) overrepresenting the frequency of violent or "sensational" crimes and (2) reducing complex social problems to simple causes (e.g., mental health of client, past leniency from the criminal justice system) (Roberts, 1992). This assertion is supported by Liska and Baccaglini's (1990) research on media coverage, which found that while homicides accounted for less than one-half of 1 percent of all index crimes, they accounted for 30 percent of written media coverage of crime issues. Similarly, the media's pronouncement of a crime wave in late 1993 and early 1994, measured in the frequency of reports on national television news broadcasts addressing crime, is suspect when compared with the relatively stable rate of crime in this country during that period. As noted by the *Washington Post,* "at a time when the nation's overall crime rate remains essentially unchanged, the three network evening newscasts doubled their coverage of crime and violence around the country [in 1993]" ("Networks," 1994). Lichter, co-director of the Center for Media and Public Affairs, offered further support for this position, noting that research on crime and media demonstrates, "People's fear of crime doesn't come from looking over their shoulders. It comes from looking at their television screens" ("Networks," 1994).

Research on the impact of media coverage and public opinion has shown that public attitudes and external information do not act totally independent of each other—that is, individuals selectively retain that information that is consistent with their existing personal ideologies and beliefs (Lord, Ross, and Lepper, 1979). Furthermore, social psychologists have demonstrated that individuals are limited by other cognitive biases, including a tendency to overgeneralize the importance of a single event to the total frequency of that event and to recall unusual rather than common events (Tversky and Kahneman, 1973). The cumulative effect of these biases is that the public develops a skewed perspective of crime from media depictions because of the nature of the reporting as well as its own cognitive limitations.

In general, the impact of media on public opinion has been considered in terms of the public's ranking of the importance of crime as a social issue, attitudes on crime, and influence on policy development. At a minimum, social science researchers have found a correlation between media coverage and public opinion on crime. For example, Page, Shapiro, and Dempsey (1987) found that short and moderate term shifts in public opinion could be documented following pro/con coverage on a specific crime topic. Besides simply swaying public opinion, media research has shown that "heavy crime show viewing promotes . . . heightened support for increased social control," "tabloid-style coverage creates the greatest support for harsher sentences," and "newspaper stories about serious crimes cause subjects to be more punitive in sentencing recommendations" (Surette, 1992:98). Furthermore, research has shown differential impacts of media format on public opinion, as written media influences factual knowledge bases while electronic media influences fear and emotion (O'Keefe and Reid, 1990).

The Public

The second corner of the crime ideology triangle is the public. According to various public opinion polls, the public is outraged with the crime problem and is demanding more punitive sanctioning of offenders (Lacayo, 1994). In response to this outcry, the media has increased coverage of crime because "crime sells," and politicians have been scrambling to appear tough on crime by selecting variations of the incapacitation and retribution themes from the menu of available crime rationales. The "get tough" rationale has been clearly manifested in the rush of politicians to introduce and enact legislation related to the current crime-fighting slogans. Interestingly, however, while public officials have eagerly attempted to satisfy the public's perceived call for a retributive get tough agenda on crime, it is worthwhile to consider the public's familiarity with and knowledge about crime and the criminal justice system.

An assessment of the public's knowledge about the criminal justice system, in general, and crime, specifically, reveals that the public's factual knowledge base of crime is suspect. When queried as to the workings of the criminal justice system, the public revealed widespread ignorance about law enforcement, sentencing, corrections, and probation/parole processes. Additionally, research has shown that the public consistently overestimates the frequency of crime, victimizations, total crimes committed, recidivism rates, and so on (Roberts, 1992:119).

Aside from overestimating the frequency of crime, researchers have found that the public formulates its estimation of future crime trends based on past experience. For example, "although crime rates have fluctuated over the past fifty years, people invariably respond . . . that crime rates are increasing . . . this is true when crime rates were increasing as well as during periods when police reports and victimization surveys indicated no change or even declines in crime rates" (Roberts, 1992:110). Roberts concluded that public opinion on crime is largely shaped by familiarity with previous trends and media coverage rather than actual crime trends.

The Politicians

Despite the public's apparent limited knowledge of the criminal justice system and crime trends, politicians rely heavily on public opinion polls in developing legislative agendas. In large part, their reliance on public opinion reflects a recognition that they are elected to represent the interests of their constituents. According to Roberts, "politicians' beliefs about the nature of public opinion are probably derived from . . . shared conventional wisdom, the perception of an association between electoral success and support for repressive criminal justice policies, and the publication of survey findings that seem to demonstrate public support for harsher sentencing" (Roberts, 1992:101). Furthermore, public opinion on crime has been shown to be critical to the future success of politicians, as it affects political campaigns, decisions in individual cases, and criminal justice policy.

Although it is clear that politicians rely heavily on public opinion in establishing their public policy agendas, it is less clear that politicians are receiving an accurate picture of public opinion. This assertion receives credence from (1) the public's unfamiliarity with criminal justice issues; (2) problems with public opinion surveys that seek to measure opinion rather than knowledge and that are often characterized by unrepresentative samples, poorly worded questions, and nondifferentiation of different offender types; and (3) the media's skewed portrayal of crime trends (Roberts, 1992:116–129). In fact, recent efforts by public opinion researchers have demonstrated that the public can and does recognize the merits of different sanctions for different offenders when presented with actual offender scenarios as well as descriptions of the available criminal justice sanctions (Public Agenda Foundation, 1993).

Perhaps more problematic than the politicians' reliance on public/media-driven policy is the public's often pervasive ignorance of legislative reforms once enacted. In 1990, Schroot and Knowles found that despite the passage of legislation to increase sentences for drug offenders that emerged from a public call for more severe sentences, a survey of state residents following legislative enactment found that 89 percent were unaware that changes had been implemented. Clearly, "the gap between legislative reform and public awareness of the reforms is counterproductive [since] legislation is frequently introduced for instrumental purposes related to the attitudes and behavior of the public" (Roberts, 1992:116). The media contributes to this gap by focusing news stories on the occurrences of crime rather than on depositions or legislative remedies. Unfortunately, public familiarity with the intent and impact of legislative initiatives is critical to the success of crime policies, especially policies grounded in a deterrence rationale that seeks to deter future criminality through evoking public awareness and fear in the proposed sanctions for committing the offense.

Aside from the impact of public opinion on policy development, researchers have also considered the impact of the media on the formation of public ideologies of crime as represented by public policies. Clearly, while politicians have access to factual accounts of crime trends, they too often rely on media coverage to identify their next legislative initiative. Examples include the establishment of the "guilty but mentally ill" plea following John Hinckley's assassination attempt on President Reagan and the "drug war" frenzy of the 1980s and early 1990s (Surette, 1992:99). This phenomenon was evidenced with the "three strikes and you're out" crusade following the Polly Klaas kidnapping and murder in California in 1994. In each instance, the media's depiction of the incident, its frequency, brutality, and inequity propelled the public to demand and the politicians to develop specific legislative and programmatic solutions to avert future occurrences of these events. Unfortunately, as has been so clearly articulated by Dr. Albert Blumstein, the current legislative flurry with regard to the "three strikes, you're out" legislation represents "the greatest wave of legislative mass hysteria since Senator Joe McCarthy frightened so many [politicians and residents]" in the 1950s ("Klaas Murder," 1994:B-1).

THE OUTCOME: THE POLITICALIZATION OF OUR SENTENCING POLICIES

The end result of the politicians' retributive get tough crime policies and the accompanying reliance on incapacitation as the most important crime control tool has been the politicalization of the crime problem. Unfortunately, this political solution to the crime problem is founded on a set of ideological beliefs that, if left unchallenged, may well bankrupt state and local governments without significantly or measurably impacting crime.

This crime hysteria will be difficult to dismantle given the efforts by the media and politicians to elevate the crime problem to new political heights. In the late 1970s, crime emerged as a prominent edifice in the political landscape with the declaration of several successive wars against this internal enemy. As Blumstein (1993) observed, getting tough on criminals was an easy way to respond to the concerns of the public and in the process get elected. Politicians were as much at home with "lock them up and throw away the key" rhetoric as they were with "apple pie," particularly since "motherhood" and the structure of the family was now up for debate.

In their effort to address the crime problem, politicians gained control over the sentencing process by shifting sentencing responsibility from judges to themselves and the prosecutors via legislation. In essence, therefore, legislators have donned judicial robes in an effort to control more directly who goes to prison and for how long. Specifically, with the politicalization of crime in the last quarter of this century, the responsibility for sentencing has been moved from the judiciary to the legislator. Whereas judicial-based sentencing establishes a system of individual justice, legislative or policy-based sentencing establishes mandates for groups of individuals. Under an individualized justice structure, although framed by limits defined by statutes or guidelines, judges issue discretionary decisions based on a consideration of all available information about the offender, the crime and its impact on the victim, and the need to effect change in the offender and/or impose sufficient controls over his or her behavior.

Policy-based sentencing, conversely, formats restricted judicial discretion through the enactment of mandatory sentencing statutes or guidelines. Sentences are imposed with little or no discretion on the part of the judge using limited criteria such as the crime of conviction and prior record. With the emergence of policy-based sentencing structures, we have moved away from utilizing sentencing as a means to administer justice befitting the crime and offender to sentencing policies grounded in overgeneralized, broad-based assumptions about the effectiveness of incarceration as a crime-control strategy.

Politicians found prosecutors to be ready allies for this shift in sentencing discretion. Prosecutors recognized that if legislatures began to restrict judicial sentencing authority, prosecutorial discretion would be enhanced through the plea bargaining and charge selection processes. The judiciary's more visible sentencing decisions became a common target of the politically active, and discretion exercised as low-visibility transactions occurring behind closed doors between attorneys slowly replaced them. Additionally, the victim advocacy groups, long estranged by the criminal justice process, and particularly by corrections, emerged as a strong, politically active constituency. Their success was largely attributable to their capacity to communicate a powerful emotional message about the effects of violence perpetrated against themselves and their families. Prosecutors and other elected officials who, along with the public, believe that more criminals should be incarcerated have made incapacitation the primary agenda, and in so doing, they have seized the opportunity to join with the victims' groups to advance their political agendas and careers. The result is the drafting of revised crime legislation calling for increased retribution via the imposition of longer, more punitive prison sentences.

The problem that has emerged from this shift toward opinion-based crime strategies is that we have so politicized the policies defining how we respond to crime that our sentencing policies are being shaped by the politics and emotion of the moment. As a result, crime policies are more frequently being grounded in ideology rather than in the methods that correctional researchers and administrators have demonstrated to offer effective correctional strategies. In recent years, our ideological response to crime in this country emerged as an oversimplified proposition—"build more prisons or put up with more crime."

During the 1980s, criminal justice officials have frequently been confronted by an emotional rather than a factual review of the events surrounding the crime problem. Unfortunately, the public responds to and is often influenced by this emotionalism, and it in turn spurs the media and public officials to further confront the crime problem and the need for systematic reform.

The current debate on the merits of "three time loser" legislation demonstrates the chain of events that can result from the nation's emotionalism and the media's reporting of the precipitating crimes ("Klaas Murder," 1994). The Polly Klaas murder case was clearly a tragic, brutal murder of a young child by a career criminal who, by anyone's account, should not have been out of prison. The electronic media's focus on the tragedy itself and attempt to place blame usually focuses attention on the criminal justice system's failure to exercise discretion. Based on simplistic notions of the criminal justice system and how it operates, the media was quick to target for blame the justice system's errors of judgment and implementation. In doing so, however, the media failed to consider flaws in the policy restraints already imposed by the legislature on judicial and corrections officials. In California, the legislature eliminated the parole releasing authority, instead choosing to address prison crowding with a mandated increase in good time. This decision resulted in the early release of inmates without the benefit of a release screen for the dangerous and violent offender. Thus in the Polly Klaas case, the offender Allen Davis was reviewed, "for parole six times during [his last term before the Klaas murder], and the board rejected him as unfit each time. But since the law dictated that he serve no more than six years, he was released on March 4, 1982" ("Klaas Murder," 1994). Clearly the California legislature had a significant role in creating the circumstance by which this career criminal was released to the streets. The media's inability to understand and/or communicate the complexity of the system or problem misinformed the public and elected officials, who in turn reacted by further restricting discretion through the enactment of "three strikes and you're out" legislation. Thus, with their proposed solution, in all likelihood they have compounded the problem that they sought to correct.

The fiscal costs of this politicalization of the Polly Klaas murder are punctuated by the recent estimate that the passage of the "three strikes and you're out" proposal in California will result in the incarceration of nearly 100,000 additional offenders and the eventual need for thirty-two new prisons at a cost of $21 billion over the next thirty years ("Three Strikes," 1994). As the inevitable fiscal crisis driven by these events approaches, California politicians will have to seek ways of reducing crowding in their system. As they have done in the past, they will look at "back door" processes to release offenders rather than acknowledge their role in creating or, at a minimum, exacerbating the problem. Elected officials in California, as elsewhere, cannot under any circumstances appear to be "soft on crime." Their continuing and incremental fine tuning of the release mechanisms may suffice for a time, at least until the next inevitable tragic event.

Regardless of what factors are fueling the fires of the current crime ideology, the fact remains that the predominant ideological proposition that fashioned our criminal justice policies in the late 1980s and early 1990s was "get tough," and if that didn't work "get tougher." The public, politicians, and to a large extent the media are fixated on the notion that the only way to address the crime problem is to arrest and incarcerate more and more offenders.

THE MYSTERY OF THE BOTTOM LINE: MYTH VERSUS FACT

Austin and Irwin (1990), in their publication entitled "Who Goes to Prison?," suggest that the substantial increases in prison population levels appear to have emerged from the assumption by the public, the media, and politicians that a majority of offenders are dangerous and, as such, should serve lengthy prison terms. Interestingly, the national crime statistics do not support this assumption: 65 percent of offenders are sentenced to prison for property, drug, and public disorder crimes rather than for violent index crimes (e.g., murder, rape, robbery, aggravated assault), and an additional 15 percent of all offenders are admitted to prison secondary to violating the conditions of their parole plan rather than for commission of an additional criminal offense (Austin and Irwin, 1990:2). Austin and Irwin (1990) further observe that "the public's fear of street crime has set off an unprecedented imprisonment binge . . . [subsequent to the] substantial increase in the major 'index' crimes (e.g., homicides, assaults, robberies, thefts, and rapes) reported to police from 1966 through 1974." Since 1974, however, while the crime rate has leveled off, the public belief that crime is increasing has not subsided (Austin and Irwin, 1990:2).

Unfortunately, the politicalization of the crime problem appears to have significantly fueled this "flawed" belief. The "get tough" on crime movement has led to attempts to equate the increased use of incarceration as a criminal justice system sanction with the resolution or, at a minimum, a reduction of the crime problem. In an attempt to convince the public that the crime issue is being addressed, federal criminal justice officials and other groups supporting the retributive get tough crime ideology have attempted to demonstrate that "there is a direct correlation between crime and incarceration rates, and the key to reducing crime is to put criminals in jail and keep them there for the full term of their sentences" ("Every Ten," 1994). This position, although based in ideology, rings true in a simplistic way to frustrated public who, similar to its elected officials, seems to be at a loss as to what to do about the crime problem. Although lip service is given to the social ills of the family, community, and economy that appear to underlie the crime problem, "social ills" are more impervious to ready-made quick fixes, and so we turn back to the individual and the notion that fear invoked as a result of either the threat of or actual punishment is somehow going to reduce the level of crime.

In a recent article entitled "Lessons from the Eighties: Incarceration Works," Block and Twist (1994) decry the changes that have occurred in America that have led to the violence that victimizes so many Americans. Specifically, the authors state that the crime problem has resulted from a breakdown in family and religious institutions. Yet the solution offered by the authors with respect to this violence—to build more prisons—does little to address declining American values. Instead, the authors' assertion that prisons will solve the values problem suggests that America's founding fathers sought life, liberty, and the pursuit of prison space. For public officials facing decreasing monies to support various social programs, the flaws in this position are becoming evident, and a recognition is emerging that the building and operation of additional correctional facilities divert the pool of public resources from schools, social welfare programs, and families—the very institutions that are the primary transmitters of societal values.

Aside from their position that prisons are the answer to the crime problem, the Block and Twist article illustrates how data presentations can be used to shape public opinion. As observed by The Sentencing Project (1994), a Washington-based think tank on criminal justice policy issues, in a recent publication entitled "Did the Growth of Imprisonment During the 1980s Work?," the Block and Twist article attempts to persuade the reader to assume a direct relationship between an increase in incarceration and a decrease in crime rate by creating a graph with disparate scales that create abnormal slopes. The end result is a graph that creates the illusion of a correlation and implied causal relationship that does not, in fact, exist. Second, the article selected offense groups consistent with its arguments rather than utilizing standardized offense categorizations as defined by the Bureau of Justice Statistics and the FBI (e.g., including narcotic drug law offenses in the violent crime category).

Throughout the country, the public, the media, and the politicians have increasingly relied on incarceration as the only seemingly viable solution to all crime problems. This reliance is based on an assumption that a singular response to crime—incarceration—can differentially impact all offenders and all crimes in the same manner. The nation's current approach to the drug offender clearly illustrates the flaws in this ideology. As suggested by Blumstein ("Don't Lock," 1993), offering incapacitation as the primary solution to the drug problem fails to acknowledge the market economy basis of drugs. Unlike the direct impact on crime realized by removing repeat violent offenders from the streets, the mandatory detention of all or most drug offenders does not impact crime in the same way. As we incarcerate one drug trafficker, the demand in the marketplace results in others being recruited into that distribution system ("Don't Lock," 1993).

Although the get tough ideology is compelling, the legitimacy of this punishment/reduced crime claim has been questioned by a number of criminologists and correctional administrators. One such opposing view emerged from a review of the relationship between incarceration and crime rates conducted by Steffensmeier (1992). After reviewing the crime rates as adjusted for the differential criminality of specific age cohorts, the study found that the unprecedented growth of prison and jail populations has not led to the expected decrease in the violent crime rate. Without a significant direct relationship between incarceration and crime rates, and recognizing the tremendous costs associated with incarceration, the study suggests that "the public should ask and deserves to be told what returns they are getting on their investments, [as] using incarceration as the primary sanction for the bulk of the offenders does not appear to be justified" (Steffensmeier, 1992:7). The study concludes that "given what criminologists do know about [the success of various criminal control sanctions (e.g., incarceration, probation, parole) perhaps] more cost-effective punishments such as intermediate sanctions or community restitution appear suitable for many non-violent offenders who disproportionately populate [our] prisons and jails" (Steffensmeier, 1992:8).

Despite the demonstrated faults in the current crime control ideology, the incapacitative model of crime control continues to reign, and prisons are seen to provide the ultimate form of punishment, short of death, that will make the miscreants change their ways. Unfortunately, this belief has placed significant pressures on correctional systems and administrators.

THE CHALLENGES OF TODAY'S
CORRECTIONAL SYSTEMS

One way to determine the impact of get tough crime politics and policies is to examine the impact that these policies have had on correctional systems and how we administer these systems. In particular, we might regard the number of individuals who are locked up as an outcome measure against which we can compare the incidence or rate of crime and the public's reaction to crime. This assertion can be illustrated by reviewing data on the status of our prison system during the 1980s and early 1990s.

There is little question that the current criminal justice policy that favors incarceration as the primary means of criminal sanctioning and offender control has resulted in the unrivaled growth in the offender population and prison overcrowding throughout the United States. Nevertheless, the recent explosion in the incarcerated population has not occurred in isolation. As noted by the National Council on Crime and Delinquency (Austin, 1991), the incarceration growth has paralleled similar growth during the 1980s in the utilization of all forms of criminal justice sanctions (including incarceration in state and county prisons and jails and community-based sanctions). Furthermore, the observed pace of growth in the use of these sanctions clearly exceeded that which was projected based on traditional offender population indices (e.g., crime-prone-age population, index crime, and arrest rates). From 1980 to 1990, reported use of probation, jail, prison, and parole sanctions for offenders increased nationally by 139, 146, 134, and 141 percent, respectively. These gains can be compared to the rather scant increases in the indices traditionally acknowledged to accurately predict the offender population levels: On a national basis, adult crime-prone-age population, adult arrests, and reported index crimes increased by 13, 34, and 8 percent, respectively, from 1980 to 1990 (see Figure 4.3) (Austin, 1991).

NCCD suggests that "the dramatic increase in the use of correctional control is neither explained by higher crime rates nor arrests, both of which only increased by 5 percent between 1980 to 1988" (Austin, 1991:2). These data clearly suggest that the significant increases observed in all forms of criminal sanctions—prisons, jails, probation, and parole—are more reflective of the impact of the government's public policy in response to the public's call for "get tough on crime" strategies than they are of increased criminality (Austin, 1991). Unfortunately, the reliance on criminal justice sanctions in the 1980s placed increasing numbers of this country's citizens under the control of the criminal justice system. According to a report prepared by the Bureau of Justice Statistics, "on any given day last year [1993] an estimated one in every 138 adult women and one in every 22 adult men were under the care, custody, and control of a corrections agency. Since 1980 probation and parole populations have

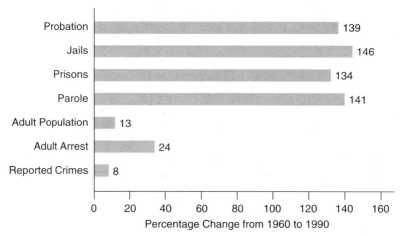

FIGURE 4.3 Overview of United States criminal justice system as compared to traditional offender population indices, 1960 versus 1990. (*Source:* National Council on Crime and Delinquency, 1990.)

grown by 163 percent, jails and prisons by 172 percent" ("Probation and Parole," 1994).

As a natural extension of the "lock them up" mentality that has swept the United States in recent years, the utilization of existing federal, state, and county criminal justice programs has outstripped the systems' capacities. The most visible example of overutilization has emerged in correctional facilities that have been required to house more and more offenders in a limited number of cells. These unrivaled increases have produced unprecedented overcrowding levels at federal, state, and county levels. Unfortunately, these levels of overcrowding are anticipated to continue for the foreseeable future. As noted by the Edna McConnell Clark Foundation, "most states have dealt with the [unprecedented] growth by building more prisons" (Clark Foundation, 1992:3). This assertion is supported by the Criminal Justice Institute, which found that in 1991 nearly 88,000 beds were currently under construction and more than 110,000 beds were in planning stages in January 1991 (Camp and Camp, 1991:41).

With the onset of this prison boom, costs associated with correctional operations have skyrocketed. The National Conference of State Legislators reports that spending increases for correctional services are twice the level of inflation, and between 1980 and 1988, state spending per $100 of personal income for corrections increased faster than any other spending category. Second, the National Conference of State Legislators has reported that spending on correctional programming has increased at a far more rapid rate than has funding for other service agencies (Yondorf and Warnock, 1989).

The Changing Roles of Correctional Administrators

Although there are thousands of correctional systems at national, state, and county levels, each with its own unique profile, these systems are also comparable in many respects. Certainly there are similarities in the forces that shape and define the activities that correctional agencies perform on a daily basis. Consistent with their role in the criminal justice system, correctional administrators have little direct up-front control over the number or type of offenders they receive into their facilities. The present growth in the offender population has required correctional administrators to further strain already crowded institutions to accommodate the increasing populations and to control appropriately, without incident, these populations once received.

There is little doubt that correctional administration has become increasingly complex as correctional populations and budgets have grown exponentially since 1980. This complexity has been further aggravated by the fiscal shortfalls of the last two decades, as correctional administrators have been asked to manage more and more offenders while staffing and facility capacity levels have failed to keep pace with the population growth. The unprecedented offender population growth has presented a number of challenges to correctional administrators, but the challenges they face as a result of budget shortfalls and inmate risk management have always existed. Simply stated, they are nothing new.

What is new is the fact that the politicalization of crime and punishment now prevalent in sentencing policy is beginning to impact the administration of day-to-day prison activities. More and more correctional administrators are recognizing that the politicians' get tough rhetoric is not going to stop with notions about who should go to prison and for how long. Beginning with the debate in Congress over banning weight lifting in prisons and eliminating education programs supported by federal Pell Grants, elected officials will not be reluctant to micromanage corrections, in particular the inmates' living conditions. The impact of the crime policy changes of the 1980s and 1990s and the increasing trend of micromanagement of correctional systems by politicians have created considerable challenges for correctional administrators.

In today's political environment, correctional administrators must be leaders in the policy arena as well as managers of the internal workings of their agencies. To realize this charge, correctional administrators must make a paradigm shift not only in how they see the system but also in how they see their roles. When the system was constructed and operated on the basis of justice meted out to individuals, the role of the correctional administrator was appropriately one of implementing programs for sentenced offenders. Correctional administrators were managing, in a positive and constructive manner, programs intended to control, rehabilitate, and punish the offender. Furthermore, there was a much closer relationship between the development and implementation of programs and sentencing practices of judges. Both correctional administrators/practitioners and judges were heavily invested in matching the needs of offenders, the demands of justice, and the capacity of prison programs to meet the requirements of individual cases. With the imposition of legislatively driven sentencing policy, this link was weakened. Correctional administrators were left with burgeoning prisons with little capacity to influence through the development of programs. In many respects, correctional administrators became the victims of a political process of which they had little understanding and still less patience.

PRISON OVERCROWDING

Without question, the most significant management challenge that correctional administrators have had to address in the 1980s and early 1990s has been that of prison overcrowding. Overcrowding has affected nearly every state in the country, and, in 1992, state correctional systems housed inmates at 154 percent of their rated facility capacity (Camp and Camp, 1993). The impact of such overcrowding has been well documented (South Carolina Department of Corrections, 1973; Paulus, McCain, and Cox, 1975; Jayewardene, McKay, and McKay, 1976; Paulus, McCain, and Cox, 1978; Farrington and Nuttall, 1980; American Correctional Association, 1981; Ekland-Olson, Barrick, and Cohen, 1983; Cox, Paulus, and McCain, 1984; Ellis, 1984; Anderson and Pettigrew, 1985; Gaes, 1985; Gaes and McGuire, 1985; Toch, 1985; Ruback, Carr, and Hopper, 1986; Canter, 1987; Kratcoski, 1988; Leger, 1988; Weiner and Keys, 1988; and Martin and Zimmerman, 1990). Crowding affects both staff working conditions as well as inmate living conditions in cells and dormitories; it limits recreation, work, and educational opportunities; and it creates difficult management problems for correctional administrators. Furthermore, as resources become increasingly strained and activities are limited, tensions between inmates and among inmates and staff are heightened and confrontations often result. These events, in turn, can result in a decrease in staff and inmate morale, staff turnover, and an erosion of institutional control. Moreover, these conditions threaten the ability of the correctional system to ensure public safety and to effect postrelease behavior through the provision of programs to the offender. The eventual outcome of this type of scenario has been vividly evidenced by the devastation and tragedy of various prison disturbances in recent years (e.g., New Mexico State Prison, 1980; Camp Hill, Pennsylvania, 1989; Montana State Penitentiary, 1991; and Lucasville, Ohio, 1993).

Aside from the specter of potential institutional riots and disturbances, widespread overcrowding has led to predictable results: Thirty-four state correctional systems are reportedly under total or partial court order, twenty-six had court imposed population caps, and nineteen had court monitors overseeing prison operations (Camp and Camp, 1993). Furthermore, this type of court intervention is expensive, as the costs of prison masters, attorney fees, and institutional staff time spent in assuring court compliance must be born by the affected jurisdiction. Equally important, court intervention removes the management and control of facilities and systems from the responsible jurisdiction or agency.

CHANGING OFFENDER PROFILES

The correctional policies of the 1980s and 1990s have not only influenced the number of offenders entering our prison systems, the levels of overcrowding, and the increased risk of institutional violence; they have also significantly impacted the profile of those offenders. These changes have posed significant challenges to correctional administrators, including addressing the needs of a changing offender population and meeting these challenges while working within overcrowded prisons with limited budgets.

The incarceration strategy of the 1980s increased the prison population in a manner that has disproportionately imprisoned select segments of society. First, according to the NCCD, "those under the control of corrections [during the 1980s] do not represent a cross section of the nation's population . . . they tend to be young . . . uneducated [individuals who are] without jobs or at best marginally employed, [and] they tend to be black and Hispanic" (Austin, 1990). In large part, the shifts in the proportions of minority offenders emerged from the nationwide war on drugs that targeted drug task forces in urban areas where minority representation is highest. Second, according to Steffensmeier (1992), another casualty of the drug war was female offenders who represented a disproportionate share of the drug commitments. In addition to disproportionately impacting minorities and females, the drug war also contributed to a significant shift in the profile of prison admissions, with nonviolent offenders representing a majority of all commitments. As demonstrated by the National Council on Crime and Delinquency in 1991, "only 18 percent of state prison inmates [were] convicted of [violent] offenses" (Clark, 1993:12).

Third, the effort to depopulate state mental facilities in the early to mid-1980s through deinstitutionalization appears to have contributed to increased incidence of mental illness in incarcerated populations. Although it is difficult to verify the impact of deinstitutionalization on correctional populations, it is interesting to note that depopulation of state mental facilities occurred concurrent to the unprecedented increases in incarceration and rising reported rates of mental disability among offenders. Further, anecdotal information from correctional administrators suggests that the number of moderately and seriously mentally ill offenders has increased during the 1980s. Finally, revisions in the sentencing structures, including mandatory minimum sentences and increased sentence lengths, resulted in increased incarceration of older offenders and a gradual increase in the average offender age. This changing offender profile poses significant security and programmatic challenges for correctional administrators.

Minority Offenders.   The increasing representation of minority offenders in our state prison systems has multiple implications for correctional administrators, including the need for culturally relevant treatment programs and the availability of oral and written translation services. Additionally, minority offenders frequently have different treatment needs than do their Caucasian counterparts. For example, an analysis of the treatment needs of state offenders in Pennsylvania found that minorities tended to report significantly fewer alcohol problems than Caucasians but higher needs for addiction intervention and anger management training in addition to educational, vocational, and work training programs.

The growing number of minority offenders also presents challenges for correctional workforces. Correctional administrators need to ensure that staff are knowledgeable and respectful of cultural and ethnic differences. One of the most effective means to ensure such awareness is to provide ongoing cultural and ethnic intimidation training and, as much as possible, to make a concerted effort to increase minority representation in the workforce. Unfortunately, successfully negotiating the challenges of increased minority representation is difficult because correctional facilities are frequently located in rural rather than urban areas, resulting in a corresponding decreased availability of minority applicants and service contractors. Given this challenge, correctional administrators may seek to decrease the cultural trauma of incarceration for minority offenders, as bedspace allows, by revisiting the concept of regional incarceration as a means to encourage family visitation and culturally relevant community-based contact. If regional placement is not feasible given capacity limitations, transportation and special visitation programs can also ease adjustment to the incarcerative experience while maintaining meaningful ties to the community.

Female Offenders.[1]   Nationally, while male offenders continue to represent approximately 95 percent of all state prisoners, the 1980s marked unprecedented growth in the female offender population. For example, in Pennsylvania commitments for female offenders increased by 176 percent, as compared with a 104 percent increase for male offenders. In particular, female offenders were most significantly impacted by the war on drugs. Similar to national trends, state prison commitments for

Caucasian and minority females in Pennsylvania increased by 1150 and 1750 percent, respectively, from 1980 to 1990, as compared to 477 percent for white males for the same period.

There is a growing concern about this significant increase in the number of females being incarcerated and the resulting disruptions of their families. More focus is being put on studying the intergenerational nature of crime and the failure of the current system to consider the impact our incarceration policies have on the children of incarcerated offenders. As a corollary, there is an increasing trend in the number of parenting programs being established as well as actual live-in programs in which mother and child may deal with the complex issues of their relationship.

In terms of administrative challenges, female offenders pose unique programming needs, particularly with respect to medical issues. In part, this tendency is attributable to the observation that female offenders tend to be older, on average, than male offenders. Furthermore, females in the general or incarcerative populations have unique medical concerns. Additionally, female offenders report a greater need for vocational training and addiction counseling (particularly for drug addictions) than their male counterparts. In terms of security concerns, female offenders pose less significant problems from a public risk or institutional assaultiveness perspective.

Drug Offenders. Substance offenders present correctional administrators with a number of security and programmatic problems. From a security perspective, substance offenders often impact security considerations following initial confinement due to withdrawal behavior and, in the long term, if they cannot adequately control their addictions during their incarceration. While it is an overgeneralization to assume that all offenders convicted of narcotic drug law violations have substance addictions, research suggests that nearly 75 percent of all offenders report drug and/or alcohol addiction histories and typically also report frequent and/or occasional use at the time of their commitment. Therefore, with the significant increases in the drug offender population resulting from the 1980s war on drugs and the reported addiction problems among offenders, correctional administrators are being challenged to increase the availability of chemical abuse treatment programs.

Offenders with addiction histories can also significantly affect health care costs, as they tend to report poor health and health practices—conditions that may result in a variety of secondary and tertiary medical problems (e.g., kidney problems, liver disorders, nutritional problems). Finally, the war on drugs incidentally contributed to the aging offender population, as the drug task force sweeps of the 1980s, in an effort to increase arrest figures, often apprehended older offenders with long histories of drug addiction. The increased admission of drug-addicted offenders to prison systems has also contributed to the increased risk of introducing more catastrophic health problems such as tuberculosis and Acquired Immune Deficiency Syndrome (AIDS), which often emerge secondary to drug addicts' abusive lifestyles.

Younger Offenders. Increased admissions of younger offenders impacts prisons from security and programmatic perspectives. Specifically, correctional research has demonstrated significant differences in institutional misconduct and assaultiveness activity in terms of severity and frequency as a function of offender age. Research has shown that inmates under thirty years old are involved in significantly more assaultive incidents than their over thirty counterparts (Gaes and McGuire, 1985b). Additionally, younger inmates are found to pose a greater public risk, particularly relative to escape risk, than offenders over thirty years old. As a result of the increased risk posed by offenders under thirty years old, these younger offenders often require more restrictive housing placements to control their assaultive tendencies. The security and assault risk of youthful offenders has been complicated, beginning in the mid-1980s, by the emergence of more organized security threat groups, or gangs, within the prison setting. As with their establishment on the streets, inmates often join prison-based security threat groups for a variety of reasons including affiliation with national or regional groups, protection, status, and involvement in prison contraband and gambling rings. Of particular appeal to younger offenders, the emergence of security threat groups presents significant problems for institutional security, given the ability of gangs to disrupt institutional order and the need to identify and separate known group members. Research by the Federal Bureau of Prisons suggests that security threat group members are five times as likely to be involved in serious institutional incidents as are nongroup members (Trout, 1992).

In addition to the need for differential handling relative to institutional security, younger offenders tend to report different programmatic needs than their older counterparts. For example, a 1987 study of state offenders in Pennsylvania found that younger inmates reported higher vocation and work training needs as well as more substantial drug addiction problems (Labecki, 1987). Recognizing that 90 percent to 95 percent of all offenders will be released from the prison system at some point in the future, correctional administrators need to consider the provision of additional skills training (e.g., parenting, anger management) that may increase offenders' likelihood for successful reintegration upon release.

Older Offenders. As a result of longer sentences and escalating numbers of offenders sentenced to life terms, our nations' prisons are housing an increasing number of older offenders. Central to any discussion of the older offender is an agreement regarding what age group or range constitutes "geriatric" in a correctional setting. As indicated by Cavan (1987), definitions of "older" tend to vary from researcher to researcher but usually fall somewhere between fifty and sixty-five years old. Older offenders pose problems that represent the antithesis of those posed by younger offenders. As such, older offenders present a unique set of administrative challenges. From a treatment perspective, and in large part due to the aging process, older offenders report significantly more medical problems than their younger counterparts. Additionally, older offenders tend to report histories of sexual assaultive behavior and a greater need for psychological intervention. Older offenders often experience "declining eyesight, increasing arthritis, reduced coordination, increased disease, medications, preoccupation, poor physical conditioning, and mental depression" (Moritsugu, 1990:43). All of these problems can complicate adjustment and survival in the incarcerative setting.

In contrast to the security problems posed by younger offenders, older offenders tend to pose fewer institutional security problems, particularly in regard to assaultive behavior. While posing fewer security risks, however, age-related deficiencies may necessitate placing older offenders in different housing arrangements designed to address their physical limitations (e.g., single versus double bunk) or in special needs units that offer them protection if they are unable to protect themselves from predatory or assaultive offenders.

Mentally Ill/Mentally Challenged Offenders.

Increasing numbers of mentally ill and mentally challenged inmates pose notable problems for correctional administrators. From a security perspective, mentally ill offenders can cause considerable disruption for staff and other inmates in general housing units. Given poor stress management skills, mentally ill individuals may demonstrate assaultive or regressive behavior. Additionally, depending on their ability to protect themselves from predatory or assaultive behavior by other inmates, mentally ill offenders require special housing in special needs units or, if their impairment so warrants, in institutional-based or outside forensic units.

From a programmatic standpoint, increasing numbers of mentally ill offenders have created the need for increased mental health programming and counseling opportunities, including programs for dually diagnosed offenders. Mentally impaired offenders also frequently require special educational programs, as they cannot successfully negotiate regulated educational offerings (i.e., General Education Degree programs). Recognizing mentally ill offenders' limited ability to recreate, institutions tend to offer them individual recreation periods, separate from the recreational opportunities offered to the general offender population. The provision of separate inmate programs specifically for mentally ill offenders clearly has considerable implications for institutional staffing levels. Furthermore, given the continuing decrease in funding for state mental facilities, coupled with the migration from long-term involuntary mental health commitments and the increasing number of older offenders, the impact of mentally ill offenders on our correctional systems is likely to continue or even increase in the foreseeable future.

Risk Management

In response to overcrowding, the increased risk of institutional violence, and the changing offender profile, correctional agencies have been forced to improve their risk management capabilities. To this end, a number of correctional agencies have attempted to develop comprehensive management information systems. These systems, often referred to as *critical indicator systems,* assist managers in identifying emerging trends, monitoring institutional climate, and increasing communications between a central office and institutional administrators (Labecki and Keyser, 1994). In addition to developing key indicator systems, correctional administrators realize benefits from developing automated security threat group (e.g., gang) management systems, individual-level misconduct tracking systems, incident-based unusual incident reporting, as well as other security-related information systems that provide administrators with the data necessary to better manage their institutions. Correctional administrators are also revising emergency plans and procedures to ensure their effectiveness in the event of an institutional disturbance. Integral to this effort is improving staff preparedness through comprehensive emergency preparedness training and revising departmental policy and organizational structure to support the emergency response effort. Aside from training and policy redevelopment, emergency preparedness efforts have been aided by the availability of specialized emergency equipment and the establishment of regular emergency drills and competitions.

PRESCRIPTION FOR CHANGE

The role of corrections administrators is changing as a result of the forces external to the agency. With the politicalization of corrections policy, most notably sentencing policies that define what is done in corrections and the "rationales" in vogue at the time, administrators can no longer simply focus on managing correctional programs. As uncomfortable as it may be, administrators must interact with and attempt to influence those who define policy: the public, elected officials, and the media. To successfully regain control over their systems, correctional administrators must be willing to deliver several important messages to the public, media, and elected officials. They must put our criminal justice policies and practices into a broader context. The lessons of the 1980s and 1990s suggest that there is no evidence that relying on crime control alone is going to solve our crime problem. More crime control, in whatever form it takes, is not the answer.

A balanced approach that equally attends to the causes of crime is the answer. Any serious attempt to address crime needs to consider the following principles:

> First, it is easier and less costly to prevent someone from doing something than it is to react after the fact.
>
> Second, solutions imposed by government from the top down do not work.
>
> Third, generally, solutions that focus simply on the individual and ignore the relational context of the individual's behavior will not work.
>
> Fourth, a decentralized criminal justice system that has its roots in the neighborhood and community has a better chance of succeeding. Our policies must invite more participation. They should encourage more creative ways to actively involve the community.
>
> Fifth, based on the community policing model, our correctional apparatus needs to decentralize and become prevention-oriented in its service delivery. We must become problem solvers rather than just reactors.

Placing our policies and practices into a broader context also means accepting the fact that sentencing and corrections are risk management endeavors. There is no simple answer, and that includes incarceration and community-based sanctions and programs. Those are not either/or propositions, and neither should be regarded as the total answer. Our sentencing policies are the crux of the issue when it comes to correctional policy. These policies define how we respond to offenders and what rationale is invoked by correctional agencies and their agents. Therefore, sentencing policies should incorporate the important values of the correctional profession and articulate the process, or at a minimum, the parameters by which these values are to be obtained. To this end, it is recommended that sentencing policy be developed around the following principles:

> *Principle 1.* Sentencing policy should be regarded as the means by which we allocate discretion within the criminal justice system. It appropriately should define the parameters within which decision makers in various parts of the system operate. It should not totally eliminate or overly restrict the discretion of one part of the system. The discretion of any part of the system should be visible and accountable as much as possible. Low visibility transactions and essentially unfettered discretion should be avoided.
>
> *Principle 2.* Sentencing policies should provide for a multiplicity of purposes and not rely on the single sentencing purpose of incarceration or incapacitation. Sentencing policies should be purposeful. They should include a continuum of sanctions that are tied as much as possible to an explicit definition of their purpose (i.e., the expected outcome

of a sanction whether it is a sentence of total confinement or a sentence to a community-based program).

Principle 3. The sentencing policy itself should be the basis for linking various sentencing purposes to different groups of offenders. It thus becomes a framework for targeting and applying appropriate sentences to different crimes and offenders.

Principle 4. When sentencing commissions or boards are established they should be done in such a way so as to (1) institutionalize a process for ensuring that our policies are insulated from the emotion and politics of the moment; (2) institutionalize a process for ensuring that our policies are drafted and revised as we become more informed by our experience and research; (3) hold decision makers accountable so that policy attends to both the justice of the individual sentence and the justice and effectiveness of our policies at the aggregate level; and (4) move away from first-generation guideline systems that address only total confinement via a mechanical formula to guideline systems that incorporate a full range of sanctions, dealing with the issue of proportionality in the sanction in a way that goes beyond the simple issue of time served. Sentencing policy must be framed to instruct and educate decision makers.

Principle 5. Finally, sentencing policy in the future should invite more participation. It must be inclusive in both substance and process and should encourage more creative ways to actively involve the community and especially the victim in the justice process. It should embrace the concept of restorative justice as a major purpose. Isolating the victim from the criminal justice and correctional process has cost us dearly. Victims must be an integral part of the agenda. In fact, righting the harm done to them needs to be the priority of the system. Any solution must realistically deal with visibly involving victims in the process and bringing to bear the resources required to meet their substantive needs.

Future endeavors to develop more effective policy-making structures must be created as a means to link informed public opinion to the political process and to create structures that will buffer policy making from the politics of the day. Creating such structures within the criminal justice agencies would facilitate a more rational consideration of the public policy questions. This assertion is based on the following observations. First, we know that an informed public has the capacity to be rational and reasonable in formulating opinions on how to punish offenders. We have also learned from experience that simply developing research data for general distribution to the media is not sufficient. In this day of the "ideological debate," the presence of a rational message in the media does not necessarily translate into votes on the House or Senate floor. One possible avenue to increase public understanding of the crime debate may be to explore other mechanisms designed to link an "informed public agenda, focus group process" with the legislative process. This was recently attempted successfully in Britain with focus groups ("Political Talk," 1994).

Second, in recent years, politicians have created various structures to buffer policy making from day-to-day politics. For example, salary commissions have been created to protect elected officials from the "political heat" attendant to granting raises to themselves and other public officials. Public utilities have established commissions imbued with policy-making authority to insulate the utilities from public debate. Perhaps correctional administrators would also benefit from a similar structure, whereby the governance structures that have policy-making authority and involve criminal justice and/or legislative representation operate as a delegated agency of a state general assembly. An effective example of this suggestion is offered in Pennsylvania with the Commission on Sentencing. The commission as a delegated agency of the General Assembly has policy-making authority in establishing sentencing guidelines. Central to the commission's effectiveness, however, is its ability to promulgate guideline changes that can be enacted without the legislature's vote. The next logical step may simply be to advance legislation requiring a fiscal note addressing the impact of any sentence modification on the criminal justice system and its resources. It may well be that we will only realize more enlightened approaches to rational policy debates when and if we can break existing paradigms on the "proper" avenues for public policy development and debate.

CONCLUSION

Correctional systems do not operate in a vacuum. Today's correctional systems and institutions are constantly affected by a myriad of influences including program decisions, administrative decisions, and other policy decisions that are often influenced and/or made by individuals outside of the criminal justice system (e.g., public, media, legislators). Developing an awareness of the impact of policy on today's correctional systems will not eliminate the challenges of correctional administration today, but it will enable administrators to better understand and, in turn, to more proactively manage their systems and the political climate. Internally, developing such an awareness and capacity to interact with outside political forces will help administrators to more effectively plan and more accurately forecast the needs of the offender population and the corresponding program, staffing, and security demands. In summary, understanding the relationship between public policy and changes in social systems, such as correctional systems, will allow administrators to more proactively manage rather than to be managed by the trends and forces that are shaping their systems.

NOTES

1. For a complete review on the issues of female offenders see American Correctional Association (1990). *The Female Offender: What Does the Future Hold?* Washington, D.C.: St. Mary's Press.

REFERENCES

American Correctional Association. (1981). *Riots and Disturbances in Correctional Institutions: A Discussion of Causes, Preventative Measures, and Methods of Control.* College Park, MD: Author.

Anderson, P.R. and Pettigrew, C.G. (1985). "Indices of Stress Associated with Prison Overcrowding." *Corrective and Social Psychiatry and Journal of Behavior Technology Methods and Therapy,* 31(1):27–32.

Austin, J. (1991). "America's Growing Correctional-Industrial Complex." *NCCD FOCUS.* San Francisco, CA: National Council on Crime and Delinquency.

Austin, J. and Irwin, J. (1990). *Who Goes to Prison?* San Francisco, CA: National Council on Crime and Delinquency.

Berman, R. (1987). *How Television Sees Its Audience.* Newbury Park, CA: Sage.

Block, M.K. and Twist, S.J. (1994). "Lessons from the Eighties: Incarceration Works." *Commonsense,* 1(2):73–83.

Blumstein, A. (1993). *Federal Prison Population: Present and Future Trends.* Verbal testimony provided to the United States House Judiciary Committee, Subcommittee on Intellectual Property and Judicial Administration, July 29, 1993.

Camp, G.M. and Camp, C.G. (1993). *The Corrections Yearbook: 1993.* South Salem, NY: Criminal Justice Institute.

Canter, D. (1987). "Implications for 'New Generation' Prisons of Existing Psychological Research into Prison Design and Use." In A.E. Bottoms and R. Light (eds.), *Problems of Long-Term Imprisonment.* Brookfield, VT: Gower Press:214–227.

Cavan, R. (1987). "Is Special Treatment Needed for Elderly Offenders?" *Criminal Justice Policy Review,* 3:213–224.

Cox, V.C., Paulus, P.B., and McCain, G. (1984). "Prison Crowding Research: The Relevance for Prison Housing Standards and a General Approach Regarding Crowding Phenomena." *American Psychologist,* 39(10):1148–1160.

"Don't Lock 'Em Up." (1993, August 8). *Pittsburgh Post Gazette:*B1.

Edna McConnell Clark Foundation. (1992). *Americans Behind Bars.* New York: Author.

Ekland-Olson, S., Barrick, D.M., and Cohen, L.E. (1983). "Prison Overcrowding and Disciplinary Problems: An Analysis of the Texas Prison System." *Journal of Applied Behavioral Science,* 19(2):163–176.

Ellis, D. (1984, September). "Crowding and Prison Violence." *Criminal Justice and Behavior,* 11(3):277–308.

Ericson, R.V., Baranek, P.M., and Chan, J.B.L. (1991). *Representing Order: Crime, Law, and Justice in the News Media.* Toronto, Canada: University of Toronto Press.

"Every Ten Minutes, a Pennsylvanian Falls Victim to a Violent Crime." (1994, January 28). News Release: American Legislative Exchange Council.

Farrington, D.P. and Nuttall, C.P. (1980). "Prison Size, Overcrowding, Prison Violence, and Recidivism." *Journal of Criminal Justice,* 8:221–231.

Gaes, G.G. (1985a). "Effects of Overcrowding in Prison." In M. Tonry and N. Morris (eds.), *Crime and Justice: An Annual Review of Research,* Vol. 6. Chicago: University of Chicago Press: 95–146.

Gaes, G.G. and McGuire, W.J. (1985b). "Prison Violence: The Contribution of Crowding versus Other Determinants of Prison Assault Rates." *Journal of Research in Crime and Delinquency,* 22(1):41–65.

Jayewardene, C., McKay, H., and McKay, B. (1976, May). "In Search of a Sixth Sense: Predictors of Disruptive Behavior in Correctional Institutions." *Crime and Justice:* 32–39.

"Klaas Murder Sparks Law on Career Convicts." (1994, May 9). *The Harrisburg Evening News:* B1.

Kratcoski, P.C. (1988, March). "The Implications of Research Explaining Prison Violence and Disruption." *Federal Probation:* 27–32.

Labecki, L.A.S. (1987). *A Statistical Assessment of Inmate Needs and Characteristics in the Pennsylvania Correctional System.* (Unpublished manuscript.) Planning, Research, and Statistics Division, Pennsylvania Department of Corrections.

Labecki, L.A.S. and Keyser, A.D. (1994). *Indicator Systems: Monitoring Institutional Climate through Correctional Management Support Systems.* (Available from the National Institute of Corrections, National Training Academy, Longmont, CO.)

Lacayo, R. (1994, February 7). "Lock 'Em Up!" *Time:*50–59.

Leger, R.G. (1988). "Perception of Crowding, Racial Antagonism, and Aggression in a Custodial Prison." *Journal of Criminal Justice,* 16:167–181.

Liska, A. and Baccaglini, W. (1990). "Feeling Safe by Comparison: Crime in the Newspapers." *Social Problems,* 37:360–374.

Lord, C., Ross, L., and Lepper, M. (1979). "Biased Assimilation and Attitude Polarization: The Effects of Prior Theories on Subsequently Considered Evidence." *Journal of Personality and Social Psychology,* 37:2098–2109.

Martin, R. and Zimmerman, S. (1990). "A Topology of the Causes of Prison Riots and an Analytical Extension to the 1986 West Virginia Riot." *Justice Quarterly,* 7(4):711–737.

Moritsugu, K. (1990). "Inmates Chronological Age vs. Physical Age." In Federal Bureau of Prisons (ed.), *Long Term Confinement and the Aging Inmate Population: December 7, 1990 Forum on Issues in Corrections:* 41–49.

"Networks Make Crime Top Story." (1994, March 3). *Washington Post:*C1.

O'Keefe, G. and Reid, K. (1990). "Media Public Information Campaigns and Criminal Justice Policy: Beyond 'McGruff.'" In *Media and Criminal Justice Policy,* R. Surette (ed.). Springfield, IL: Charles C Thomas.

Page, B., Shapiro, R., and Dempsey, G. (1987). "What Moves Public Opinion?" *American Political Science Review,* 81:23–43.

Paulus, P.B., McCain, G., and Cox, B.C. (1975). "Some Effects of Crowding in a Prison Environment." *Journal of Applied Social Psychology,* 5:86–91.

Paulus, P.B., McCain, G., and Cox, B.C. (1978). "Death Rates, Psychiatric Commitments, Blood Pressure and Perceived Crowding as a Function of Institutional Crowding." *Environmental Psychology and Nonverbal Behavior,* 3:107–116.

Paulus, P., McCain, G., and Cox, V. (1981, December). "Prison Standards: Some Pertinent Data on Crowding." *Federal Probation,* 45(4):48–54.

"Political Talk Therapy." (1994, June 5). *Washington Post:* Editorial Section.

"Probation and Parole Population Reach New Highs." (1994, September 11). News Release: United States Department of Justice.

Public Agenda Foundation. (1993). *Punishing Criminals: Pennsylvanians Consider Their Options.* New York: Edna McConnell Clark Foundation.

Roberts, J.V. (1992). "Public Opinion, Crime, and Criminal Justice." In M. Tonry (ed.), *Crime and Justice: A Review of Research,* Vol. 16. Chicago: University of Chicago Press: 99–180.

Ruback, R.B., Carr, T.S., and Hopper, C.H. (1986). "Perceived Control in Prison: Its Relation to Reported Crowding Stress and Symptoms." *Journal of Applied Social Psychology,* 16(5):375–386.

Schroot, D.G. and Knowles, J.J. (1990). *Ohio Citizens Attitudes Concerning Drug and Alcohol Use and Abuse: General Findings.* Columbus, OH: Governor's Office of Criminal Justice.

The Sentencing Project. (1994). *Did the Growth of Imprisonment During the 1980s Work?: The NRA and the Misuse of Criminal Justice Data.* Washington, D.C.: Author.

South Carolina Department of Corrections. (1973). *Collective Violence in Correctional Institutions: A Search for Causes.* Columbia, SC: South Carolina Department of Corrections.

Steffensmeier, D. (1992). *Incarceration and Crime: Facing Fiscal Realities in Pennsylvania.* University Park, PA: Center for the Study of Law and Society, Pennsylvania State University.

Surette, R. (1992). *Media, Crime, and Criminal Justice: Images and Realities.* Pacific Grove, CA: Brooks/Cole.

"Three Strikes, Who's Out?" (1994, May 16). *The Sunday Patriot News:* B6.

Toch, H. (1985). "Warehouses for People?" *Annals of the American Academy,* 487:58–72.

Trout, C.H. (1992, July). "Taking a New Look at an Old Problem. *Corrections Today:* 62, 64, 66.

Tversky, A. and Kahneman, D. (1973). "Availability: A Heuristic for Judging Frequency and Probability." *Cognitive Psychology,* 5:207–232.

U.S. Department of Justice, Bureau of Justice Statistics. (1988). *Historical Statistics on Prisoners in State and Federal Institutions: Year End 1925–86* (Report no. NCJ-111098). Washington, D.C.: U.S. Department of Justice.

Weiner, R.E. and Keys, C. (1988). "The Effects of Changes in Jail Population Densities on Crowding, Sick Call, and Spatial Behavior." *Journal of Applied Social Psychology,* 18(10):852–866.

Yondorf, B. and Warnock, K.M. (1989). *State Legislatures and Corrections Policies: An Overview* (Criminal Justice Paper no. 2). Denver, CO: National Conference of State Legislatures.

Zucker, H. (1978). "The Variable Nature of News Media Influence." In B. Ruben (ed.), *Communication Yearbook,* Vol. 2. New Brunswick, NJ: Transaction Books:225–240.

FIVE

Prison Overcrowding and the War on Drugs

Why We Should Legalize Marijuana

SAMUEL M. RICHARDS
The Pennsylvania State University

INTRODUCTION

The issue of legalizing marijuana is examined in the light of the impact of the war on drugs. The chapter bases the case for legalization on the costs and futility of government efforts to criminalize marijuana. Drawing on the history of the politicalization of hemp, continued criminalization of the drug, it is argued, has resulted in overcrowded prisons, an underground drug economy and criminal subculture, and the diversion of resources that could be better directed to fighting violent crime and the eradication of other social problems.

The author wishes to thank Brad Bernstein, Ted Alleman, and especially Laurie Mulvey for comments on earlier versions of this chapter.

It is old news to argue that our criminal justice system is besieged by problems. Every critically thinking commentator writing about the courts, police, and prisons discusses the need for change and reform. Indeed, many argue that we have gone beyond the possibility of reform and that we are greatly in need of a radical restructuring of the way "justice" is administered and laws are upheld in this country.

Throughout this book, numerous problems related to the corrections system are discussed. Overcrowding of prisons is one example. Clearly the prison housing situation in this country is in a crisis state, as we cannot build jails and prisons fast enough (Selke, 1993). In 1990, our state and federal correctional facilities were filled at 123 percent capacity, while jail housing stood at 101 percent capacity (Sourcebook-92, 1993:617). In 1991, there were 18,304 prisoners housed in local and county jails due to overcrowding in state facilities, and this number is expected to continue to grow (Sourcebook-92, 1993:605). Record overcrowding will surely remain a problem regardless of how many prisons we build, because the amount of criminal activity tends to be proportionate to the amount of space available for incarceration. In other words, if the space is available, more criminals will simply be sought out and arrested.

This problem should not be dismissed offhandedly. Besides what this means about our definition of criminal activity, overcrowding gives rise to other related stresses, including the inability of prisons to meet the basic needs of prisoners (food, shelter, safety, etc.). Not meeting basic needs of prisoners also leads to increased stress in the social interactions among prisoners, and between prisoners and guards. This may be a central component of a punitive corrections system; however, such strained interactions shape the consciousnesses of prisoners, most of whom return to the community with a high degree of anger and resentment fueled by years of inhumane life behind the walls. Clearly, the stresses and strains that are built up in prison life shape prisoners' actions when they return to the streets. Quite simply, this is an inefficient way to curb crime.

Overcrowding also necessitates placing an emphasis on the punishment of prisoners and not on their reform, because it means more resources must be spent on the control of inmates. In fact, with few exceptions, there is virtually no serious attempt to guarantee that those who leave correctional facilities will not return to them. And, with greater frequency, violent offenders are likely to find themselves back on the streets before even *they* believed possible. In 1990, for example, it was estimated that felons who were convicted of murder would serve only 43 percent of their total sentences.

There is little funding for reform programs because the public does not see the logic behind spending money on this—largely because there has been no serious public debate of the social, economic, and political benefits of curbing the recidivism rate in this way. Within the current ideological climate regarding "justice," a person gets one chance to "make it" and criminals should be harshly punished as quickly as possible. However, we do not act on this ideological belief because we do not want to pay the costs of seeing it materialize. The outcome of this inconsistency is "turnstile justice," in which criminals repeatedly enter and exit the system, usually according to whimsical bureaucratic necessities that have more to do with economic and political needs than with the need to carry out the law.

Clearly this is not an efficacious way to address the problem of crime. Packing people into jails and prisons and then releasing them into the community without skills and basic opportunities that would allow them to change is a recipe for disaster. Currently, recidivism rates soar upward to 70 percent (BJSAR-87, 1988:70). This means that although the justice system may be "managing" criminal activity, it is certainly not curtailing it.

This strain on the criminal justice system is only likely to worsen, because there is an increasing polarization of social classes in this country. Greater proportions of wealth and income flow to the few who are very wealthy, while a growing population of marginalized people have access to less and less (Barlett and Steele, 1992). This situation leads to greater social, economic, and political inequality, which is likely to fuel increasing resentment and conflict between groups and, ultimately, criminal activity, including violent criminal activity.

One way to control the problem of increasing crime (and violence) is to create economic and political opportunities for disenfranchised people through widescale socioeconomic and political reform. But, unfortunately, such reform is unlikely to occur soon to any great extent and so it is pointless to discuss as a realistic option. Another way to contain crime and violence is to give police more power, coupled with more weapons and greater discretionary flexibility when using them. Unfortunately, this is likely to lead the police (and courts) to curb more and more basic liberties of the people. Such a trend could lead to the frightening possibility of the creation of a neo-fascist police state.

So it would appear that we need to search for rational changes that will both address the problem of crime and keep violence under control without undermining the basic democratic structures that still exist within our political and legal institutions.

One way to do this is to find ways to reduce some of the current strains on the criminal justice system in order to maximize its ability to function in an efficacious way. This is a prodigious task, to be sure. But in thinking about it, we need to pose some serious questions: How can there be communities or neighborhoods that police fear entering? What are police and courts spending resources on that is more important than controlling such apparently "out of control" violence? Where is all the money going?

One answer is that a large portion of criminal justice funds is spent fighting illegal drugs. Although some crime associated with illegal drugs is violent, a far greater portion of it is victimless (i.e., the only person who may suffer harm is the perpetrator). In other words, drug usage and trafficking do sometimes result in violent behavior and crimes against innocent people. In fact, television news viewers in every major city see eyewitness accounts of drug-related violence almost every night. Although this is a distorted vision of reality, as it represents a small segment of the illegal drug trade and only a fraction of the illegal drug users, it is enough to prod the American public to demand that something be done immediately.

But there is no simple solution, and indiscriminately arresting any illegal drug users, buyers, and sellers only forces us to spend scarce resources on many people who are committing victimless crimes. This funnels resources away from violent criminal activity, which, incidently, would likely decrease, many argue, if all drugs were made legal (see Ostrowski, 1989). As such, it seems that one place to start when thinking about how to reduce the strain on the criminal justice system would be to rethink how we deal with such victimless crimes as drug possession and distribution.

This chapter focuses on the degree to which legalizing marijuana might help to reduce the strain on the criminal justice system by freeing monetary and human resources to deal more effectively with both lowering the recidivism rate and curbing violent crime.[1] In making this argument, this author takes the position that we are spending a great deal of scarce resources trying to control a problem (i.e., marijuana smoking) that may not be of critical import for the long-range future of this country.

IDEOLOGY AND THE "WAR ON DRUGS"

Before proceeding it is important to acknowledge some points about drugs in general and marijuana in particular, because the debate over drugs in the United States has been fueled by rhetoric at the expense of logical and rational discourse. Most of what people in this country tend to think about the drug debate is a reflection of either flashy news stories that emphasize shallow ideas and simplified solutions or political rhetoric by politicians who are trying to keep their jobs.

This rhetoric has blinded us to the fact that we live in a drug-addicted society and that some of the most antidrug citizens cannot go without their own daily "fixes" of coffee or chocolate. The most deadly legal drugs of choice, however, are alcohol (accounting for approximately 150,000 annual deaths, in addition to its contribution to half of all highway deaths and more than half of all murders) and tobacco (accounting for another 300,000 to 400,000 deaths on an annual basis).[2] In addition to these drugs is a veritable supermarket of "mood elevators" that the medical establishment dispenses by prescription. These include Xanex, Prozac, and others. Millions of Americans take these drugs on a regular basis, and many (if not most) of these users are somehow addicted to them in one form or another, although the term *addiction* is rarely applied to these "wonder drugs" (Kramer 1993).

When people such as John Lawn (a former administrator for the DEA) state that "[drugs] are not bad because they are illegal, they are illegal because they are bad," few question the foundation of such a premise. However, when we realize that a society's norms and values are socially constructed, such statements can only be viewed as patently false. In other words, some drugs are illegal because some powerful people want them to be illegal. Likewise, other drugs are legal because some powerful people decide they should be legal. In fact, if we bother to read and understand our history, it is clear that legalizing one drug and criminalizing another are arbitrary matters based on who holds the power to determine laws and, hence, to set norms.[3] Therefore, the legal status of a drug is *not* a reflection of the danger of the drug itself. In fact, using the word *drug* to refer *only* to illegal drugs is evidence of the degree to which citizens are uninformed of the politicalization of drugs in our country's history.

Let me proceed to the case of marijuana in particular, a plant that is viewed by many as inherently "evil." I will discuss how this is a relatively recent label that largely emerged because a few powerful people were successful in shifting public policy for what appears to be private gain.

BREAKING DOWN OUR IDEOLOGICAL BARRIERS TO CHANGE: A BRIEF HISTORY OF MARIJUANA IN THE UNITED STATES

The marijuana plant, or hemp—as it has been called on this continent for most of the past four centuries—has played an important role in U.S. history largely because its stem produces one of the strongest and most durable fibers known to human beings. Hemp fiber has been said to be lighter, softer, warmer, more water absorbent, and much more durable than cotton.[4] For this reason, hemp supplied approximately 80 percent of the world's rope, twine, and cordage until 1937. In addition, approximately 80 percent of the world's paper—including the first draft of the Declaration of Independence—was made from hemp until the late 1800s. The uses of this plant go far beyond those just identified. Others include using hemp oil for paint, lighting, fuel oil, medicine, food preparation, and (exceptionally clean) biomass fuel.

In the early years of the colonization of this continent, laws were passed *mandating* farmers to grow hemp. In fact, the U.S. government grew hemp during World War II to manufacture high-quality rope and textiles. (Accordingly, in 1942, the U.S. Department of Agriculture made a film called *Hemp for Victory* that extolled the benefits of hemp.) All of our so-called founding fathers grew hemp or strongly supported its dissemination throughout America because it was such an important resource. This group includes George Washington, Thomas Jefferson, and Benjamin Franklin, who started one of this country's first hemp paper mills.

Marijuana is one of the world's oldest natural medicines, with references dating back thousands of years. In the latter half of the 1800s, hemp comprised half of all medicine sold, with little fear of its intoxicating effects. In fact, marijuana was prescribed for more than one hundred separate illnesses, including multiple sclerosis, nausea, asthma, epilepsy, arthritis, headaches, menstrual cramps, and excessive bleeding (Cohen and Stillman, 1976). This drug continues to help many people when other medicines fail. Some people with diseases such as multiple sclerosis, for example, report that their conditions have "dramatically improved" and that they are in fact "recovered" if they smoke marijuana regularly (Leaflet, 1993). The medicinal use of this plant has changed dramatically in the past century, however, and because marijuana is illegal this information is no longer public knowledge.

Until the beginning of the twentieth century, the leaves and flowering buds of this plant were not ingested to produce intoxicating effects; most people were simply not aware of how to use the plant as an intoxicant. However, people definitely experienced its mind-altering properties, particularly when a tincture of marijuana was prescribed medicinally, as it so often was throughout the nineteenth century.[5] So what has happened to the status of marijuana in such a short period of time? Why is a plant that was once so highly regarded that laws were passed to force people to grow it now seen as an "evil menace"?

From Useful Resource to Evil Menace

Politicians and people associated with the legal establishment will generally point to problems associated with marijuana ingestion as people began using it in this way on a wider scale shortly after World War I.[6] They argue that this intoxicant was producing a "crazed" population and that this fear led to a crusade against hemp and, ultimately, to the passage of a bill in 1937 outlawing the plant in the United States. This is the official story.

However, as is always the case, the unofficial story is not so straightforward. Many historians offer alternative explanations as to why hemp is now illegal that generally focus on two different sets of factors. First, many politicians and law enforcement officials had an economic interest in seeing hemp banned. For example, Harry J. Anslinger, author of the 1937 anti-marijuana bill and head of the Federal Bureau of Narcotics and Dangerous Drugs (later the FBN) from 1933–1963, had powerful family members and friends who would gain virtually unlimited wealth—what has now turned out to be billions of dollars—if hemp was no longer available for public and commercial use. His uncle-in-law, who named him to the FBN post, was Andrew Mellon, whose bank was literally supported by the DuPont Corporation. This is the same corporation that, rather coincidentally, patented nylon and the wood-pulp paper sulfide process in 1937! (Remember that at this point in time, hemp was still our principal source of rope and paper.) If hemp had remained legal, the DuPont Corporation would surely not be a household name today. There were many other similarly powerful people and corporations that spent untold thousands (or perhaps millions) of dollars lobbying powerful politicians to pass the bill to outlaw hemp (see Bonnie and Whitebread, 1974; Herer, 1993).

The second set of factors involves the fact that marijuana became an intoxicant of perceived "deviant" subcultures (i.e., the black and Hispanic communities) before whites smoked it on a wider basis. Many argue that the government wanted the power to attack so-called "undesirables" of minority communities and used this behavior as their rallying point. The Hearst newspapers regularly featured stories of the evils of marijuana, blaming "marijuana-intoxicated Blacks and Mexicans for many heinous crimes that were being committed against Whites" (Lusane, 1991:37). (Coincidentally, William Randolph Hearst also stood to earn a second fortune if hemp were banned because he owned millions of acreage of uncut forest in the West. Hemp paper made his land and the billions of trees that were on it nearly worthless.)

So is marijuana bad because it is illegal or is it illegal because it is bad? In thinking about your answer, consider this: Marijuana became a popular intoxicant only *after* it was outlawed. In trying to ban hemp for other reasons, Anslinger and others inadvertently popularized its recreational uses through propaganda used to inflame the public discourse surrounding the plant. Moreover, when one considers the fact that marijuana use is not a "problem" (i.e., not widely smoked, let alone abused) in places where it is not strictly illegal (e.g., Holland), one has to wonder if there would be a marijuana problem if it had never been made illegal. But let's turn to the known risks of ingesting marijuana to understand particular health effects that may further call into question its legal status.

What We Know About the Risks of Smoking Marijuana

Proponents of marijuana legalization commonly argue that marijuana has never directly caused a human death (Weil and Rosen, 1993:118) and that it does not lead to the degree of aggressive behavior that is commonly linked to alcohol. Certainly people have killed themselves and others while high on marijuana, but not at the same rate as with alcohol-related suicides and homicides. For example, although we do not know how many highway deaths are related to marijuana, estimates place the number *well below* the number of people killed as a direct result of drinking alcohol. And while there is no reliable data on the amount of violence and destruction associated with marijuana use, it is widely accepted that marijuana-caused violence pales in comparison to violent behavior directly induced by alcohol. Moreover, there is *very conclusive* evidence of the harm to the body (and mind) that is caused by drinking alcohol, smoking tobacco, and ingesting in one form or another a wide variety of unregulated or semiregulated drugs and other chemicals that are commonly added to our food, water, and air. So why the differential regulatory status of these drugs?

One explanation is that people simply assume that marijuana is harmful: "It is an illegal drug so it must be bad." Another explanation is that antimarijuana researchers have vigilantly persisted in their desire to find harmful effects of this drug and widely disseminate their findings with the help of the government and police agencies. Such researchers have postulated a wide range of medical risks associated with ingesting marijuana, including possible damage to brain function and human fetal development; effects on the immune system, chromosomes, and sex hormones; and the increased risk of lung diseases, including cancer (for particularly heavy smokers). Although some of these researchers claim to have identified causal relationships between ingesting marijuana and harming the body (e.g., Jones, 1983; Inciardi and McBride, 1991; Nahas, 1991), the results of a long list of studies remain inconclusive. For every study claiming marijuana is harmful, there is one that arrives at the opposite conclusion, maintaining that "there is absolutely no risk" associated with ingesting this plant (see also Zimmer and Morgan, 1997). These studies remain, according to one researcher's comments, "a series of fragmented hypotheses and jigsaw conclusions in which people continue to 'suspect,' 'postulate,' and 'hypothesize' that the chemicals in the hemp plant may be linked to health problems. But there is simply no hard evidence." Quoting *The Harvard Medical School Mental Health Letter* (1987:2), "Studies [of the health effects of marijuana] are often conflicting and permit various views of marijuana's possible harmfulness. This complicates the task of presenting an objective statement about the issue." Consequently, one cannot make the absolutist claim that marijuana is dangerous. And, indeed, one would be hard-pressed to even rank marijuana as one of the more harmful of the drugs widely used by the American public.

So it does not seem logical that marijuana is illegal simply because it is dangerous. With this in mind, it is not difficult to conclude that we are a people with a somewhat distorted understanding of the true dangers that face us as a nation. Quite simply, we too often accept what we are told without question.

Let us now turn to the issue of the illegal status of marijuana as it is related to the criminal justice system in the United States and calculate the cost of our apparent collective misperception.

DRUG AND MARIJUANA USE AND PROSECUTION IN THE UNITED STATES

Marijuana Use in the United States

Approximately 67.4 million Americans twelve years old and over had tried marijuana as of 1991, and 9.7 million reported that they had used it within the past month (NHSDA, 1993). This represents a large number of potential "criminals"—almost one quarter of the U.S. population![7] However, marijuana use does appear to be on the wane. In 1979, 30.9 percent of Americans twelve to seventeen years of age reported having tried it compared with only 13.1 percent in 1991 (NHSDA, 1993). Similarly, the number of people who used it "in the prior month" dropped from 16.7 percent to 4.3 percent during this same period. These figures represent a significant decline.

Whether the number of users will continue to decline remains to be seen. While we can be fairly certain—given the rising numbers of high school students who are against smoking pot—that there are fewer regular marijuana smokers today than just a decade ago, it is difficult to ascertain the validity of data based on self-reporting. In our punitive antidrug climate, most illegal drug users are reluctant to admit to anyone, especially an anonymous caller, that they "do drugs."

The Office of National Drug Control Policy estimated that in 1990, $8.8 billion was spent on marijuana and $40.4 billion was spent on all illegal drugs (WAUSID, 1991). Other sources claim that the second figure is actually much higher. The National Narcotics Intelligence Consumer's Committee estimated that black market sales of illegal drugs were about $80 billion in 1980, and certainly much higher by the end of the decade (NIE, 1980). James Ostrowski (1989) argues that what people currently spend on illegal drugs is approximately ten times the price of these drugs if they were legal. If we accept the more conservative figure for what is spent on marijuana ($8.8 billion), this means that in 1990 approximately $7.7 billion went toward bolstering a black market—a market that is linked to organized crime syndicates in the United States and abroad.[8]

Arresting and Incarcerating Drug and Marijuana Offenders in the United States

In late 1980, the beginning of the Reagan/Bush/Quayle period in American history, a new political climate took hold in the United States. This climate was marked by a polarization of issues, people, and groups. Life was either black or white, good or bad; there rarely seemed to be a gray area of indecision. If someone or something was not good, then it was bad and needed to be controlled. It was determined that the most effective means of control was to funnel more monies into the criminal justice system. The war on drugs emerged from within this new climate and it gave rise to an unprecedented increase in the amount of money spent on combatting illegal drugs. And, quite naturally, it also resulted in an unparalleled increase in the number of drug criminals at the federal, state, and local levels.

Federal Courts.   In 1980, the Bureau of Justice Statistics reported that 5135 people were arrested and convicted for federal drug offenses in the United States and that 72 percent of them went to prison (BJSNU, 1992). By mid-1991, these numbers had increased threefold. Nearly 20,000 defendants were disposed of in U.S. district courts for illegal drug crimes. Of these, 16,346 were convicted (Sourcebook-92, 1993:516). This represents a 218 percent increase for convicted federal drug offenders in twelve years.

In 1991, 4377 (or 26 percent) of all federal drug convictions involved marijuana (Sourcebook-92, 1993:516). Drawing on data from 1989, we can approximate that nearly three quarters of these arrests and convictions were for distribution, import, and/or sale, while the other 25 percent were for the possession of marijuana (BJSNU, 1992).[9]

Of the 16,346 convicted drug defendants in 1991, 14,382 (88 percent) were imprisoned after they were sentenced to serve an average of 95.7 months (see Table 5.1). In 1991, drug offenders represented over one third of all federal offenders sentenced to prison and almost one half of all federal convicts who actually spent time in federal prison.[10] Of the 4377 federal marijuana convictions in 1991, 3566 actually resulted in time spent in a federal penitentiary. Their average sentence was 68 months (BJSNU, 1992). This is a lot of time to serve, particularly for crimes of possession.

When these numbers are put into context they are somewhat startling. Looking at Table 5.1, by 1991, marijuana offenders spent more time

TABLE 5.1 Defendants Sentenced in U.S. District Courts for Selected Crimes—1991

General Offenses	Total Number Imprisoned	Number Serving Less Than 6 Mo.	Number Serving 13–35 Mo.	Number Serving More Than 60 Mo.	Average Months Sentenced
Murder (1st)	73	1	9	43	176.8
Murder (2nd)	12	0	1	7	139.9
Manslaughter	54	4	21	14	50.6
Assault	266	68	53	45	51.2
Embezzlement	571	213	137	28	20.0
Sexual Abuse	137	9	35	60	92.4
Total Drugs	14,382	839	2,828	6,708	95.7
Marijuana	3,566	420	1,047	977	68.0

Source: Sourcebook of Criminal Justice Statistics—1992, p. 516.

in federal prison on average than people convicted of manslaughter and assault, both violent crimes, although they do not always involve violence with intent. Moreover, on average, they spent three times as much time in prison as "white-collar" criminals (Sourcebook-92, 1993). For example, Charles Keating received only a ten-year sentence for stealing more than a billion dollars from U.S. taxpayers—and he will probably be out in only five years. By comparison, people get ten to twenty years for selling a fraction of the marijuana that was grown by Thomas Jefferson each year. In fact, only about 5 percent of our criminal justice budget goes toward curtailing the elite deviance—white-collar crime—that costs the taxpayers several tens of billions of dollars each year; considerably more than the amount we pay for the uses and abuses of all currently illegal drugs. This alone says a good deal about the social construction of the "evil drug scourge."

State and Local Jurisdictions.

Drawing on data from more than 10,000 law enforcement agencies across the country and compiled by the FBI's Uniform Crime Reporting Program for state and local jurisdictions, there were 1,066,400 arrests for drug law violations in the United States in 1992, out of more than 14 million total arrests (UCR-92, 1993:216).[11] Thirty-two percent of these arrests (or 342,314) were for marijuana violations—approximately 271,900 (25.5 percent) were for marijuana possession, and 70,400 were for its sale and/or manufacture (UCR-92, 1993:216). These figures represent a sharp decline from the beginning of the decade. In 1981, for example, 400,300 (almost 70 percent) of all state and local drug arrests were for the violation of marijuana laws (Sourcebook-83, 1984:415). Even then, however, people arrested for breaking marijuana laws were five times more likely to be charged with possession than for the sale and/or manufacture of marijuana. This means that law enforcement agencies spend most of their antimarijuana resources tracking down people who are committing a victimless crime. And, by and large, most of those arrested represent a cross section of the population; they are not who we think of when we think of "criminals."

Data from the state courts point to a dramatic increase in the number of people incarcerated because of state felony drug offenses during the 1980s. The proportion of drug offenders in state prisons increased from 6 percent in 1979 to 22 percent in 1991, an increase of 144 percent. In 1990, there were 274,613 felony drug convictions in state courts in the United States, or one third the total convictions (Sourcebook-92, 1993:527). Of the 168,360 drug-trafficking convictions, 16,613 (approximately 2 percent of the total state court felony convictions) were for marijuana. Approximately 0.6 percent (or about 5000) of the total felony convictions were for marijuana possession (FSSC-90, 1993).[12]

The number of drug offenders in local jails increased from 10 percent of the total average jail population to 23 percent of the total (a 147 percent

TABLE 5.2 Drug Offenders in Local Jails

Current Offense	1983 Percentage	Total	1989 Percentage	Total
	100	227,541	100	386,845
Any Drug Offense	10	22,754	23	88,989
Trafficking	4	9,102	12	46,437
Possession/Use	5	11,377	10	38,684
Other Drug Crimes	1	2,275	1	3,868

Sources: Drugs and Crime Facts, 1992, p.18. and *Sourcebook of Criminal Justice—1992*, p.590. *Note:* The numbers next to the percentages are approximations calculated from percentages.

increase) between 1983 and 1989 (Table 5.2). By 1991, the average daily population of local jails had increased to 422,609 from 227,541 in 1983 (Sourcebook-92, 1993:592).

Assuming that the percentages for total number of drug offenders increased incrementally to 25 percent by 1991, this means that approximately 100,000 were people incarcerated in local jails for drug crimes at any point during that year. It would be impossible to estimate the number of these who were marijuana offenders, however, since states vary so widely in their marijuana laws and how they choose to enforce them.

The Costs of Criminalizing Marijuana

To understand the real burden on the justice system of controlling illegal drug use in general, and marijuana in particular, let's turn to the costs of this offensive. In 1991, the U.S. federal government spent $10.8 billion to control the spread of drugs in this country (Sourcebook-92, 1993:19–21). Looking at Table 5.3, by 1993 this number soared to more than $12 billion, and President Clinton requested $13.1 billion for federal drug control programs in 1995. Approximately half of these monies are spent to fund the drug control activities of the federal, state, and local criminal justice systems, including the enforcement of marijuana laws.

A small percentage of federal funds goes directly to the Domestic Cannabis Eradication/Suppression Program that was established to ensure a coordinated marijuana control effort between governing bodies at the federal, state, and local levels. In 1982, the DEA Cannabis Investigation Section distributed $843,340 to 101 state and local law enforcement agencies for this purpose. By 1991, however, this number increased to $13.7 million, although in 1992 it dropped to $10 million (CIO, 1992:12). In 1992, 12,369 marijuana arrests were made by state and local governments with the funding and organizational initiatives of this program. This accounted for about

TABLE 5.3 Federal Drug Control Spending

Function	FY 1993 (Millions)
Drug Treatment	2,339.1
Education and Community Work	1,556.5
Criminal Justice System	5,685.1
International Activities	523.4
Interdiction	1,511.1
Research	499.1
Intelligence	150.9
Total	12,265.3

Source: NDCSBS, 1994:3.

4 percent of the total marijuana arrests that year (Sourcebook-92, 1993:468).

In addition to these monies, state and local taxes are spent fighting drug use. In 1991, for example, state and local spending on drug control reached $15.9 billion, although this included $3.2 billion in federal drug grants (see Table 5.4). This was nearly a 13 percent increase over the $14 billion spent during the previous fiscal year. The bulk of this spending ($12.6 billion, or 79 percent) was for criminal justice activities (as opposed to health care and education) and represented 16.5 percent of the total justice system budgets for state and local governments that year (SLSDCA, 1993:9).

It is impossible to ascertain the precise percentage of the billions that are spent arresting and incarcerating marijuana offenders, since data on the number of people arrested or incarcerated at the local level are either unreliable, scarce, or simply nonexistent. But we can calculate a rough estimate based on the number of arrests for marijuana crimes at the state

TABLE 5.4 State and Local Spending on Drug Control in 1991 (in Millions)

Activity	State	Local	S + L
Justice	5,501	7,118	12,619
Police	637	3,585	4,223
Courts	469	980	1,449
Corrections	4,342	2,486	6,827
Other	53	68	120
Health Care	1,611	1,173	2,784
Education	340	163	503
Total	7,451	8,455	15,907

Source: SLSDCA, 1993, p. 3.

and local levels compared to other drug crimes. During 1991, 28 percent of arrests for drug crimes at the state and local levels were for marijuana possession and trafficking (Sourcebook-92, 1993:458). Using a figure of $10 billion[13] for state and local drug control, this would mean that in 1991, state and local governments spent as much as $2.8 billion arresting 282,800 people who were caught possessing cannabis or selling it to one another, as well as incarcerating some of those in this group who were convicted. This means that during that year, with 16.5 percent of the total justice system budgets of state and local governments (or $76.3 billion) spent on controlling drugs, perhaps as much as 4.6 percent of their total budgets was spent enforcing marijuana laws.[14] In addition to these monies spent was a percentage of the 1991 federal drug budget that was used to arrest these 282,800 and convict another 4377 marijuana users and traffickers. The total amount that we spent to arrest, prosecute, and incarcerate marijuana offenders in 1991 may have been in the range of $3–4 billion![15]

With respect to the costs of incarceration in particular, state and local governments spent $27.8 billion during 1991. People incarcerated for drug-related crimes cost $6.8 billion, or 24.5 percent of the total corrections budget (SLSDCA, 1993:9). It is impossible to determine the percentage of this amount that went toward housing marijuana offenders, given the lack of marijuana incarceration data for local jails. However, we can begin to calculate the cost of our current marijuana policies by examining the cost of keeping a person behind bars, a topic that is regularly debated in media circles.

To begin, prisons are very expensive structures to build. When all costs are totaled, the price of building one prison bed averaged $53,100 in 1991–1992 (Christie, 1993:99). So simply building more prisons when space runs out is an expensive answer to our crime problem. The total construction, operation, and maintenance cost of prisons was nearly $11.5 billion in 1990 (Samana, 1994:456). This came out to an average of $15,513 that year to keep one prisoner confined to a federal or state prison (Samana, 1994:456).[16] Jail housing during 1990 was almost $13,000 per prisoner per year across the nation. These costs are expected to continue to escalate rapidly.

Returning to marijuana incarceration data for federal prisons, in 1991 there were 3566 prisoners sentenced to serve an average of 68 months in prison. At a cost of $15,513 per year, this figures out to be about $310 million just for incarceration of these offenders.[17] Earlier we saw that approximately 21,600 marijuana law offenders were convicted in state courts in 1990. Using a conservative number of 20,000 we can estimate the cost of housing these felons to be close to $6 million in 1990.[18] At the local level data are simply inestimable. But the point has been made—it is costly to arrest and house marijuana offenders.

By all measures, this is a great deal of money to spend trying to eliminate an activity that has been a part of human existence for perhaps

10,000 years. As Weil and Rosen write, "Drugs are here to stay. History teaches us that it is vain to hope that drugs will ever disappear and that any effort to eliminate them from society is doomed to failure" (1993:1). So we have to question the origins and functions of maintaining such a policy, compared with the potential value of legalization.

As a point of comparison, let me conclude by referring to some data on the economics of marijuana decriminalization in California.[19] (On January 1, 1976, the state of California began fining people who were caught possessing an ounce or less of marijuana $100.) For California taxpayers, this new law has been very lucrative. In 1985, for example, there were 40,761 citations issued for marijuana possession, which resulted in more than $4 million in collected fines for the state treasury. The estimated cost of arresting and bringing to trial each of those offenders would have been approximately $2,875 per person, or $117 million total. Between 1976–1985, it is estimated that decriminalizing marijuana saved California taxpayers up to $100 million annually in arrest, court, prison, and parole costs. Because not all possession arrests during this period would have led to imprisonment and, ultimately, parole, these numbers are somewhat inflated. But even if only a handful of the possession charges had made it to court, the savings were (and have continued to be) significant and represent funds that the state's law enforcement agencies could use to address other crime problems, including violent crimes.

CONCLUSION

This chapter has focused on the actual costs of our current marijuana policies. It is difficult to quantify such costs because many factors simply cannot be translated into monetary figures. For example, James Ostrowski (1989:11–12) discusses how drug prohibition stimulates crime in a wide variety of ways. Two that stand out are that it forces users into regular contact with professional (and often violent) criminals, and it encourages people (particularly the young) to become criminals—indeed, it defines them as such—by creating a profitable black market in drugs. These costs must be considered as well.

The main argument, however, is that fighting drugs in general and marijuana in particular is costly and utilizes criminal justice resources that could and should be used in other areas of crime fighting. One important component of this argument has been that marijuana offenders take resources (including prison and jail space) away from efforts to combat violent criminals. Ostrowski accurately sums up this problem:

Because of the sheer lack of prison space, violent criminals frequently are given deals, probation, or shorter terms than they deserve. Then they are back on the streets, and often back to serious crime . . . In a world of scarce prison resources, sending a drug offender to prison for one year is equivalent to freeing a violent criminal to commit 40 robberies, 7 assaults, 110 burglaries, and 25 auto thefts. (1989:21)

Using these figures and a conservative figure of 140,000 marijuana offenders currently in prisons or jails across the country, a very large number of violent criminal acts are committed that could otherwise be averted.

Sentencing in marijuana offenses gets out of control because laws were enacted by representatives who did not understand the scope and nature of the actual problem. This is usually because they have been blinded by the rhetoric of people like former Los Angeles Police Chief Daryl Gates, who stated that casual drug users (including marijuana smokers), "ought to be taken out and shot" (TDC, 1990). He called this the "smoke a joint, lose your life" criminal justice approach. As a result of political short-sightedness and people who reason like Daryl Gates, we have a great many extreme laws that lead to absurd sentences. Consider the case of the fifteen-year-old Idaho boy who found himself facing five years to life for selling $40 worth of marijuana to a friend on school property. Or consider the hundreds of people who fight a daily battle with cancer, AIDS, and other terminal illnesses who smoke marijuana because the drug relieves nausea and pain and are then prosecuted when they are caught. People facing death have been hauled into court and sentenced to jail, sometimes for many years. This does not make sense and reflects an antidrug strategy that is totally out of control.

Most of the violence that is currently associated with illegal drugs would not exist if these drugs were not illegal. For example, we do not see such violence associated with the distribution of alcohol (except, of course, when people consume it). Most of the "war on drugs" tends to be fought in places where there is absolutely no link to violence. As one person who is serving ten years for selling five "hits" of LSD remarked when asked his opinion about DEA agents regularly arresting people at rock concerts for illegal drug use and trafficking, "What would you rather do? Round up a bunch of teenagers in a parking lot, or go wading into a crack den in the inner city?" (Buchanan, 1994:36). So, who is really being hurt by these current policies? Who is truly benefitting?

Finally, it is of utmost importance to keep in mind that there is no perfect policy to deal with how any drugs should be consumed and regulated; that is, there are pros and cons to every public policy decision. However, drugs will always be with us in various forms and there is *nothing* that we can do to change this. We must search for a solution that will maximize the pros and minimize the cons. I have argued that our best option is to take a look at our priorities and to redefine our view of the drug war in line with common sense and rational understanding rather than reactionary short-sightedness. Only in this way can we efficaciously address serious criminal activity.

NOTES

1. One question that might immediately come to mind is, why not legalize other drugs that are currently illegal? Why only marijuana? I respond to this by saying that I think we should give some serious thought to a more wide-scale legalization policy and consider legalizing all currently illegal drugs. The arguments for doing so seem to make a great deal of sense (Greenspoon, 1977; Friedman and Szasz, 1992; Trebach and Inciardi, 1993). However, marijuana seems to be the most benign of the drugs that are currently illegal, in part because it is the least addictive and all-around the least dangerous, an issue I will briefly address in the following section. Thus, it provides a relatively "safe" place to look for new ways to resolve the drug problem (and prison overcrowding problem) in this society.

2. These figures do not include the incalculable millions of dollars that are spent each year in health care and property costs incurred because of alcohol and tobacco abuse.

3. The same sociological process applies to other areas of life as well. For example, in Nazi Germany it was a capital offense to help a Jewish person. From our sociohistorical distance, we can clearly see that this law was based on the preferences (and prejudices) of a particular group, not on "divine truth."

4. Most of the information for this section was taken from Herer (1993). I encourage readers who are interested in this subject to read this very well-documented book.

5. When George Washington was president, he wrote to a friend that he had found that separating the male and female hemp plants produced plants that were much stronger.

6. Weil and Rosen (1933:115–116) and others argue that hemp smoking was probably first practiced by African slaves brought to Brazil and elsewhere in the Caribbean as part of religious ritual practices. This knowledge slowly moved north into Mexico and was introduced into the United States by Mexican migrant workers after the war. One has to question, however, why slaves transported to Brazil were the only slaves with this knowledge or why Europeans never heard of this practice after years of trade on the African continent. The fact is, we simply do not know how many Americans smoked marijuana in the past and how often they did so. It is certain, however, that fewer people smoked the plant than do today.

7. By contrast, approximately 84.6 percent of Americans (approximately 210 million) over the age of twelve have tried alcohol at least once, while just over 50 percent used it in the last month (NHSDA, 1993).

8. This represents another way in which the prohibition of marijuana serves to *increase* crime.

9. The reason for this is that federal authorities pursue people who cross state lines with drugs, which usually involves larger amounts. The assumption—which is reflected in the penalties tied to drug laws—is that people are always selling (and not using) larger amounts of illegal drugs.

10. This represents a rather drastic increase from the previous decade. In fact, during the years 1980–90 there was a 72 percent increase in the average prison sentence of federal drug offenders (BJSNU, 1992). By 1992, 41,314 of the 70,465 prisoners incarcerated in federal penitentiaries (nearly 60 percent) were committed because of a federal drug offense (Sourcebook-92, 1993:636).

11. This is *arrests* and not *individuals,* as one person is often arrested more than once in a year (sometimes for the same crime). But these are not multiple charges; one person arrested for marijuana *and* underage drinking at a single point in time counted as two different arrests.

12. Again, as with federal marijuana crimes, people caught with larger amounts of the plant are assumed to be traffickers.

13. State and local governments spent $12.6 billion in 1991 paying for drug control (i.e., directly curbing drug consumption and trafficking). Since approximately $2.6 billion of that was from federal drug control grants, we can estimate that approximately $10 billion was spent by these governments in 1991 toward direct drug control measures and not other related activities (i.e., education).

14. These are very approximate figures since, in most state and local jurisdictions, marijuana is handled less severely than other drugs (particularly narcotics and cocaine) regardless of whether the penalties appear similar on the books. In other words, marijuana law offenders

are more likely to get a quick plea bargain, less likely to spend time behind bars, or, if they do, less likely to complete their sentence.

15. Fines (e.g., payment of court costs) levied against marijuana offenders may help to offset the costs of apprehending and incarcerating them. However, these fines represent a relatively negligible "return payment" to governing bodies. At the same time, a larger and larger percentage of the operating revenues of law enforcement agencies come from taking property away from people convicted of drug crimes. In 1990, for example, 94 percent of all state police departments, 38 percent of all local police departments, and 51 percent of all sheriffs' departments received money or goods from a drug asset forfeiture program (DCF, 1993:12). In 1992, for example, $69.3 million in assets were seized through the DEA's Domestic Cannabis Eradication/Suppression Program, and other assets were seized by law enforcement agencies not operating under this program (Sourcebook-92, 1993:468). This is a more significant amount of money but it still does not repay taxpayers. But a series of recent court cases and the fact that Janet Reno, the current attorney general, is opposed to asset forfeitures for drug crimes, may have begun to pave the way toward curtailing these forfeiture programs.

16. On average, in 1990, federal penitentiaries were slightly more costly than state prisons, and the average housing costs of the latter ranged from $30,302 for Minnesota to $7557 for Arkansas.

17. 3566×5.6 years $\times \$15,513 = \$310$ million.

18. On average, approximately 41 percent (or in this case 8200) of all felony convicts were sentenced to state prisons that year with an average sentence of four years and three months, while 37 percent (7,400) went to jail with an average sentence of six months ($7400 \times .005 = 37$; $8200 \times .0425 = 348$; $385 \times \$15,513 = \$6$ million). I use the 20,000 figure because marijuana offenders are somewhat less likely than other offenders to be incarcerated.

19. These data were published by an organization called the Marijuana Study Group and distributed in a pamphlet outlining the pros and cons of legalization.

REFERENCES

Barlett, D.L. and Steele, J.B. (1992). *America: What Went Wrong?* Kansas City, MO: Andrews and McMeel.

Bonnie, R. and Whitebread, C. (1974). *The Marijuana Conviction.* Richmond: University of Virginia Press.

Buchanan, R. (1994). "The Heads and the Feds," *Details*:36.

BJSAR-87. (1988). *Annual Report, 1987.* Washington, D.C.: Bureau of Justice Statistics.

BJSCVUS-92. (1994). *Criminal Victimization in the United States, 1992.* Washington, D.C.: Bureau of Justice Statistics, U.S. Department of Justice.

BJSNU. (1992). *Bureau of Justice Statistics, National Update.* Data obtained from Federal Criminal Case Processing, 1980–89 with Preliminary Data for 1990. NCJ-130526.

Christie, N. (1993). *Crime Control as Industry: Towards GULAGS, Western Style?* London: Routledge.

CIO. (1992). *Cannabis Investigations Overview,* from the 1992 Domestic Cannabis Eradication/Suppression Program pamphlet. Drug Enforcement Agency.

Cohen, S. and Stillman, R. (1976). *Therapeutic Potential of Marijuana.* New York: Plenum Books.

DCF. (1993). *Drugs and Crime Facts, 1992.* Washington, D.C.: Bureau of Justice Statistics, U.S. Department of Justice.

DCJS. (1992). *Drugs, Crime, and the Justice System: A National Report.* Washington, D.C.: Bureau of Justice Statistics, U.S. Department of Justice. NCJ-133652.

Friedman, M. and Szasz, T.S. (1992). *On Liberty and Drugs: Essays on the Free Market and Prohibition.* Washington, D.C.: The Drug Policy Foundation Press.

FSSC-90. (1993). *Felony Sentences in State Courts, 1990.* Washington, D.C.: Bureau of Justice Statistics, U.S. Department of Justice. Bulletin NCJ-140186.

Greenspoon, L. (1977). *Marijuana Reconsidered* (2d ed.). New York: Bantam Books.

Harvard Medical School Mental Health Letter. (1987). Boston, MA: Department of Continuing Education of Harvard Medical School, Vol. 4, No. 5.

Herer, J. (1993). *The Emperor Wears No Clothes.* Van Nuys, CA: HEMP Publishing.

Inciardi, J.A. and McBride, D.C. (1991). "The Case Against Legalization," in J.A. Inciardi, (ed.), *The Drug Legalization Debate.* Newbury Park, CA: Sage.

Jones, R.T. (1983). "Cannabis and Health." *Annual Review of Medicine,* 34:247–258.

Kramer, P.D. (1993). *Listening to Prozac: A Psychiatrist Explores Antidepressant Drugs and the Remaking of the Self.* New York: Viking.

Leaflet. (1993). *The Leaflet: Special Medical Issue.* NORMAL Newsletter, Vol. 22, No. 1, March.

Lusane, C. (1991). *Pipe Dream Blues: Racism and the War on Drugs.* Boston, MA: South End Press.

Nahas, G. (1991). *Keep Off the Grass.* Middlebury, VT: P.S. Eriksson.

NDCSBS. (1994). *National Drug Control Strategy: Budget Summary.* Washington, D.C.: Office of National Drug Control Policy, Executive Office of the President.

NHSDA. (1993). *National Household Survey on Drug Abuse: Highlights 1991.* Washington, D.C.: USGPO. U.S. Department of Health and Human Services, Substance Abuse and Mental Health Services Administration.

NIE. (1980). "Narcotics Intelligence Estimate." The National Narcotics Intelligence Consumer's Committee, Technical Report.

Ostrowski, J. (1989). "Thinking About Drug Legalization." Policy Analysis Working Paper no. 121. Washington, D.C.: CATO Institute.

Samana, J. (1994). *Criminal Justice* (3d ed.). St. Paul, MN: West Publishing.

Selke, W.L. (1993). *Prisons in Crisis.* Bloomington: Indiana University Press.

Sourcebook-92. (1993). *Sourcebook of Criminal Justice Statistics, 1992.* Washington, D.C.: Bureau of Justice Statistics, U.S. Department of Justice. NCJ-143496.

Sourcebook-83. (1984). *Sourcebook of Criminal Justice Statistics, 1982.* Washington, D.C.: Bureau of Justice Statistics, U.S. Department of Justice.

SLSDCA. (1993). *State and Local Spending on Drug Control Activities.* Report From the National Survey of State and Local Governments, Office of National Drug Control Policy, Executive Office of the President, Washington, D.C.

TDC. (1990, September 7). "L.A. Police Chief Endorses Shooting Casual Drug Users." *The Daily Collegian.*

Trebach, A.S. and Inciardi, J.A. (1993). *Legalize It? Debating American Drug Policy.* Washington, D.C.: American University Press.

UCR-92. (1993). *Crime in the United States, 1992.* Washington D.C.: Uniform Crime Reports, U.S. Department of Justice, Federal Bureau of Investigation.

Weil, A. and Rosen, W. (1993). *From Chocolate to Morphine: Everything You Need to Know About Mind-Altering Drugs.* New York: Houghton Mifflin Co.

WAUSID. (1991, June). "What America's Users Spend on Illegal Drugs." (Technical paper.) Washington, D.C.: Office of National Drug Control Policy.

Zimmer, L. and Morgan, J.P. (1997). *Marijuana Myths Marijuana Facts: A Review of the Scientific Evidence.* New York: The Lindesmith Center.

SIX

Crowding and Correctional Change

STAN STOJKOVIC
University of Wisconsin-Milwaukee

JOHN KLOFAS
Rochester Institute of Technology

INTRODUCTION

This chapter provides a comprehensive overview of the issue of correctional crowding. Defining the various types of prison crowding and their effects, the discussion reviews court cases that have ruled on crowding and the emerging redefinition of crowding as a managerial problem. Finally, current strategies for confronting crowding in local jails and state prisons are reviewed.

No problem in the history of American corrections has been as costly and disruptive as the current wave of crowding in jails and prisons. Since the late 1970s, the crowding of correctional facilities has been recognized as one of the most significant problems facing criminal justice (National Institute of Justice, 1988). Surveys of criminal justice officials and policy makers regularly show that police, prosecutors, and judges share concerns about the impact of correctional crowding on the entire criminal justice system (Gottfredson and McConville, 1987). Crowding has led to dramatic increases in spending for jail and prison construction as well as to the increased use of alternatives and the development of other pre- and postincarceration strategies (Stojkovic and Lovell, 1992). Despite these effects, the populations of prisons and jails continue to grow at unprecedented rates (Bureau of Justice Statistics, 1992). In this chapter we examine the problem of correctional crowding by focusing on how the concept has been defined, how it affects contemporary institutions, and how some people have a stake in the ongoing debate over prison and jail crowding.

DEFINING CROWDING

Concern with crowding has not been limited to corrections. Educators have focused on crowding in classrooms, and recreation professionals have been concerned with the crowding of parks and other recreational facilities (see Klofas, Stojkovic, and Kalinich, 1992). What links such diverse fields is interest in trying to understand how many people is too many people for any given resource. That is, the concern is that facilities may be used beyond their capacities. This approach to crowding, then, focuses our attention on such issues as how we can define crowded conditions, identify the adverse effects of crowding, and develop methods of mitigating these effects.

Measures involving people and space are the most common approaches to operationalizing the concept of crowding. In corrections, the search for objective measures of crowding has produced several approaches, including (1) design capacity, (2) rated capacity, and (3) operational capacity.

Design capacity refers to the number of inmates a prison or jail may hold as determined by a facility's architects. Architects determine capacity figures by examining building codes, health codes, and other national architectural standards. For example, the standard of air quality relates to how many individuals may occupy a given cell for a period of time given the air flow in the institution. Such standards are promulgated for the efficient use of confinement space consistent with the proper functioning of the institution.

Rated capacity is a measure that is determined by correctional officials, usually based on standards put forward by state agencies or national professional organizations such as the American Correctional Association (ACA) or American Jail Association (AJA). Rated capacity deals with such issues as square footage per cell, recreational space available, and adequacy of medical facilities. These standards may also include the number of officers necessary to adequately manage and supervise the inmate population. Accreditation through professional associations can depend heavily on meeting such standards. Oversight agencies operate in many states. The power of these agencies varies widely from simply reporting inadequacies to actually closing facilities.

Operational capacity is a less formal term that is often larger than design or rated capacity and is defined by correctional administrators as the number of inmates that can be managed appropriately within a facility. The operational capacity of an institution is often determined through the subjective interpretations of correctional officials who are concerned with the direct effects of crowding on the operation of the facility. Crowding, for example, may preclude the use of recreational space for some offenders. Instead, space may be needed to house the inmate population. In this way, the ordinary operation of the institution is disrupted because of crowding. Crowding is problematic for correctional managers and the operational capacity of the institution has been exceeded when daily operational activities cannot take place.

Upon close examination, it is easy to find problems with these attempts at objective measurement of crowding. The measures provide little information about conditions within facilities and are susceptible to wide interpretation and manipulation. As Bleich (1989) has stated, "Whether a prison can accommodate an increase in its population cannot be determined simply by counting floor tiles or beds. Rather the answer may depend in large part on the configuration of the sleeping units, the composition of the population, the types of programs provided, and the levels of staffing." As early as 1937, the Bureau of the Census abandoned the use of capacity measures in assessments of crowding because of the difficulty in determining the "normal capacity" of prisons and jails (see Bleich, 1989:1141).

Although they remain the most prominent measures, there is a growing recognition of the inadequacy of capacity-based crowding measures. At the same time, there is an increasing recognition that the concept of crowding is also related to individual, institutional, and political interests. In this sense crowding may be better understood by examining how it is used than by defining it simply as an objective construct that incorporates measures of the number of people occupying a given space. We return to this problem after considering some of the changing approaches to understanding jail and prison crowding.

Effects of Crowding

One of the reasons some people support capacity-based definitions of crowding is the belief that when crowding reaches a certain level there are distinct physiological, behavioral, and psychological effects. Studies have demonstrated that these effects occur in laboratory animals, and social scientists have identified effects in crowded housing and other facilities. Only recently have studies of correctional facilities attempted to document the impact of crowding.

The physiological effects of crowding have been examined in several studies. Identified effects have included elevated blood pressure levels

(D'Atri, 1975; D'Atri et al., 1981), an increase in complaints of illness among inmates (McCain, Cox, and Paulus, 1976), and serious health concerns, such as coronary problems (Carr, 1981). In addition to health-related concerns, research has also identified social as well as behavioral problems produced by institutional crowding. These types of problems relate to the overall adjustment problems experienced by prisoners as a result of crowding.

Behavioral problems caused by crowding include increased assaults and disciplinary infractions among inmates (Zausner, 1985). The research on these effects, however, is problematic (Porporino and Dudley, 1984; Innes, 1987; Fry, 1988). Much of the research suffers from a lack of consistency in the definition and measurement of crowding. Moreover, there is much room for interpretation with regard to crowding and behavioral problems among confined populations. Useem and Kimball (1989), for example, argue that when examining serious institutional events, such as riots and violent assaults, much can be explained by prison officials' lack of administrative control. Crowding, therefore, may be a factor associated with serious institutional violence, yet other causes may be more significant. A similar view is offered by other researchers.

Gaes and McGuire (1985) report that high levels of inmate violence occur within institutions that have a high population density, yet their findings lack generalizability, since the prisons studied were at the federal level. Given the considerable differences that exist between federal and state prisons, we need to be cautious about these conclusions. A similar view must be taken when examining violence and overcrowding from an international perspective (see Farrington and Nuttall, 1985).

Research on the psychological effects of crowding is even less clear. While some have argued that increased psychological stress occurs as a result of the general experience of incarceration, this is different from saying that crowding has a definitive psychological effect on the prisoner population. Teplin (1990) has found that recently admitted jail inmates have mental illness rates that are two to three times those of the general population. Such a high incidence of mental illness, however, may be due to a number of factors, including preexisting conditions, and not simply to the level of jail crowding. Furthermore, research has not been able to identify the specific relationship between crowding and mental illness. A similar criticism can be levied against those who suggest that crowding is also strongly correlated with other psychological problems, such as increased levels of anxiety, suicide, and depression (Gaes, 1994).

When the research on the effects of crowding is closely examined, it would seem to support the abandonment of "normal capacity" measures. Although the research has shown some effects, in such areas as illness and violence, the studies have not produced strong or consistent findings. In one review of the literature, Gaes (1985) argues that only two basic conclusions could be drawn. First, dormitory housing produces higher illness reports than other forms of housing and, second, crowding can produce elevated assault rates. More important, however, he also notes that "unfortunately, while deeply held views about the effects of crowding are common, the core scientific knowledge on which informed opinion must be based is small and is constrained by methodological limitation that caution against generalizing from it" (1985:69). More recently, Gaes (1994:358) has suggested that even his two basic findings may not be valid. It seems that there is little basis for describing universal effects of crowding. Instead, Gaes argues, the way administrators react to population increases may be more important than the increases themselves.

Crowding and the Courts

The limitations of the measures used to assess crowding at the institutional level have also been recognized by the courts. In cases dealing with jail and prison crowding, the Supreme Court has appreciated the complexity of institutional crowding and has rejected approaches based solely on capacity. In *Bell* v. *Wolfish* (441 U.S. 520 [1979]), the Court ruled on, among other things, the constitutionality of the "double bunking" of pretrial detainees. While the decision focused on the absence of punitive intent by officials, the Court also considered the fact that inmates were provided adequate room for sleeping, were detained for relatively short terms, and were allowed out of their cells for substantial periods each day.

In *Rhodes* v. *Chapman* (452 U.S. 347 [1981]), the Supreme Court considered the double bunking of prison inmates. For crowding to result in constitutionally prohibited cruel and unusual punishment, conditions would need to "involve the wanton and unnecessary infliction of pain" or "be grossly disproportionate to the severity of the crime warranting imprisonment." As Justice Brennan described in a concurring opinion, the Court used a "totality of circumstances test" and found no constitutional violation. Among the factors considered by the Court in *Rhodes* were the amount of time inmates spent out of cells and the quality of food, ventilation, programming, and inmate safety.

In decisions before and after *Bell* and *Rhodes,* lower courts have found constitutional violations in some crowded institutions. Plaintiffs in these cases delineated, with varying degrees of specificity, the harmful effects of crowding in their particular institutions (see Thornberry and Call, 1983). Although remedies have often been linked to capacity by requiring reductions in prison or jail populations, the cases make it clear that measures of crowding based solely on capacity are of limited value. And, the problem is not only that judicial perspectives on crowding are not adequately reflected in measures of crowding. As the director of the jails division of the National Institute of Corrections, Michael O'Toole (personal communication, March 16, 1990) has noted that it is common wisdom among corrections professionals that two institutions may be filled equally beyond their design or rated capacities and still be very different places in which to work or live.

In further recognizing the difficulties with objective measures of crowding, recent court decisions have emphasized administrative expertise and perspective in managing correctional facilities. In *Wilson* v. *Seiter* (1991), the Supreme Court ruled that for an inmate to prevail in an allegation that crowding comprises cruel and unusual punishment, there must be a showing of deliberate indifference by prison administrators. As Gaes (1994:332) suggests, this makes it more difficult for inmates to succeed in prison conditions suits involving overcrowding.

FROM HUMANENESS TO MANAGERIAL EFFICIENCY

The case law in this area illustrates the changing nature of thinking about correctional crowding. While institutional crowding has increased and decreased before in the United States, the debate over its significance is distinctly modern. In the early period of current population increases, many scholars and reformers argued that our society should not tolerate conditions in prisons and jails that did not meet some general standard of humaneness (e.g., Irwin, 1980). The concern was not with specific deleterious effects but rather with some general notion of quality of life and standards of decency. As experience with crowding continued, there was a shift of focus to concern with the specific effects of crowding. Crowding was problematic only to the extent that it was presumed to contribute to such problems as violence, suicide, or poor health. In this sense, the moral argument gave way to empirical considerations.

The failure of research to produce convincing evidence of specific deleterious effects (Gaes, 1985:146), however, is leading to another redefinition of crowding problems. The deference to administrative expertise suggests that even crowding-related problems are less relevant than an unwillingness to address the specific adverse effects that an administrator recognizes in his or her institution. The focus has shifted from crowding as a moral problem, to an empirical problem, to a managerial problem. This current view is underscored in a recent assessment of the importance of crowding. As Gaes (1994:359) notes: "There are many institutions that are crowded; however, for the most part, those prisons that are orderly and meet basic needs have avoided litigation or have won conditions suits brought against them."

With the focus shifting to managerial responses to overcrowding, concerns about the quality of life for prisoners assume a back seat to managerial prescriptions. Concerns over proper management techniques have become the major topic for correctional administrators. Even among researchers, this shift in focus has produced a number of studies aimed at improving the quality of prison and jail management (Dilulio, 1987, 1991; Useem and Kimball, 1989:227; Johnson, 1995; Wright, 1995), as well as specific management suggestions based on empirical examinations of the crowding phenomenon.

One management-based approach to crowding is provided by Klofas, Stojkovic, and Kalinich (1992:178), who present a model that identifies specific variables of interest to administrators (see Figure 6.1). To develop the model, jail experts from across the country including sheriffs, jail administrators, and jail inspectors, met in a focus group for the purpose of exchanging information on what crowding means in their facilities. The model they proposed specifies variables associated with problematic crowding. Under this model, correctional crowding is difficult for jail administrators only when visible problems are produced.

As indicated in Figure 6.1, there are eight variables related to the severity of prison crowding: (1) number of inmates and jail capacity; (2) timing issues related to the days and times of the week when crowding becomes an issue; (3) fluctuations in the number of inmates admitted to jail; (4) composition of the inmate body, such as the proportion of inmates with mental health problems or other illnesses; (5) characteristics of the jail, including the structure and design of the institution; (6) disruptions of jail routines due to overcrowding; (7) primary management issues that jail administrators face, such as the effect of crowding on staff stress and the necessity of staff overtime to run the jail; and (8) relationships with outside agencies and organizations. Taken together, these variables provide a means of defining the severity of crowding from a managerial perspective and may also assist managers to develop policies and practices to better run their facilities.

FIGURE 6.1 A model of the severity of jail crowding.

Severity of Crowding =

Number of Inmates and Jail Capacity

+

Timing Issues

+

Intake Fluctuations

+

Composition of Inmates in Population

+

Characteristics of the Jail

+

Disruption of Jail Operations

+

Management Issues

+

Relationships with Outside Agencies and Organizations

Such a model offers hope to correctional administrators in specific ways. The model allows managers to focus on particular issues that they confront on a daily basis and to identify strategies that would be unique to their institutions. In this way, managers have a method to determine the unique problems they face and to proceed in a proactive fashion when facing a crowded institution. Moreover, with emphasis being placed on the importance of management in dealing with correctional crowding, the model provides a conceptual and empirical basis for both current and future attempts to address crowding.

CROWDING IN JAILS

The approach to managing crowding discussed previously was developed with the expertise of jail administrators from across the country. The model provides a foundation for understanding crowding in other correctional facilities, but it also describes the unique problems facing U.S. jails. The differences between jails and prisons mean that these institutions deal with different types of crowding problems and that we can also expect differences in efforts to solve these problems.

In jails across the country, the biggest challenges result from the complexity of the inmate population. Among jail inmates can be found unarraigned offenders in holding tanks, having just been arrested. Others will be awaiting trial. Still others will be held for a variety of miscellaneous reasons including violations of probation, violations of parole, and civil confinement for nonpayment of child support. Some inmates are held by federal detainer and include accused criminals and illegal immigrants.

Finally, about a third of inmates may be serving sentences in local jails. Within each of these categories there can also be male and female inmates, young and old, healthy and infirmed, and sophisticated criminals and the naive or misfortunate. The daunting task of jail administrators is to manage this complex human mix.

Managing jails is made all the more difficult in crowded conditions, especially in light of the requirement that many categories of offenders be kept separate. Not only must men and women be kept apart, but often so too must the accused and the convicted. In addition, jail classification systems attempt to separate first-time offenders from experienced criminals, and those who seem likely to be victimized from their potential predators. Jail staff frequently face other demands too. Often they must isolate co-defendants, members of rival gangs, and those believed to carry some contagious illness.

The task of management is further complicated by the fact that the myriad decisions needed to divide the inmate population appropriately must be made and remade swiftly and with limited information. The proximity of the street to the jail means that crowding strikes quickly, often with little notice. Police sweeps, prostitution details, and even minor crime waves can bring many new inmates to jails at almost any time. With them comes little information to assist in their separation and sorting. Criminal histories, mental health problems, medical conditions, and other problems are often undocumented or unknown as staff must assess inmates for their placement within the jail.

The jails' unique problems of crowding can be seen clearly when inmates representing such a range of legally relevant categories and conditions arrive at an overpopulated facility. Maintaining the appropriate divisions and ensuring proper care may mean that crowding is experienced differently in different parts of the jail. At one time cellblocks for women may be jammed beyond capacity while elsewhere there is room. At another time pretrial inmates may suffer while sentenced offenders have elbow room. And, too, staff must frequently move inmates, regularly transforming the jail as the population mix changes.

Since the population of the jail responds to many changes in crime and the criminal justice system, there is some regularity to its ebb and flow. Jail populations go through regular cycles that affect their crowding problems in annual, weekly, and even daily patterns. Since the vast majority of inmates are unarraigned or awaiting trial, jail populations reflect the annual cycles of criminal behavior and police enforcement. The warm weather of summer brings with it large numbers of people arrested in street sweeps of prostitutes, drug users and dealers, and other criminals that Irwin (1985) has termed "rabble." In cold months the holiday season may bring not only the spirit of gift giving but also opportunities for larceny and other crimes. Accused perpetrators of these offenses will swell the ranks of jail inmates. These cycles mean that the population of some jails will change significantly over the course of a year.

Change also occurs on a weekly basis. In communities without night court or weekend sessions, jail populations grow over weekends. That can mean that jails that are crowded at five o'clock on Friday will be bursting at the seams by Monday morning. Those problems can be further complicated if jails must also supervise offenders serving weekend sentences. Even on a daily basis, the jail population may fluctuate significantly. As crime and enforcement activity increase through late evening and early morning hours, the jail feels the effects of increasing arrests, only to find numbers falling as inmates are released on bail or released on recognizance (ROR) the next morning. And, too, there may be morning surges as local lockups transport the evening's catch to the central jail to await arraignment. The jail, then, because of its proximity to the street, is subject to frequent increases and decreases in its population that can greatly affect the problems associated with crowding.

The rises and falls of the jail population make it clear that jails are greatly influenced by activity throughout the rest of the criminal justice system. Studies show that the processing of criminal cases from arrests through pretrial release decisions has had the greatest impact on jail population and subsequent crowding (Monroe County Study, 1994). A study of the jail inmates in Rochester, New York, for example, revealed that from 1980 through 1993 the jail population grew by more than 350 percent, while the crime rate remained nearly flat and the number of arrests grew only slightly. Although correctional populations may grow by increased admissions to the jail or through increases in the length of stay, the latter appears to have the most significant impact. In Rochester, the average length of stay increased by more than 50 percent in the last decade.

In many jails, the greatest increases in length of stay and in the overall occupancy of cell space have come from inmates whose custody is not controlled by local authorities. Parole violators and inmates who have been sentenced for felonies but not yet transferred to state prisons are of particular concern for local jail officials. Those categories of offenders demonstrate the link between crowding in state prison systems and the crowding of local jails (Stojkovic, 1986).

Although increases in the length of stay in local jails may have greatly influenced the size of the inmate population, it does not mean that all inmates stay in jail for long periods. In fact, the processing function of jails appears to be far more significant than the holding function (Klofas, 1991). That is revealed by the fact that for most inmates admitted to jail, the stay can be very brief. In the Rochester study, 35 percent of newly admitted inmates stayed fewer than four days. By the end of a week, 50 percent of the inmates had been released and over two thirds of inmates were released in fewer than two weeks. Findings of this type are suggestive of the extent to which public safety is served by the short stays experienced by most inmates. They also raise questions about the efficacy of expensive programs of jail expansion to address crowding, and they suggest alternative approaches.

Analysis of the jail population and length of stay suggests that crowding problems can be addressed effectively through analysis and reform of case processing in criminal justice. The long-term solution to crowding may depend on changing the way local criminal justice systems do business rather than on the construction of new cell space. This can mean reconsidering the circumstances that warrant admission to jail. It means increased use of citation and release mechanisms, streamlining processing through preset bail, and expediting bail procedures and assisting inmates to raise bail. It may also mean developing a system of graduated custody and supervision programs for some pretrial inmates who need not be kept in jail.

A wide variety of innovations have been developed across the country in efforts to manage the size of jail populations through improved case processing. Jails now routinely assess their populations to track inmates who may have fallen through the cracks or suffered other reasons for delay.

Pretrial diversion programs use community supervision and treatment as alternatives to jail (McShane and Krause, 1993). Custody of some offenders is maintained through electronic monitoring and home confinement in lieu of incarceration (McCarthy, 1987). Day reporting programs have also been developed in efforts to ensure an accused offender will return to court (National Institute of Justice, 1992). Similar programs are also increasingly used as sanctions for misdemeanants who might otherwise be sentenced to brief periods in local facilities. In light of the brief but costly stay that most jail inmates experience, these alterations to case processing are sensible and effective. In many jurisdictions, their effectiveness is also improved by the creation of special warrant units to arrest and place in secure custody those who do not comply with the requirements of the new programs.

Concern with jail crowding, then, is revolutionizing the practice of criminal justice in many communities. Where once the police, the judiciary, and releasing authorities rarely spoke with each other and never engaged in joint planning, it is now common for administrators from across the criminal justice system to come together and consider the shared impacts of their individual offices (Weiss, 1991). And, too, there have been developments in information processing through which the effects on the jail population can be examined for individual judges, courts, and police agencies. It is becoming routine for local criminal justice planning groups to examine data on the processing of cases and to work together to control the growth of jail populations while ensuring the safety of the public.

CROWDING IN PRISONS

Prison crowding presents a number of concerns and problems that differ from those tied to jail crowding. The most visible difference between prisons and jails is the type of offender housed in them. Prison inmates, with their longer sentences, require different types of programs and services than jail inmates. As a result, it is common for prisons to spend large sums of money on programming that addresses the problems and needs of the inmate population. More often than not, these needs require a long-term commitment on the part of the institution. Thus, the prison has to approach the offender much differently than does the jail.

One of the most pressing problems that arises concerning crowding and prisoner management relates to the issue of classification. Prison classification requires that inmates are assessed early in their confinement to determine the level of security that is required, as well as the type of treatment services and medical or mental health services that may be needed (VanVoorhis, 1994). Such a procedure is often hampered when, because of crowding, correctional officials are unable to provide either the security necessary to satisfactorily manage inmates or the programming necessary to meet their treatment needs. Duffee (1989), for example, has discussed how during severe space shortages, prison classification committees utilize available space regardless of prisoners' treatment needs. Since the most space exists in maximum security prisons, it is not uncommon for low security offenders to be housed in prisons where security is higher than necessary. Research has shown that most inmates require medium security placements, but because of the oversupply of inmates and the undersupply of prison space, classification committees often overclassify prisoners (Austin, 1983).

This situation is exacerbated by not only a large number of offenders being sent to prisons, but also by the type of offender being housed within correctional institutions. As documented by the Bureau of Justice Statistics (1993), the growth in prison populations has been more than 200 percent over the past fifteen years, with drug offenders being the single largest group, making up more than one third of new admissions to prison. Couple this fact with the reality that many of these offenders will be serving long prison sentences and it is easy to see that crowding will pose an even greater strain on the resources of prisons for years to come. Another important point is that research has identified drug offenders as the most difficult to manage and control (Flanagan, 1983).

From a management perspective, prison populations have become increasingly more challenging to manage. Additionally, many of these drug offenders will require long-term treatment strategies to deal with their drug addictions. In most prison systems, however, resources committed to drug treatment are sparse (Clear and Cole, 1990). Most important, many of these offenders are being sent to institutions for long sentences under newly developed sentencing strategies. Beginning with the advent of federal sentencing guidelines instituted in the mid-1980s, there have been attempts to increase the length of sentences among offenders. One of the most profound changes in sentencing laws has been the creation of the "three strikes and you're out" legislation promulgated at both the federal and state levels.

The state of California has the most stringent three strikes and you're out laws, calling for immediate imposition of prison sentences from twenty-five years to life if convicted of a third felony. The immediate effect on local criminal justice systems has been dramatic increases in jail populations. It is estimated that in Los Angeles County alone there are more than 5000 additional inmates in local jails because of the three strikes initiative (State of California Analyst's Office, 1994). Since many of these offenders may receive rather lengthy sentences if convicted, they are opting for jury trials instead of traditional plea bargains. The enormous impact on crowding will be felt by the entire system of criminal justice, yet jails and prisons will have the most pronounced effects on their operations stemming from the new legislation.

Crowding will continue to be a major problem for most states well into the next century. According to the California Department of Corrections (1994), if present trends continue, the state will have to build and maintain twenty-five additional prisons to accommodate another 125,000 inmates, doubling its current prison population from 125,000 inmates to close to 250,000 inmates. The effects of crowding will only get worse, and if other strategies are not implemented in the near future, the crowding situation will most likely worsen for most prison systems across the country. Therefore, many are advocating a comprehensive plan of alternative mechanisms to handle offender populations, consisting of both "front door" and "back door" approaches.

Front door strategies often center on attempts to reduce the prison population by focusing on those offenders who do not require some type of incarcerative response by the criminal justice system. This usually means approaches that emphasize the removal of individuals from the criminal justice system well before a decision is made to incarcerate them. *Diversion* as a front door strategy has been developed and implemented extensively within both state and federal criminal justice systems over the past twenty-five years. Diversion attempts to "weed out" those offenders who pose the least threat to society and provide them with the least restrictive alternatives to incarceration.

Programs like electronic monitoring and intensive probation are designed to enable offenders to stay in their communities to serve their sentences. The state of Wisconsin, for example, has instituted a Department of Intensive Sanctions that is designed to keep prison populations and the attendant crowding to manageable levels. Under this strategy, offenders are placed in small groups—usually consisting of twenty or fewer offenders—and are supervised closely by monitoring agents. The offenders are still considered inmates in the sense that they are under the authority of prison officials, yet they serve a majority of their sentences in the community. Any infraction of department rules can lead to immediate placement in a correctional facility. In this way, the department has attempted to control prison populations by selecting those inmates who pose the least threat to the community and monitoring their behavior under a set of rules that limits their activities (Wisconsin Department of Corrections, 1992).

Whereas the primary intent of front door strategies is to reduce the number of offenders received by prisons, *back door strategies* employ approaches that attempt to release inmates from institutions in a safe and efficient manner. These approaches are sensitive to prison officials' need to manage crowded facilities. More often than not, back door strategies attempt to prevent crowding conditions in advance of crisis situations. The most widely used and well-known back door strategy is parole. *Parole* as a release mechanism has been around for more than 120 years in U.S. prisons. Prison wardens are the most receptive toward expanded paroling strategies, since they enable prison managers to adjust their populations in times of need.

Although a useful strategy to reduce crowded prisons, the concept of parole has been severely attacked and criticized on both moral and empirical grounds. On moral grounds, critics have argued that parole is an anachronistic correctional approach that has outlived its usefulness. These critics argue that the history of parole in America is an inglorious one, citing problems with its conceptualization as well as its moral underpinnings. Ardent critics like Morris (1974), Fogel (1975), and VonHirsch (1976) have all argued that the moral basis for parole is centered, in part, on a faulty notion of prediction of human behavior. These critics suggest that punishment can be imposed on people only for what they have done, not on what they might do. In addition, they have documented the many abuses that have occurred with parole, suggesting that prisoners are forced to play a "game" with parole officials in order to obtain early release (Manocchio and Dunn, 1970). Such a process is blatantly immoral, according to critics, and therefore should be abolished and not condoned as an acceptable penological practice.

Notwithstanding these moral objections to parole, empirical criticisms may be more devastating. Current research suggests that many offenders released on parole fare poorly in the community and that as many as one third return to prison within a three-year period subsequent to release (Bureau of Justice Statistics, 1994). Such evidence is disconcerting to prison officials who see parole as an important strategy for reducing crowded correctional institutions. In spite of protests by correctional administrators, parole is under continued attack by many, including politicians who can conveniently pander to the fears of citizens when a parolee commits a particularly heinous crime. As a result, state and federal legislatures have attempted to either severely restrict parole or to abolish it outright (Irwin and Austin, 1994). Several states have chosen to select the latter approach, having a direct impact on the crowding situation in their prisons.

Another controversial back door strategy is *good time credit* for prisoners. This strategy is intended to provide incentives to inmates to act appropriately while incarcerated. Through a good time program, prisoners are allowed a number of days off their sentences if they act in accordance with institutional rules and regulations. There are wide variations across the country with regard to the number of days off an inmate can receive for good behavior. The incentive, however, is obvious to the inmate, but in addition, the institution is able to use such efforts to reduce the size of the inmate population. Advocates of good time programs argue that they are necessary for the long-term management of both prisons and prisoners.

Prisoners benefit from the potential reduction in sentence, while the institution benefits through a reduction in the size of the prisoner population. Critics, however, argue that such programs undermine the moral legitimacy of the criminal sentence and the sentencing judge and send a wrong message to offenders. Current proponents of "truth in sentencing provisions" argue that good time programs are manipulated by both prisoners and prisons officials to meet narrow self-interests to the detriment of public safety and the integrity of the sentencing process. Regardless of the interest served, many states rely on a practical program of early release for prisoners who conform to institutional rules. Moreover, it is equally clear that prison administrators would have a difficult time managing their facilities if there were no good time programs available. Current efforts designed to significantly alter or reduce good time credits given to prisoners would have demonstrable negative effects on the management of crowded correctional institutions.

A final back door strategy employed to reduce crowding in prisons is the use of *half-way houses* in the community for those offenders who are at the end of their sentences. This strategy to reduce overcrowding in prisons has been effectively used for the past thirty years across the country (Smykla, 1984). Such an approach seeks to identify those offenders who pose the least threat to society and can be managed safely and securely in the community. Recently attempts have been made to use this strategy to reduce the number of people in prison who are an enormous cost to institutions and because of some illness or disability may be more appropriately supervised in the community. Examples of this may include some elderly offenders and HIV-infected inmates.

Some states have attempted to deal with HIV-infected inmates by providing early release and placement in the community in half-way houses. Many of these offenders are in the advanced stages of AIDS and often have little time to live. Supporters of this strategy note the tremendous cost such offenders place on prisons, and that in a time of scarce prison resources such a strategy is both cost effective and humanitarian. Whether this strategy will gain in momentum remains to be seen, yet there is no doubt that HIV-infected inmates and full-blown AIDS cases pose a significant threat to the operation of prison facilities today and into the next century. The half-way house as a back door strategy to reduce the number of prisoners who suffer from debilitating diseases is one that many states and the federal government will have to consider seriously. This same strategy has also been proposed for the growing number of older inmates who will be confined for long periods of time (Durham III, 1994), well past the time they represent a danger to society.

Through the use of these types of front door and back door strategies, correctional administrators attempt to deal with the problems caused by crowding. Taken together these strategies have proven effective in aiding correctional officials in the day-to-day operations of their prisons. Each strategy provides both direct and indirect benefits to correctional managers, yet no single strategy will be able to solve the prison crowding problem. Instead, a combination of approaches seems a more reasonable course of action. Additionally, by combining these strategies, correctional administrators are also able to meet the varying interests and concerns that are represented in the crowding debate. It is those interests and the uses of correctional crowding that now direct our attention.

CORRECTIONAL CROWDING: A PANORAMA OF INTERESTS

The transformation of the issue of crowding from one of concern of humaneness to one of effects and management illustrates the importance of examining correctional crowding in a larger context. Consistent with that, Bleich (1989:1180) has argued that correctional crowding is a social construction that cannot be defined in a moral or political vacuum. As crowding has become detached from an objective analysis of institutional conditions, then, it is important to consider how and in whose interests the concept has been used. Over the past fifteen years, specific interests have advanced the issue of crowding with the hope of obtaining discernible benefits. Among the parties with interests in the crowding issue have been prisoners, prison reformers, correctional professionals, a growing corrections industry, and aspiring politicians.

For some prisoners, the concern has been the degree to which crowding could be used to promote public concern about prison conditions, to encourage court-ordered reform, and to make a case for early release and alternative sentences. Although the courts have been reticent about requiring wholesale change, there have been notable victories. The interests of prisoners have also been reflected in the increasingly public discussion of diversion of nonviolent and drug offenders from prisons. In the long run, the visibility of the crowding issue may be more important than actual consequences of litigation.

Prison reformers have also promoted their interests by using crowding. For them, crowding has been the platform from which to advocate policies of humanitarian reform. Similar to prisoner groups, prison reformers have been appealing to the courts for redress concerning the crowding issue. Sometimes successful, they have struggled to shape the debate over crowding on ideological grounds. Those reformers have attempted to use the issue of crowding to send a political message to the community about the harmful effects of prison crowding on inmates and on society as a whole. A convincing example of this is the proliferation of lawsuits that have arisen because of the use of high security prisons across the country, such as Pelican Bay in California (Irwin and Austin, 1994:91–114). Reformers have long been concerned with what they regard as inhumane conditions in such facilities. Increasingly, reform groups are returning to the language and method of humanitarianism, thereby avoiding the limitations of empirical analyses of the issue.

Correctional professionals, including heads of departments of corrections and wardens, have also used crowding to promote their interests. Some administrators may recognize that claims of crowding may excuse some of management's problems in troubled facilities (Dilulio, 1987:3). For others, crowding can garner new resources through the modernization and expansion of prison systems. Even county sheriffs have seen antiquated facilities replaced by modern megajails often accompanied by new courtrooms, prosecutors' quarters, and other facilities. Although crowding persists, budgets and personnel roles have expanded dramatically. States are also looking toward much greater expansion. In California, for example, officials are planning a doubling of prison capacity to meet the demand. The state is considering the construction of twenty-five more prisons to handle the influx of new inmates (California Department of Corrections, 1994:5). Under these conditions, the crowding issue may be the trump card in the process of competing for resources in a struggling economy.

Intimately tied to this expansion of prisons is the burgeoning corrections-related industry. Similar to the military-industrial complex of the 1950s, we have seen an enormous growth in business and industry related to corrections in the last fifteen years. The proportion of state and federal revenue spent on corrections has almost tripled across the country over the past fifteen years (Irwin and Austin, 1994:13). In some states, including California, Wisconsin, and Michigan, correctional budgets have far outpaced spending on education and other social services. Many of these funds have gone to architects, builders, food contractors, medical suppliers, and others, all of whom have developed special services for corrections. The management of prisons and jails by private contractors may still be in its infancy, but business in ancilliary industries is booming. Crowding plays a direct role in expanding the correctional landscape and in the growth of the resulting business and financial empires.

Finally, correctional crowding has been tied to a variety of political interests. Fear of crime, responded to and fostered by simplistic rhetoric, has encouraged politicians to seek concrete solutions. As the crime issue has become increasingly politicized, the debate has focused almost entirely on getting tougher. Politicians have demonstrated their "toughness" by passing legislation to put more people in prison for longer periods of time. And they have demonstrated their toughness in tolerating if not promoting declining conditions in prison. Recent debates over such topics as weight lifting in prison and funding for inmate education illustrate the way prison conditions have found their way into political discourse. Where get tough legislation has collided with demands for cost control, overcrowding and declining conditions have been the result.

An analysis of correctional crowding, therefore, can benefit from a consideration of the constellation of interests served. This type of understanding can help widen the discussion of correctional crowding and can help us formulate questions that we might not consider if crowding were viewed simply in terms of prison and jail capacity.

CONCLUSION

The modern era of correctional crowding began in the mid- to late-1970s and has continued unabated. Since it began we have seen prison and jail populations grow by more than 300 percent. That growth has continued to outstrip the expansion of capacity. It seems very likely, given the current social and political climate, that correctional populations will continue to grow and that the expansion of prison and jail capacity through construction will not keep pace. Important lessons, then, may be found in understanding crowding not only in a narrow technical perspective but in a larger social context.

The earliest concerns about crowding centered on perceptions of deteriorating jail and prison conditions. Empirical examination changed the course from broad humanitarian concerns to the consideration of specific effects. Even that concern may be giving way to a focus on how crowded facilities can be better managed. Similarly, addressing crowding grew from a focus on square footage, to attention to legal requirements, to the manner in which the criminal justice system itself may be changed to better manage jail and prison populations.

As analyses have moved back and forth from the broadly philosophical to the pragmatic and from a narrow institutional to a system focus, however, it has also become clear that still wider contexts are important. The enormous growth in jail and prison populations and the vast resources that have gone into maintaining them do not exist in a vacuum. They have been shaped by our concerns with the quality of American life and by our own vision of morality. As our society confronts the issues of growing diversity and declining prosperity for many, the crowding of correctional facilities provides one view of our interests and priorities. The state of our correctional facilities provides a perspective on the state of the American character at the end of the twentieth century (Kalinich and Embert, 1995).

REFERENCES

Austin, J. (1983). "Assessing the New Generation of Prison Classification Models." *Crime and Delinquency,* 29(4):561–576.

Bell v. *Wolfish,* 441 U.S. 520 (1979).

Bleich, J. (1989). "The Politics of Prison Crowding." *California Law Review,* 77(5):1125–1180.

Bureau of Justice Statistics. (1992). "Prisoners in 1991." Washington, D.C.: U.S. Department of Justice.

Bureau of Justice Statistics. (1993). "Prisoners in 1992." Washington, D.C.: U.S. Department of Justice.

Bureau of Justice Statistics. (1994). "Comparing Federal and State Prison Inmates, 1991." Washington, D.C.: U.S. Department of Justice.

California Department of Corrections. (1994). "Budget Summary and Projections for the California Department of Corrections." Sacramento, CA: California Department of Corrections.

Carr, T. (1981). "The Effects of Crowding on Recidivism, Cardiovascular Deaths and Infraction Rates in a Large Prison System." (Unpublished doctoral dissertation, Georgia State University.)

Clear, T. and Cole, G. (1990). *American Corrections* (2d ed.). Pacific Grove, CA: Brooks/Cole.

D'Atri, D. (1975). "Psychophysiological Responses to Crowding." *Environment and Behavior,* 7(2):237–252.

D'Atri, D., Fitzgerald, E.F., Kasl, S., and Ostfeld, A. (1981). "Crowding in Prison: The Relationship between Changes in Housing Mode and Blood Pressure." *Psychosomatic Medicine,* 43(1):95–105.

DiIulio, J., Jr. (1987). *Governing Prisons: A Comparative Study of Correctional Management.* New York: The Free Press.

DiIulio J., Jr. (1991). *No Escape: The Future of American Corrections.* New York: Basic Books.

Duffee, D. (1989). *Corrections: Practice and Policy.* New York: Random House.

Durham III, A. (1994). *Crisis and Reform: Current Issues in American Punishment.* Boston: Little, Brown and Co.

Farrington, D. and Nuttal, C. (1985). "Prison Size, Overcrowding, Prison Violence, and Recidivism." In M. Braswell, S. Dillingham, and R. Montgomery Jr. (eds.), *Prison Violence in America.* Cincinnati, OH: Anderson Publishing Co.

Flanagan, T. (1983). "Correlates of Institutional Misconduct Among State Prisoners." *Criminology,* 21(1):29–39.

Fogel, D. (1975). ". . . We Are The Living Proof . . .": The Justice Model for Corrections.* Cincinnati, OH: Anderson Publishing Co.

Fry, L.J. (1988). "Continuities in the Determination of Prison Overcrowding Effects." *Journal of Criminal Justice,* 16(3):231–240.

Gaes, G. (1985). "The Effects of Overcrowding in Prison." In M. Tonry and N. Morris (eds.), *Crime and Justice: An Annual Review of Research.* Chicago: University of Chicago Press.

Gaes, G. and McGuire, W. (1985). "Prison Violence: The Contribution of Crowding versus Other Determinants of Prison Assault Rates." *Journal of Research in Crime and Delinquency,* 22(1):41–65.

Gaes, G. (1994). "Prison Crowding Research Reexamined." *The Prison Journal,* 74(3):329–363.

Gottfredson, S. and McConville, S. (eds.). (1987). *America's Correctional Crisis: Prison Populations and Public Policy.* New York: Greenwood Publishers.

Innes, C. (1987). "Population Density in State Prisons." *Bureau of Justice Statistics: Special Report.* Washington, D.C.: U.S. Department of Justice.

Irwin, J. (1980). *Prisons in Turmoil.* Boston: Little, Brown and Co.

Irwin, J. (1985). *The Jail: Managing the Underclass in American Society.* Berkeley, CA: The University of California Press.

Irwin, J. and Austin, J. (1994). *It's About Time: America's Imprisonment Binge.* Monterey, CA: Wadsworth.

Johnson, R. (1995). *Hard Time: Understanding and Reforming the Prison* (2d ed.). Monterey, CA: Wadsworth.

Kalinich, D. and Embert, P. (1995). "Grim Tales of the Future: American Jails in the Year 2010." In J. Klofas and S. Stojkovic (eds.), *Crime and Justice in the Year 2010.* Monterey, CA: Wadsworth.

Klofas, J. (1991). "Disaggregating Jail Use: Variety and Change in Local Corrections Over a Ten-Year Period." In J. Thompson and G. Mays (eds.), *American Jails: Public Policy Issues.* Chicago: Nelson-Hall Publishers.

Klofas, J., Stojkovic, S., and Kalinich, D. (1992). "The Meaning of Correctional Crowding: Steps Toward an Index of Severity." *Crime and Delinquency,* 38(2):171–188.

Manocchio, A. and Dunn, J. (1970). *The Time Game: Two Views of a Prison.* Beverly Hills, CA: Sage.

McCain, G., Cox, V., and Paulus, P. (1976). "The Effects of Prison Crowding on Inmate Behavior." Washington, D.C.: Law Enforcement Assistance Administration.

McCarthy, B. (ed.). (1987). *Intermediate Punishments: Intensive Supervision, Home Confinement, and Electronic Surveillance.* Monsey, NY: Criminal Justice Press.

McShane, M. and Krause, W. (1993). *Community Corrections.* New York: Macmillan.

Monroe County. (1994). "The Jail Utilization Team Report." Rochester, NY: Department of Public Safety.

Morris, N. (1974). *The Future of Imprisonment.* Chicago: University of Chicago Press.

National Institute of Justice. (1988). "Nation's Jail Managers Assess Their Problems." Washington, D.C.: U.S. Department of Justice.

National Institute of Justice. (1992). "Day Fines in American Courts: The Staten Island and Milwaukee Experiments." Washington, D.C.: U.S. Department of Justice.

Porporino, F. and Dudley, K. (1984). "An Analysis of the Effects of Overcrowding in Canadian Penitentiaries." Ottawa: Ministry of the Solicitor General of Canada.

Rhodes v. *Chapman,* 452 U.S. 347 (1981).

Smykla, J. (1984). *Probation and Parole: Crime Control in the Community.* New York: Macmillan.

State of California Analyst's Office. (1994). "Crime in California." Sacramento, CA: Legislative Analyst's Office.

Stojkovic, S. (1986). "Jails versus Prisons: Comparisons, Problems and Prescriptions on Inmate Subcultures." In D. Kalinich and J. Klofas (eds.), *Sneaking Inmates Down the Alley: Problems and Prospects in Jail Management.* Springfield, IL: Charles C Thomas Publisher.

Stojkovic, S. and Lovell, R. (1992). *Corrections: An Introduction.* Cincinnati, OH: Anderson Publishing Co.

Teplin, L. (1990). "The Prevalence of Severe Mental Disorder Among Male Urban Jail Detainees: Comparison with Epidemiological Catchment Area Program." *American Journal of Public Health,* 80(4):663–669.

Thornberry, T. and Call, J. (1983). "Constitutional Challenges to Prison Overcrowding: The Scientific Evidence of Harmful Effects." *Hastings Law Journal,* 35(23).

Useem, B. and Kimball, P. (1989). *States of Siege: U.S. Prison Riots, 1971–1986.* New York: Oxford University Press.

VanVoorhis, P. (1994). *Psychological Classification of the Adult Male Prison Inmate.* Albany, NY: State University of New York Press.

VonHirsch, A. (1976). *Doing Justice: The Choice of Punishments.* New York: Hill and Wang Publishers.

Weiss, W. (1991). "New Approach to Local Government Corrections." *American Jails,* V(5):46–61.

Wilson v. *Seiter,* 111 S. Ct 2321 (1991).

Wisconsin Department of Corrections. (1992). "Intensive Sanctions: Manual for the Wisconsin Criminal Justice System." Madison, WI: Wisconsin Department of Corrections.

Wright, K. (1995). *Effective Prison Leadership.* Binghamton, NY: William Nell Publishing Co.

Zausner, S. (1985). "Unusual Incident Report 1984 Calendar Year." Albany, NY: State Department of Correctional Services.

SEVEN

Unit Management and the Search for Excellence

JAMES HOUSTON
Appalachian State University

INTRODUCTION

The task of corrections is becoming ever more difficult. This chapter delineates a more rational way of ensuring the security and delivery of services in a correctional institution. Unit management has proved to be an effective way to enhance staff job satisfaction and promote institutional tranquility. Finally, a model unit program is proposed to illustrate the flexibility of unit management as an approach to managing a correctional institution.

Today there are approximately 1 million people incarcerated in U.S. prisons (Allen and Simonsen, 1998). Many of these prisons are overcrowded, dangerous warehouses; on the other hand, others are well-managed institutions that are a credit to the community. Nevertheless, one conservative estimate is that U.S. prisons siphon off in excess of $20 billion

---

This chapter draws heavily on chapter 15 in J. Houston. (1994). *Correctional Management: Functions, Skills, and Systems.* Chicago: Nelson-Hall.

a year (McDonald, 1989). Such an investment demands a prudent and just return for each dollar spent. However, that return is questionable not only in terms of how well the inmate population is served, but also in regard to staff needs and the efficient allocation of resources.

The effective management of a complex organization such as a prison requires the implementation of an approach to management that recognizes the multidimensionality of the organization. As a consequence, correctional executives must implement a system that effectively integrates inmate supervision and service delivery to a diverse and often violent inmate population while recognizing the needs of employees.

Traditionally, prisons have relied on a pyramidal type of organizational structure, with most decisions and policy moving from top to bottom. Little has been written about the management style of early prison administrators, but historical anecdotes document a paramilitary organizational structure to accomplish stated objectives, keeping convicts segregated from the rest of society.

As European feudal society began to break up in the twelfth century, "many people were cut loose from the land and from the two basic social organizations of the agricultural society, the family and the tribe" (Irwin, 1985). These increasing numbers of "rabble" needed to be controlled, and that task was left to the sheriff and the military.

The prison system in America reflected its European roots. The military continued controlling the masses and was given responsibility for implementing the 1717 Act of Parliament. This law authorized the transportation of convicts from England to the American colonies for the purpose of being sold as bond servants to colonial planters (see Tappan, 1960; for a discussion of early U.S. federal prisons, see Keve 1991). The colonists also brought with them the tradition of the sheriff and his responsibility for operating the gaol (jail). With the sheriff came the paramilitary approach to prison management.

Prior to the U.S. Civil War, jails were organized haphazardly, and the punishment of criminals was considered primarily a local matter. Prisons that serve a large area such as a state are an American invention. As more traditional methods of punishment such as flogging declined, the prison in America gained in popularity. The paramilitary approach to management was an attractive and efficient way to allocate scarce resources in these institutions. For example, in the early nineteenth century, de Beaumont and de Toqueville found a paramilitary management structure in the U.S. prisons they visited. *The Rules and Regulations for the Connecticut State Prison* clearly illustrates this structure with the warden at the top of the management pyramid and the deputy warden, overseers, and watchmen performing all duties and tasks as may be directed by the warden (de Beaumont and de Toqueville, 1833).

Eventually, however, corruption, administrative abuses, and patronage led to reforms and the establishment of boards of administration charged with the responsibility to control and manage all state prisons (Tappan, 1960). The National Congress on Penitentiary and Reformatory Discipline held at Cincinnati, Ohio, in 1870 stated:

> It is now commonly acknowledged that no prison system can be successful, to the broadest and most desirable extent, without some central authority at the helm, to give unity and efficiency to the whole prison administration of the state. (E.C. Wines, ed.)

Zebulon Brockway believed that there should be unity of spirit and identity of aim (1871/1970). He advocated an organization that was pyramidal in shape, with final authority residing at the top of the structure. Ultimately, boards of correction delegated management responsibility to the respective wardens and superintendents, and it was they who developed the various policies and procedures. This highly centralized form of management lent itself well to the paramilitary structure that efficiently carried out the orders of the warden or superintendent.

In 1946, the American Correctional Association issued its *Manual for Correctional Standards,* which stated there and through its subsequent editions that each agency should be headed by a chief executive, implying a paramilitary structure fanning out below each state director of corrections (ACA, 1966).

Thus, while there have been many changes in American prison institutional discipline, classification, sentencing structure, and programming, little has changed in the approach to management of prisons during the last 150 years. It was not until the 1970s that the U.S. Bureau of Prisons pioneered a new approach to management and revolutionized the way many corrections executives view correctional management today.

TRADITIONAL MODELS OF ORGANIZATIONAL MANAGEMENT

Scientific management, based on Frederick Taylor's system for achieving the maximum possible efficiency of machines and workers, gave way to the classical school of management. The classical school focused on organization structure and how best to structure resources and personnel to achieve organizational goals. The classical school gave way to the human relationists and their emphasis on relationships. Their primary contribution was recognition of the workplace as a social experience just as it is a vehicle to attain organizational objectives. The systems approach appeared during World War II and viewed the organization as the sum total of its parts. A problem in one part of the system affected the rest of the organization.

Exploitative Authoritative	Benevolent Authoritative	Consultative	Participative Group
system one	system two	system three	system four

FIGURE 7.1 Likert's management systems. (*Source:* Adapted from R. Likert. (1967). *The Human Organization: Its Management and Value.* New York: Harper and Row.)

Managers discarded very little of the various models of organization, as each had its merits. However, they all seem to have come together during the 1960s when, it was believed, Rensis Likert (1967) discovered that the informal structure of the organization was more important than the formal structure. He suggested some important aspects of the informal structure that can modify, supplement, or replace the more traditional structural designs used in business and government (Figure 7.1).

Likert found that the lowest producing departments fall to the left of the continuum and that the departments falling to the right of the continuum are the highest producing departments; that is, they can be described as system three or four organizations, in which employees participate more. Further, when employees were asked what kind of organization they worked in, they usually described a system two or three, a more authoritarian structure. When asked to describe the kind of organization they would like to work in, they usually described a system four.

According to Likert, three things appear to explain the success of system four management: supportive relationships, group decision making and group methods of supervision, and high performance goals for the organization. The success of system four organizations demonstrates that the organization is a tightly knit, effectively functioning social system. This system is composed of interlocking work groups with a high degree of group loyalty among members and favorable attitudes and trust between superiors and subordinates. A system four work group includes a superior and all of his or her subordinates. Each subordinate, in turn, is a superior for subordinates at the next lower level in the organization. This linking pin function is necessary for the effective functioning of the organization. Clearly, the functional unit fits neatly into the system four scheme.

UNIT MANAGEMENT DEFINED

The decision by the U.S. Bureau of Prisons to adopt unit management as a management structure and operating philosophy reflected a general trend in the 1970s to decentralize organization. Many private companies as well as organizations in the public sector learned that their structure was too rigid to quickly adapt to market conditions or public need. During this period, there also began a movement toward the adoption of work teams to improve service delivery and to allow greater input into decision making by the rank and file.

Unit management springs from notions about decentralization; its adherents point to two central arguments (White, 1936):

- Certain matters may be handled better at the local level and should remain there.
- Administrative officials at the center may act in an arbitrary and capricious manner.

Since its inception, the U.S. Bureau of Prisons had been a traditional pyramidal agency, with the director sitting at the top and the layers of the organization spreading out beneath him or her. Policy and budgetary decisions reflected a top-down approach that often failed to allow for input from lower levels.

By 1970, the U.S. Bureau of Prisons (BOP) recognized two needs that would drive the adoption of unit management (Toch, 1992). One was to reduce tension and violence in many institutions and to protect weaker inmates who are prone to more predatory inmates. The second need was to deliver effective programs for those inmates with a history of substance abuse. The Narcotic Addict Rehabilitation Act (NARA) units were already proving to be successful, and the BOP recognized a need to devise programs that effectively delivered services to those inmates who had histories of substance abuse but did not qualify for a NARA unit.

Unit management was an idea whose time had come. It was time for a paradigm shift. Roy Gerard, Robert B. Levinson, and then director of the U.S. Bureau of Prisons Norman Carlson embarked on a journey that has revolutionized prison management (Gerard, 1991). The result has been an approach to prison management that incorporates the basics of sound management principles. Staff are allowed more input into organizational decision making and direct contact with inmates, which results in a more humane prison environment.

According to the U.S. Bureau of Prisons, a *unit* is defined as a small, self-contained inmate living and staff office area, which operates semiautonomously within the confines of the larger institution (Unit Management Manual, 1977). The essential components of a unit are

- A smaller number of inmates (50–120) who are assigned together permanently.
- A multidisciplinary staff (unit manager, case manager[s], correctional counselor[s], full- or part-time psychologist, clerk typist, and correctional

officers) whose offices are located within the inmate housing unit and are permanently assigned to work with the inmates of that unit.

- A unit manager with administrative authority and supervisory responsibility for the unit staff.
- A unit staff with administrative authority for all within-unit aspects of inmate living and programming.
- Assignments of inmates to units based on age, prior record, specific behavior, specific behavior typologies, need for specific type of correctional program (such as drug abuse counseling), or on a random-assignment basis.
- A schedule that includes work in the unit evenings and weekends, on a rotating basis, in addition to the presence of the unit correctional officer.

Prior to the implementation of unit management, Bureau of Prison's institutions, similar to most state correctional institutions today, were arranged hierarchically with functions arranged by department. That is, a separate department head supervised similar functions. Faulty communications between departments were often the result. The Federal Correctional Institution (FCI) at Terminal Island, California, is a good example of how organizational functioning was improved by the implementation of unit management.

In 1976, the Bureau of Prisons decided to implement unit management at FCI, a unique institution that was actually two institutions under one warden. The northern part of the institution housed approximately 600 men, and the southern end of the institution about 150 women inmates. As a consequence, there were duplicate services and departments for both men and women. One advantage of the implementation of unit management was the consolidation of all services.

The warden appointed a committee comprised of two units for women and four units for men to implement unit management. Included was a drug program unit for men and one for women under one unit manager. The remaining units were for general population inmates with no special services other than those normally required for all inmates of the institution. There were a number of personnel problems to be worked out, but once those were decided, unit managers were selected, dormitories were rehabilitated and converted into cubicles for inmate privacy, and office space for staff was constructed.

Inmates with histories of drug abuse or serving NARA sentences were assigned to a drug program unit. The men's drug program unit housed approximately 100 male inmates; the female drug unit housed approximately 80 inmates. Otherwise, there were approximately 120 inmates assigned to each unit by alphabet. Each unit contained two case managers, four correctional counselors, a secretary, and one unit manager who was responsible for supervision of all activities in the unit. While no official data were collected, the general view of staff in the institution at the time was that supervision was more effective, staff appreciated the opportunity to be proactive, disciplinary reports decreased, staff morale rose, and rapport with inmates increased.

CLASSIFICATION AND HISTORY OF UNIT MANAGEMENT

Unit management is the evolutionary product of the classification process in prisons. Classification is defined as "a method by which diagnosis, treatment planning, and the execution of the treatment program are coordinated in the individual case" (Loveland, 1960:623). Classification grew slowly, first with the segregation of the sexes and children from adults. Gradually, institutions began to add educational and spiritual programs along with vocational training. Many states had relatively sophisticated classification systems by the 1930s, when the U.S. Bureau of Prisons instituted classification as a central intake procedure.

As the BOP grew, classification was introduced as the primary prisoner management tool (Keve, 1991). Until the 1930s, the Bureau of Prisons utilized only rudimentary classification procedures. By that time, new institutions had been constructed so that prisoners of varying age groups could be designated to different institutions, with female prisoners going to Alderson, West Virginia. By the 1950s, the Classification Committee— composed of the associate warden, captain, superintendent of education, chaplain, superintendent of industries, and the chief of classification and parole—was the vehicle for inmate classification. Undoubtedly, many inmates agreed to program participation because of intimidation fostered by the amount of "brass" in the room.

Treatment Team

During the early to mid-1960s, the concept of the *treatment team* began to take shape. The treatment team consisted of a group of staff (case manager, liaison officer, and teacher) who were responsible for the classification, periodic program review, and all other inmate case management matters. The liaison officer, a position developed from the research of Glaser (1964), was assigned to work with the case manager to handle much inmate contact and was also required to work with the correctional officers in the inmates' cell house or dormitory. From that position evolved the correctional counselor, a nondegreed position assigned to work directly with the team, the inmate, and the inmates' work and housing supervisor.

Unit management and the treatment team appeared to be made for each other. However, unit management as a concept in the Bureau of Prisons had an even earlier beginning (BOP, 1977) at the National Training School for Boys (NTS) in Washington, D.C., where inmates on one caseload were moved into one housing unit, and an interdisciplinary staff worked with them as they implemented a counseling and recreational program. Based on the success of this effort, the entire institution was reorganized according to this model.

In 1963, the Federal Youth Center at Englewood, Colorado, established a unit system featuring unit officers and a separate case manager for each unit. However, it wasn't until the Kennedy Youth Center at Morgantown, West Virginia, opened in 1969 that unit management got off the ground as a means to organize an entire institution.

The earliest units were specialized entities designed to handle substance abusers and difficult-to-manage inmates. For example, the Narcotic Addict Rehabilitation Act of 1966 (NARA) delegated to the U.S. Bureau of Prisons the responsibility for drug treatment of certain eligible felons who had committed their offenses in order to support serious heroin habits. Those units established the basic rules for unit functioning.

In 1968, the first NARA unit was established at the Federal Correctional Institution (FCI), *Danbury, Connecticut.* Shortly afterward, other units were established at the FCIs at Terminal Island, California, and Milan, Michigan, and in the early 1970s, Fort Worth, Texas, and Lexington, Kentucky. Additionally, a number of drug abuse programs were established in a number of FCIs and penitentiaries, followed by an alcoholism unit at FCI Fort Worth and the S.T.A.R.T. unit at the U.S. Penitentiary at Marion, Illinois, for the most intractable inmates.

The experience at the Kennedy Youth Center that had been preceded by the Narcotic Addict Rehabilitation Act (NARA) units and followed by the various drug abuse programs established by the Bureau of Prisons in the 1970s proved that the idea of unit management would work. It ultimately worked in a variety of settings—penitentiaries and the less-secure federal correctional institutions (FCIs). Treatment teams replaced the old classification committees and inmates came to be viewed as members of the team and allowed input. Previously, inmates were faced by all top managers in the institution; now they were included as team members with the staff who were supposed to know them best.

How Unit Management Works

In a *unitized* institution, newly arriving inmates meet with a unit correctional counselor within twenty-four hours of their arrival to compose a preliminary visiting list and discuss any concerns and fears. During the initial orientation period, medical, psychological, and educational testing

Team Meetings

Team meetings are informal meetings with the case manager, correctional counselor, a representative of the education department, and often a psychologist and the unit manager sitting in. Prior to the meeting, the correctional counselor meets with the inmate and develops a visiting list and discusses other areas of concern. In the meantime, the inmate is subjected to a variety of psychological, medical, and educational tests to aid the team in developing a program for the inmate at the time of initial classification.

Before the meeting the case manager obtains a printout of all inmates due for action that week. On the day of the meeting, the case manager sees that inmates are able to meet with the team and that they will arrive at the meeting site at the designated time. The informality of the session promotes cooperation between inmates and staff, and all program decisions are arrived at jointly; other matters, such as custody level, are not an issue for negotiation. It is not uncommon for a team to spend all day in session meeting with inmates and conducting discussions. After inmates are through with their session, they return to their work assignment or cell house.

A record of all decisions is maintained by a member of the team and the decisions are later entered into the management information system for later retrieval. The advantage of the team approach is that staff listen to the inmate in all matters of importance to him or her, the decisions are explained, and even if the inmate does not agree, hostility is likely to be blunted.

is completed and inmates are moved into their units. Within a short time (usually one to two weeks), inmates meet with their team to develop programs that attempt to meet their needs relative to education, counseling, and employment upon release. Other concerns such as custody and institutional work assignment are also addressed. Periodically, inmates are brought before the team for review of their program and custody classification. There may be some variation depending on the institution, but the process has remained basically the same for at least fifteen years.

The advantage of unit management is that staff are able to follow inmates closely, physically see them daily, and interact on a more equal level as individuals and human beings. In addition, decisions are made on the unit, inmates have a say in those decisions, and there is the added flexibility of programming. This proactive approach has, in many instances, brought unruly and mutinous institutions under control.

Roy Gerard (1991), one of the originators of unit management, offers what he calls "commandments" for the successful implementation and operation of units:

1. *The concept of unit management must be understood by and have the support of top-level administration.* Unit management threatens the established hierarchical order. Many executives and supervisors do not want their position or authority challenged or changed and see unit management as a threat. In many ways it is a threat. Power is redistributed, information flows to the unit manager, and security and case management decisions are made by unit staff members. Executives and supervisors need to be able to see the advantages without worrying about their role. Such a view requires commitment to the organization and a strong sense of personal security.

2. *There must be a table of organization that has unit managers at a "department head" level, giving them responsibility for staff and inmates assigned to their unit.* On this table the unit managers and the head of security report to the same supervisor.

3. *The unit's population size should be based on its mission; that is, a general unit can house from 150 to 250 inmates and a special unit can house from 75 to 125 inmates without negatively affecting the unit mission.* Ideally, staffing should reflect the following:

	General Unit	Special Unit
Unit Manager	1	1
Case Manager	2	2
Correctional Counselor	2	2
Secretary	1	1
Mental Health	1/2	1

Part-time education, recreation, and volunteer staff.
Twenty-four-hour coverage of correctional officers.

4. *Inmates and unit staff should be permanently assigned to the unit; correctional officers should be stationed on the unit for a minimum of nine months.* The administration of an institution is tempted to move inmates around for a number of reasons. However, anecdotal evidence reflects that when inmates are responsible to the same staff over a prolonged period of time, the staff and inmates come to know each other well enough that inmates exhibit fewer problems. Unit management divides the large number of inmates into small, well-defined, and manageable groups whose members develop a common identity and close association with each other and their unit staff.

5. *In addition to correctional officer coverage, unit staff should provide twelve-hour supervision Monday through Friday and eight hours on each weekend day.* At the FCI, Terminal Island, the warden established a work schedule that required case managers and correctional counselors to work two evenings per week. In addition, all unit managers were required to work at least one evening per week and one weekend per month. The advantage of this schedule is that case managers, counselors, and unit managers are available to meet the needs and work schedules of inmates in their unit. A tertiary advantage is that more staff are available for supervision of inmates. This work schedule is in use in nearly all U.S. Bureau of Prisons' institutions as well as many state institutions that have implemented unit management.

6. *Staff offices should be located on the unit or as near to it as possible.* Access is the key to success. Availability of unit staff to inmates reflects the decentralized nature of the institution and increases the accessibility of staff. It increases the frequency of contacts and the intensity of the relationship between staff and inmates, resulting in

1. Better communication and understanding between individuals
2. More individualized classification and program planning
3. More valuable program reviews and program adjustments
4. Better observation of inmates, enabling early detection of problems before they reach critical proportions
5. Development of common goals that encourage positive unit cohesiveness
6. Generally a more positive living and working environment for inmates and staff

A Model Unit Management Program

The establishment of unit programs is a policy matter left up to the warden, assistant wardens, and the respective unit managers (in consultation with staff). Some units may offer only required services relative to case management needs and minimal individual counseling as called for by individual circumstances. It is likely that these types of units will be found in institutions for older, more sophisticated inmates. However, for younger inmates and for inmates with special needs such as substance abuse, a program can be devised that attends to the needs of the inmates.

A successful unit program is hinged on a unit plan, and it is important that all staff participate in developing the unit plan. This is much like a master plan that defines "unit missions and goals, describes programs, defining (sic) responsibilities, prescribes how the unit will evaluate its operation" (BOP, 1977). One approach is to divide the day into equal segments from 8:00 A.M. to 9:00 P.M. Assuming adequate space for group counseling and executive approval of the program, the inmate can be required to fill each segment of the day constructively. The following sample program illustrates the options available to unit staff:

8:00–10:00 A.M.	Work (industries)
10:00–12:00 noon	Work (industries)
12:00–1:00 P.M.	Lunch (cell time)
1:00–3:00 P.M.	School (GED)
3:00–4:30 P.M.	Group counseling
4:30–6:00 P.M.	Count, cell time, supper
6:00–7:30 P.M.	Group counseling
7:30–9:00 P.M.	Self-help group (tutoring, parent effectiveness training [P.E.T.], etc.)

This schedule is arrived at in consulation with inmates at the time of classification and periodic reviews, and it allows unit staff to maintain close watch over the activities of inmates. In addition, as one segment of the program is completed (e.g., GED), another activity can be inserted into the vacant time slot.

Some critics may point out that programs and security do not go well together and as a consequence, programs are given short shrift in favor of security. The problem is not that programs and security are incompatible, but rather that programs are imposed on the security framework. The advantage of unit management is that security is part of the approach, and programs and security are viewed from the same side of the fence. In this plan, unit staff are full partners in security efforts by demanding accountability from inmates regarding their conduct for eleven hours out of the day.

THE EFFECTIVENESS OF UNIT MANAGEMENT

It is difficult to state exactly how many systems have implemented unit management, as there have been no nationwide surveys. However, Table 7.1 illustrates which states are believed to have implemented unit management.[1] The table includes the states of Connecticut, Georgia, Iowa, Missouri, and New York, all of which have provided no information.

The impact of unit management on institutions has been spectacular in some instances and more subtle in others. Staff generally believe that they are included in the decision-making and planning processes. Inmates,

TABLE 7.1 Unit Management in the United States

State	Date Begun	Facilities—Number and Percentage in Unit Management		Size Range (avg.) Ideal	Staffing Pattern	Staff/Inmate Ratio
Connecticut	—	—	—	— —	—	—
Georgia	—	—	—	— —	—	—
Iowa	—	—	—	— —	—	—
Michigan	1973	24/24	100%	120/450/175/200	3	1:58
Missouri[a]	—	—	—	— —	—	—
Nebraska	1979	6/6	100%	82/130/100/100	7	1:14
New York City (June)	—	—	—	— —	—	—
New Hampshire	1986	1/1	100%	25/200/150/175	4.5	1:33
North Carolina	1982	2/11	18%	93/120/110/100	4	1:28
Ohio	1986	13/17	75%	150/400/250/300	6	1:42
Oklahoma	1986	13/13	100%	120/180/150/150	6	1:25
South Carolina	1982	4/10	40%	126/312/150/150	5	1:30
Tennessee[b]	1988	0/14	—	— 160 —	6	1:27
Virginia	1985	1/10	10%	72/100/72—	3	1:24
Bureau of Prisons	1965[c]	47/47	100%	150/400/250/200	6	1:42

[a]Obtained from other sources.
[b]The NIC provided the information with no explanation as to how Tennessee could claim to have units, but show no institutions involved.
[c]The 1965 date reflects the BOP's first experiments with the forerunner of Unit Management at the National Training School.

Note: In 1996, the Wisconsin Department of Corrections conducted a national survey and found 27 states using unit management (Wisconsin Department of Corrections National Survey, 1996).

Source: Correspondence with the National Institute of Corrections (April 1992).

on the other hand, believe that they have close interaction with staff and are given the opportunity to participate in unit processes. Overall, in those institutions that have implemented unit management, it has been found that few areas are unaffected by its use.

The U.S. Bureau of Prisons assessed the impact of unit management as it is implemented in many institutions. Bureau of Prisons' researchers found that inmate assaults on other inmates in intermediate adult institutions decreased, and that overtime pay decreased, not only during disturbances but during other more tranquil periods. In addition, abuse of sick days declined (Rowe et al., 1977). Further research was conducted by the U.S. Bureau of Prisons (BOP, no date) using Rudolf Moos's Correctional Institutions Environmental Scale (CIES). The CIES was administered to staff and inmates at the Federal Correctional Institution, Milan, Michigan, both prior to implementation and afterwards, revealing remarkably *favorable results,* including greater inmate satisfaction with programs and increased job satisfaction by staff.

Unit management has also been implemented in Australian prisons. Robson (1989) reports that the implementation of unit management has been found to be more efficient and cost effective in one institution. He also notes that unit management appears to have reduced vandalism, negative behavior, and assaults. Pierson (1991) reports that Missouri implemented unit management with success, but there have been modifications in the concept to allow for budget constraints; for example, units house from 150 to 300 inmates instead of the number advocated by Levinson and Gerard. Nevertheless, Pierson reports the same advantages of unit management as does the U.S. Bureau of Prisons.

The latest and most recent evaluation of unit management was completed by the Ohio Department of Corrections in 1991 (Executive Summary, Ohio DOC, 1991). Central office staff conducted interviews and on-site reviews at twenty of the department's twenty-two institutions. With few exceptions, the report concludes that

> We have found it [unit management] to be both an effective and efficient means of addressing the concerns of managing an expanding inmate population while remaining sensitive to community expectations and the responsibilities we share with our legal system. Since the transition to unit management, we have observed a marked improvement in the overall operation of our institutions. The report found improvement in a variety of areas. (p. 3)

The authors of the report note the proactive approach of unit management and conclude that escapes drop significantly, inmates are held more responsible for their behavior, nonsecurity staff are more involved and more knowledgeable of security measures, the multidisciplinary team approach responds to inmate needs more quickly, and the overall delivery of services is improved. In addition, line staff are more aware of management's expectations, the custody-treatment staff dichotomy is reduced, and in general the overall experience of staff is expanded.

The Ohio experience is an excellent example of the commitment necessary by executive staff if unit management is to succeed. Obviously, initial interest is in the area of inmate management, but as the U.S. Bureau of Prisons and the Ohio Department of Corrections found, the importance of involving staff in "everything" is just as important as good inmate management.

SUMMARY

Corrections today is faced with seemingly insurmountable problems. Overcrowding, gangs, shrinking budgets, a better educated workforce, and a more difficult to manage inmate population are just a few of the issues that must be faced by the corrections manager. Unit management is an approach to managing a correctional institution that takes advantage of sound management principles and efficiently delivers services to the inmate population.

Involving staff in policy decisions, recognizing their achievements, and building a climate that fosters camaraderie and excellence are the qualities that serve the public and promote quality control. Communication, classification, program planning, inmate observation, and other activities are more easily monitored for quality.

Unit management is both a management approach and a service delivery vehicle. It grew out of the U.S. Bureau of Prisons' need to reduce tension and protect weaker inmates as well as to provide a vehicle to deliver substance abuse programs. Early units such as the NARA and the Drug Abuse Program units proved that the concept would work and provided the impetus to expand unit management throughout the U.S. Bureau of Prisons.

Today, fourteen states, besides the BOP, claim to use unit management, and the concept appears to be growing internationally as well. The success of unit management, where implemented, can be attributed to the ability of staff to better relate to inmates, increased staff job satisfaction, and increased program flexibility.

NOTES

1. Until the publication of *Correctional Management: Functions, Skills, and Systems* (Nelson-Hall), no information was available on how many jurisdictions claimed to utilize unit management. A call to the National Institute of Corrections revealed that no one had made an effort to determine how widespread the use of unit management had become. I am grateful to Patricia Scholes for her work in putting together most of the information that appears in Table 7.1. However, the reader is cautioned to view the table with some skepticism because some jurisdictions may be using something they call unit management, but it may not conform to the definition of Gerard et al.

REFERENCES

Allen, H.E. and Simonsen, C.E. (1998). *Corrections in America* (8th ed.). Upper Saddle River, NJ: Prentice Hall.

American Correctional Association. (1966). *Manual of Correctional Standards*. College Park, MD: Author.

de Beaumont, G. and de Toqueville, A. (1833, 1970). *On the Penitentiary System in the United States and Its Application in France*. Philadelphia: Carey, Lea & Blanchard. Reprinted by A.M. Kelly.

Brockway, Z.H. (1871/1970). "The Ideal of a True Prison System for a State." In E.C. Wines, D.D., LL.D., (ed.), *Transactions of the National Congress on Penitentiary and Reformatory Discipline*, Albany: Weed, Parsons and Co., Printers. Reprinted by the American Correctional Association.

Business Week. (1970, June 8). "The Push for Quality":130–144.

Executive Summary. (1991, December). "A Report Prepared Pursuant to Amended Substitute House Bill 298." Columbus: Ohio Department of Corrections.

Gerard, R.E. (1991, April). "The Ten Commandments of Unit Management." *Corrections Today:*32, 34, 36.

Glaser, D. (1964). *The Effectiveness of a Prison and Parole System.* Indianapolis: Bobbs-Merrill.

Irwin, J. (1985). *The Jail: Managing the Underclass in American Society.* Berkeley: University of California Press.

Keve, P.W. (1991). *Prisons and the American Conscience: A History of U.S. Federal Corrections.* Carbondale, IL: Southern Illinois University Press.

Levinson, R.B. and Gerard, R.E. (1973). "Functional Units: A Different Correctional Approach." *Federal Probation,* 37(4):8–15.

Likert, R. (1967). *The Human Organization: Its Management and Value.* New York: Harper and Row.

Loveland, F. (1960). "Classification in the Prison System." In P. Tappan (ed.). *Crime, Justice, and Correction.* New York: McGraw-Hill.

McDonald, D.C. (1989). "The Cost of Corrections: In Search of the Bottom Line." In National Institute of Corrections, *Research in Corrections.* Boulder, CO: National Institute of Corrections 2(1).

McGregor, D. (1960). "Theory X and Theory Y." In D.S. Pugh. (1984). *Organization Theory* (2d ed.). New York: Penguin Books.

Pierson, T.A. (1991, April). "One State's Success with Unit Management." *Corrections Today:*24, 26, 28, 30.

Robson, R. (1989). "Managing the Long Term Prisoner: A Report on an Australian Innovation in Unit Management." *The Howard Journal* 28(3):187–203.

Rowe, R., Foster, E., Byerly, K., Laird, N., and Prather, J. (1977). *The Impact of Functional Unit Management on Indicies of Inmate Incidents.* (Unpublished research report by the U.S. Bureau of Prisons.)

Skolnick, J. (1993). *Justice Without Trial: Law Enforcement in Democratic Society* (3d ed.). New York: John Wiley and Sons, Inc. Skolnick discusses the elements of authority and danger relative to the role of the police officer, but his notions of solidarity among police officers also have merit in a discussion of staff solidarity vis-a-vis inmates. The existence of potential danger and the inherent authority of staff members creates a press to look to each other for mutual support. See also Kauffman, K. (1988). *Prison Officers and Their World.* Cambridge, MA: Harvard University Press; and Lombardo, L.X. (1981). *Guards Imprisoned.* New York: Elsevier.

Tappan, P.W. (1960). *Crime, Justice, and Correction.* New York: McGraw-Hill.

Toch, H. (1992, Winter). "Functional Unit Management: An Unsung Achievement." *Federal Prisons Journal,* 2(4):15–19.

U.S. Bureau of Prisons. (1977). *Unit Management Manual.* Washington, D.C.: U.S.B.O.P.

U.S. Bureau of Prisons (1975, September). *Preliminary Evaluation of the Functional Unit Approach to Correctional Management.* (Unpublished report by the U.S. Bureau of Prisons.)

U.S. Bureau of Prisons (no date). *Position Paper on Functional Units.* (Unpublished document.)

Webster, J.H. (April, 1991). "Designing Facilities for Effective Unit Management." *Corrections Today:*38, 40, 42.

White, L.D. (1936). "The Meaning of Principles in Public Administration." In J.M. Gaus, L.B. White, and M.E. Demock (eds.), *The Frontiers of Public Administration.* Chicago: University of Chicago Press.

Wines, E.C., D.D., LL.D. (ed.). (1871). "The Present Outlook of Prison Discipline in the United States." In E.C. Wines, D.D., LL.D. (ed.), *Transactions of the National Congress on Penitentiary and Reformatory Discipline,* Albany: Weed, Parsons and Co., Printers. Reprinted by the American Correctional Association, Washington, D.C., 1970.

EIGHT

Postsecondary Correctional Education

The Imprisoned University

JON MARC TAYLOR
Missouri Department of Corrections

RICHARD TEWKSBURY
University of Louisville

INTRODUCTION

Postsecondary correctional education is the natural extension of, and most recent addition to, the 200-year-long progression in the field of correctional education. Since the founding of the first prison college program in the 1950s, the expansion of these educational opportunities has been prodigious, reaching, by 1990, nearly 800 programs throughout the fifty-two American correctional systems. This expansive growth, however, has not been without criticism ranging from academe to the highest political officers in the land.

This chapter reviews (1) the history of the growth of postsecondary correctional education; (2) the common criticisms raised in opposition to providing these educational programs; (3) examples and reviews of the political debates revolving around these opportunities; (4) synoptic analysis of the programming's evaluations; (5) institutional impact; and

(6) reviews of the costs, funding structures, and the projected return on society's investment for the provision of postsecondary education for prisoners.

"The most hopeful trend in prison work, in America today, is the growing realization that the term in prison can be made into an educational experience" (Craig, 1983:102). The natural progression of this educational experience extends to offering convicts the same, albeit physically restricted, opportunities to earn a college degree from fully accredited institutions of higher education. This chapter reviews the history, criticisms, debates, successes and failures, and cost analysis of postsecondary correctional education (PSCE). The authors believe that PSCE is a highly efficient and cost-effective means to manage, (re)habilitate, and (re)integrate offenders as productive, tax-paying, and law-abiding citizens.

IN THE BEGINNING

Since 1844, when the first secular school teacher was hired to work in the Eastern Penitentiary of Pennsylvania (Roberts, 1972),[1] education programs modeled after traditional structures have consistently expanded in scope and depth within the confines of the keep. For the next century, correctional education grew from tutoring in the three R's to accredited prison high school programs. By the 1930s, the philosophy behind correctional education had come to be best summarized in the Correctional Law of New York State: "The objective of prison education in its broadest sense should be the socialization of the inmate through varied impressional and expressional activities, with emphasis on inmate needs" (Englehardt, 1939:33).

The roots of the expansive network of postsecondary correctional education programs can be found in Illinois and California fewer than forty years ago. In 1956, Southern Illinois University matriculated the nation's first inmate college class (introductory journalism) in the State Penitentiary at Menard. The next year, courses in English, government, philosophy, and speech were also offered. By 1962, a fully accredited curriculum was in place, and by 1969, a degree program similar to the basic general studies program available on the main campus was functioning at the prison (Marsh, 1973). A decade after the commencement of higher education at Menard, a baccalaureate degree program (funded by a Ford Foundation grant) was begun at San Quentin prison in California. The University of California at Berkeley offered a fully accredited curriculum emphasizing the social sciences: psychology, sociology, criminology, English composition, algebra, and calculus (Adams, 1968).

Stuart Adams, the San Quentin-Berkeley program project director, evaluated the program and identified nine critical issues that to this day continue to distinguish or plague most prison college programs. Adams (1968:15) found that

1. College-level programs can operate in the penal setting.
2. Programs seldom failed on their own accord.
3. Inmate-students performed academically as well as, or even surpassing, students in on-campus programs.
4. Programs provided a stimulus for other education programs in prisons.
5. Consistent positive attitude and behavior changes could be observed in inmate-students.
6. These programs reach only a small percentage of the inmate population.
7. Funding is the most critical problem facing postsecondary correctional education.
8. Library resources are extremely inadequate for research purposes.
9. Poor classroom conditions detract from the educational experience.

In conclusion, Adams found it more practical to offer two-year, rather than four-year, degree curriculums in the penal setting.

The Office of Economic Opportunity initiated what was to become known as Project NewGate at the Oregon State Penitentiary in 1967. By 1969, this program had expanded to five states and was a more ambitious and comprehensive approach than any other PSCE program of the time (Baker, Irwin, Haberfeld, Seashore, and Leonard, 1973). The uniqueness of Project NewGate was that it instituted a near total therapeutic environment by establishing self-contained scholastic programs inside the prison. This in turn operated on a milieu therapy philosophy of immersion in academic endeavors with the intellectual and psychological growth of the inmates as primary goals. This objective was in harmony with the rehabilitative zeitgeist of the era. Project NewGate programs exemplified such a philosophy. As Craig (1983:29) comments, "the emphasis had shifted solely from the importance of keeping an offender isolated from the community to the importance of returning to society a rehabilitated man." The end goal, as Reagen and Stoughton (1976) noted, was to invoke a metamorphosis in a social liability and change him into a social asset.

The Project NewGate program not only offered postsecondary classroom instruction to the inmate-students, but also academic counseling, extracurricular activities, and psychotherapy sessions. Upon release, paroled students were sent to campus half-way houses for academic as well as community transition programming. Decreasing living and tuition stipends, administrative services, and psychological counseling were provided to the students (Baker et al., 1973). By 1972, a seventh NewGate program had been established and thirty-one states had begun the process of establishing Project NewGate programs. In 1974, however, the NewGate Resource Center ceased operating under the aegis of the National Council on Crime and Delinquency because of the termination of federal funding.

The comprehensive NewGate programs were not the only PSCE opportunities available. Although by 1965 only a dozen on-site PSCE programs existed (Herron, Muir, and Williams, 1984), by 1968 Humphreys's (1972) survey of 590 prisons reported that ninety-four institutions provided college program opportunities to inmates, with seventy-four (79 percent) being exclusively via correspondence and twenty (21 percent) through some form of on-site and study release programs. The growth of these educational opportunities continued even as the rehabilitative ideal faded and the just deserts model gained ascendancy. In 1970, 6 percent of the national prison population was enrolled in PSCE programs. By 1977, enrollment had increased to 10 percent of the prison population (Bell et al., 1979). These percentages, although fluctuating over the years and the ever-expanding prison population, translated into prolific expansion for PSCE sites. At the beginning of the 1980s, there were 350 programs with more than 27,000 enrolled inmate-students (Littlefield and Wolford, 1982). By the end of the decade, Stephan (1992) noted that there were 772 prison college programs operating in 1287 correctional facilities with more than 35,000 enrolled students. These opportunities ranged from certificates to associate degrees to baccalaureate and even graduate degrees.

For nearly forty years, postsecondary correctional education continued to expand until eventually over 90 percent of the U.S. correctional systems offered some form of PSCE opportunities (Ryan and Woodard, 1987).[2] Yet in 1993, the states of California, Michigan, Nebraska, New Jersey, and in 1994 Missouri and Florida, shuttered their prison college programs due to funding restrictions. The lesson here is that no correctional program, regardless of its successes or viability, is immune to the political process.

CRITICISMS OF PSCE

The critics of postsecondary correctional education have raised various objections to the idea of providing educational opportunities for prisoners. Some of these criticisms focus on governmental funding of prisoner education programs, the apparent ineffectiveness of higher education in reducing recidivism, and the financial cost of such efforts. These criticisms are examined in the following sections. Here we analyze the following objections: (1) Correctional systems lack the public and legal mandates to offer such programs; (2) these opportunities are fundamentally inappropriate for prisoners; and (3) all that PSCE programs do are produce smarter criminals who in turn prey upon the society that provided them with their education.

"The correctional movement of this century," Quinney (1979:349) comments, "has counted on the prison as a center for rehabilitating offenders as well as confining them." Over the years, the public has affirmed rehabilitation as a major goal of the correctional system. Harris Polls in 1968 and 1982 (cited in Cullen, Skovron, Scott, and Burton, 1990), in 1984 in a *Judicature* article (Gottfredson and Taylor), twice in 1987 in a Bureau of Justice Statistics survey, and in nationwide focus groups for the Public Agenda Foundation (Doble, 1987:12) all revealed that the public believed that "a goal of the prison system should be to rehabilitate offenders." This public desire for offender rehabilitation is found in most of the states' constitutions, bills of rights, and correctional laws (Rotman, 1986). The Indiana State Constitution, for example, expressly specifies that "the penal code shall be founded on the principles of reformation, and not vindictive justice" (*Burns Indiana Statutes Annotated, Constitution,* 1990).

Yet this public sentiment is largely lost in the rhetoric of politics. Part of the problem, however, reports Roberts (1992), is that the "myth" that the public seems to be singularly punitive in its response to crime is due mainly to the limits of most public opinion surveys, which ask questions that are too simple based on worst-case scenarios. Both Gottfredson and Taylor's (1984) and Clark's (1985) studies of policy makers' interpretations of public criminal justice opinion found that these decision makers erroneously assumed the public to be singularly punitive in its approach to crime control. "Despite politicians' and criminologists' continual attempts over the past fifteen years to undermine its legitimacy," Cullen and others (1990:15) report in their analysis of support for correctional treatment, "the public believes that rehabilitation should be a goal of corrections."

Others have argued that it is just inappropriate for prisoners to receive college educations. Senator Ernest Hollings (D-SC) proclaimed during the debate over Pell Grant funding eligibility for prisoners that he believed "in education in prison, but not at the higher education level" (*The Congressional Record–Senate,* 1991). The senator did not elaborate on why he believed this, but as the former governor and current senior senator of his state, he is an influential force in the determination of public policy. Governor William Weld (R) of Massachusetts similarly objects to PSCE as a matter of principle. Despite any demonstrated rehabilitative effectiveness and cost-efficiency of such programs, he commented that "it seems to me that it's a confession that we can be successfully blackmailed by people saying 'Well, we're going to commit serious crimes unless you not only feed, clothe, and house us at your expense, but give us a great education to persuade us not to return to a life of crime.' (I say) NO" ("60 Minutes," 1991).

These two examples highlight that some people object to PSCE opportunities simply because of the fact that the students are prisoners. The rationality of the wide-ranging benefits accruing from prison college programming is superfluous to these critics, which leads one to wonder whether the motivating force behind this objection is a prejudice based upon the scarlet "F" (for felon) imposed on all inmates.

However, the argument that the provision of PSCE programs exceeds corrections' mandate for the provision of rehabilitative opportunities is in conflict with legal strictures and the manifested general public sentiment. Since education is the rehabilitation/treatment program most favored by the public (Cullen et al., 1990), advanced educational opportunities are clearly within the purview of correctional administration.

Perhaps the most insidious set of objections to PSCE is that when acknowledging successes in reducing recidivism, critics attribute this result to the assumption that inmate-students are now just "smarter criminals" and thus are harder to catch (*New Encyclopaedia Britannica,* 1983). In fact, "the conventional wisdom has been that we need to educate the criminal by helping to learn to read, to write or acquire job skills," observes Stanton Samenow (1986:44); however, "what we may well produce is criminals with an education of job skills," but still criminals nonetheless. What this rationalization overlooks in regard to postsecondary education, as opposed to secondary and vocational paradigms, is the cognitive dynamic at work in higher education.

Andrews, Bonta, and Hoge (1990) contend that it is crucial to have a psychological understanding of criminal conduct to implement effective correctional treatment. Canadians Ross and Fabiano (1980) conclude from their review of forty years of empirical research that a considerable number of offenders experience delays in the development of cognitive skills that are crucial to social adaptation. These cognitive deficits manifest themselves in individuals' inabilities "to conceptualize the consequences of their behavior and [they] are unable to use means-ends reasoning to achieve their goals" (Ross, Fabiano, and Ewles, 1988:30). Such a conclusion reflects the earlier reasoning of Kohlberg (1970) that such adaptive insufficiencies "could lead to criminal behavior."

It is in these cognitive-social deficiencies, not in general intelligence, in the ability to deal with interpersonal conflicts, to comprehend other points of view, and adaptive prosocial manners that higher education lends itself to (re)habilitation. As early as 1955, Cressey expressed the need to focus on the attitudes, motives, and rationalizations of criminal behavior. It is in the revision of certain cognitive deficiencies that Volpe, Waksman, and Kearney (1985), and others (Duguid, 1981; Arbuthnot, 1984), believe that higher education provides the means to correcting criminal behavior. Postsecondary education accomplishes this task, as Tope and Warthan (1986:76) explain:

A liberal education is one which offers that student an awareness of social dynamics. For those who lack the basic cognitive finesse to make conscious judgements which are consensual with the morality of our society, liberal education can help him fill this void, particularly for those inmates who possess the equivalence to a high school education and wish to proceed to post-secondary schooling. By igniting the spark which starts the maturation process for a criminal, education frees the inmate from the confines of irrational judgement-making and promotes the mental and emotional transformation from adolescence to that of a communally functioning adult.

Hans Toch (1987) postulates that education is a regenerative tool for "chronically maladaptive" offenders. PSCE assists in transforming the way inmate-students view the world, and as Thomas (1983) notes, can change how they act within it. Furthermore, as Scharf and Hickey (1976:107) suggest, if an offender "leaves prison with the same social conscience with which he entered, he faces a continuing probability of remaining morally alienated from society and its institutions." It is here, with the organized exposure to and development of a more mature sense of values (Homant, 1984), that the distinction between higher education and secondary schooling and vocational training occurs. Thus, as Taylor (1994a) notes, "prison college programs do not turn out better educated criminals; rather, they assist in elevating those involved individuals' cognitive development to new levels, enlightening their world perspective, and enhancing their moral development." Those who object to PSCE because it turns out better educated criminals (who presumably can more efficiently victimize the community), do not comprehend the mediating mechanism by which higher education can provide the impetus for change in the offenders' worldview, morals, and values. It is by virtue of the cognitive change, rather than simply vocational skill training as presented in the rational choice theory of offender rehabilitation (Orsagh and Marsden, 1985),[3] that the provision of postsecondary education opportunities for prisoners eventually protects the community. This protection is a product of an altered psychological schemata to a more prosocial mode. This alteration represents what former Attorney General Ramsey Clark (1970:220) intended when he said, "the end sought by rehabilitation is a stable individual returned to community life, capable of constructive participation and incapable of crime." As we shall see, PSCE programs provide this service.

POLITICAL CONTROVERSY

The most prolific objections to prison college programs have come from the political arena and do not necessarily concern the provision of educational opportunities themselves, but rather the provision of public funding for financing inmates' participation in PSCE programs. Public outcries, and politicians' rhetoric, about the impropriety of granting taxpayers' dollars to convicted offenders for purposes of financing higher education have led to growing widespread concerns about the existence of PSCE programs as they currently exist. The issue of state funding of prisoners' college educations has not only caused political outcries, but has also fueled repeated debates in Congress regarding federal funding for such programs.

In 1985, a New Hampshire inmate, attempting to enroll in a college program in order to meet the court offered sentence reduction for exceptional rehabilitative achievement, petitioned the court to order the Department of Corrections to cover whatever educational expenses were not met by other financial aid sources. The state's supreme court ruled that an incarcerated offender had no right to a free college education when "a talented law-abiding citizen of the state . . . had no right to a state-funded college education" (see *Corrections Digest,* 1986). Two years later, the Indiana Senate approved legislation excluding incarcerated felons from applying for state-funded higher education grants, with one senator questioning: "It's hard for me to believe what I'm hearing. We're going to deny an 18 year old from a family of 12, whose father earned only $20,000 and give it to an axe murderer?" (Niederpruem, 1987). The month the Indiana bill was signed into law, a federal court ruled that excluding only incarcerated felons from a program funded by tax dollars was discriminatory and thus unconstitutional ("Judge Says Indiana," 1987).

Beginning in 1991, senators and representatives from both political parties have repeatedly introduced legislation in Congress to exclude "any individual who is incarcerated in any federal or state penal institution" from qualifying for Pell Grant assistance (*The Congressional Record–House,* 1992). The primary argument behind this proposal appears to be that as prisoners receive Pell Grants, a substantial number of needy or otherwise deserving students would go without financial assistance and therefore be unable to complete their education. If this can be shown to be the case, then the argument against funding inmates' educations may be politically viable. As we will show here, however, an analysis of the argument, including the facts cited and reasoning applied, clearly reveals the fallacy behind the proposed legislation.

The original force behind the exclusionary legislation was Senator Jesse Helms (R-NC), who fulminated on the Senate floor that "the American taxpayers are being forced to pay taxes to provide free college tuition for prisoners at a time when so many law-abiding, tax-paying citizens are struggling to find enough money to send their children to college" (*The Congressional Record–Senate,* 1991:11330). The senator, however, failed to mention four critical points that clarify the validity and applicability of this argument. First, Congress has never fully funded the Pell Grant program. In fact, in fiscal year 1991–1992, Congress actually *reduced* the appropriation by $14 million (Blumenstyk, 1991). Second, dollars for financial aid in higher education in the 1980s, when adjusted for inflation, actually *decreased* (Zyble, 1990). Third, inflation-adjusted tuition increases of 141 percent at state schools and even more at private schools occurred during the 1980s (*The Washington Spectator,* 1992). Finally, incomes for working and middle-class households have stagnated. These four elements can be cogently argued as having a greater influence on families' abilities to pay college tuition than money being provided to inmate-college students. These facts, added with the infinitesimal proportion of Pell Grant dollars that goes to inmates, bring this issue into focus in a slightly different manner from that proposed by Senator Helms.

Representative Thomas Coleman (R-MO) declared during a House of Representatives debate over his co-sponsored legislation[4] that 100,000 prisoners received Pell Grants during the 1991–1992 academic year (*The Congressional Record–House,* 1992), and in 1993 Senator Kay Hutchinson (R-TX) stated that in 1991–1992 inmates "received as much as $200 million in Pell funds" (*The Congressional Record–Senate,* 1993:15746). The interesting aspect of these claims is that there is simply no way they could be true. For example, if Thomas is correct, then one out of every eight inmates is a college student (U.S. Department of Justice, 1992b), which is simply not the case. Only one of every 100 inmates has a college education (Greenfeld, 1985). In 1990, it was reported that there were 35,000 inmate-college students in the United States (Stephan, 1992). If the 35,000 inmate-college students were each awarded the $1500 average inmate-student grant, this would equate to only one quarter of the $200 million claimed by Senator Hutchinson.[5]

Wisconsin's Republican Representative Gunderson lamented that millions of "the most needy students among us" are denied Pell Grants, and by eliminating prisoners' eligibility at least some deserving students would then receive aid (*The Congressional Record–House,* 1992). This is true. If inmates do not get this money, then we may presume it will be redirected to other financially needy students. However, this argument presupposes that prison inmates are neither needy nor deserving students. Instead, it is implied that only traditional students are deserving, and that a substantial number of such students would benefit from the exclusion of inmate-students. More than 60 percent of inmates were living below, at, or near the poverty line before their incarceration, however, with over one-half being racial minorities (Innes, 1988). Furthermore, between 60 and 80 percent of inmates had not completed their high school educations prior to incarceration (Greenfeld and Minor-Harper, 1991), or they are illiterate (Bell, Conrad, and Suppa, 1984). This leaves little question regarding whether inmates are among the most needy of our nation's students. During the 1993–1994 academic year, 4.5 million Pell Grants were awarded to 5.5 million applicants.[6] It is also a common practice, however, for financial aid counselors to have even those they know to be ineligible for federal assistance apply for Pell Grants, so they can then utilize the evaluations in their own aid disbursement decisions. As such, these practices serve to inflate the pool of applicants denied Pell Grants, thereby inflating the supposed "crisis" in the grant program.

Fewer than 30,000 inmates receive Pell Grants, meaning that prisoners account for about one half of 1 percent of all grant recipients. The Pell Grant program was created in 1972 to assist the children of the poor and working class (targeting families with less than $15,000 annual income) (Hutchinson, 1993). Considering this objective, and the previously noted demographics of inmate-college students, it is clear that the Pell Grant program *is* achieving its mandate. As Lawyer and Dertinger (1993:52) observe, "where else would we find, in such large numbers, individuals who are so educationally, economically, and socially disadvantaged?"

Representative Bart Gordon (D-IN), the co- and continuing originator of the House bill to exclude inmate Pell Grant eligibility, objects to prisoners' participation since he believes they were not intended for the grants and should use other rehabilitation program dollars to fund their educations (Berkey, 1993). The problems with the representative's reasoning are twofold. First, during the debate concerning the Higher Education Reauthorization Act, several senators commented on the expansiveness and inclusiveness of the Pell Grant program, without mentioning prison exclusion (*The Congressional Record–Senate,* 1992). Senator Kennedy (D-MA) commented that "one of the central goals of this legislation was to increase access to higher education for *all* Americans" (*The Congressional Record–Senate,* 1992:1950). Senator Daschle noted that the legislation "improves educational access for *all* Americans" (*The Congressional Record–Senate,* 1992:51950). Senator Durenberger observed that "we do need to make higher education more accessible for *every* American student (The Congressional Record–Senate, 1992:1961). Senator Graham (R-TX) concluded that ensuring access to higher education for *all* segments of society helps equalize opportunities for *all* people to pursue and achieve the American dream (*The Congressional Record–Senate,* 1992).[7] Thus, Representative Gordon's argument that Pell Grants were not meant for prisoners does not appear to be supported by Senate intent. Second, Gordon's call to replace Pell Grants with other funding sources is criticized by David Evans, Senator Pell's (D-RI) staff director, who states that he does not accept the argument: "It's the way of getting out of it. Take money from here and get it from somewhere else. There are no excesses of money at the federal level" (Berkey, 1993b:A5). Supporting Evans's observation, the representative has not presented a plan or means to replace Pell Grant funding if it should be cut off. And, as previously cited, the $70 million allocated to offender education programming is already committed. Lastly, Gordon calls for the tracking of prisoners to see if higher education indeed pays off when inmates are released from prison (Berkey, 1993b). This is a commendable idea, but one that fails to recognize the current state of knowledge regarding PSCE. Representative Gordon has been repeatedly briefed (by these authors and others) on the effectiveness and efficiency of PSCE. Additional research is welcomed, but not in place of funding for continued PSCE programming.

If the facts and figures do not support the program's critics, then what are the motivating factors driving this as a political issue? Besides reasons of obstinacy and punitiveness, as shown by Governor Weld's objections to PSCE in general, two theories have been advanced: political posturing and racism. Excluding prison inmates from Pell Grant eligibility to achieve the minimal gain for traditional students can easily be classified as an example of "sixty-second management" of the nation's higher education funding dilemma (Boyte, 1991). Such a technique can be described as the political culture of the quick fix: crisis management with a short-term calculation of gain. "Whatever the problem," according to Carl Sagan and Ann Drayan (1991), "the quick fix is generally to shave a little freedom off the Bill of Rights." Political reporter William Greider (1991) calls this political strategy coming from our nation's capital "scapegoating," which he describes as looking for minority segments to blame when things go badly and decline is visible. The call to ban prisoners from Pell Grants can thus be seen as attention-getting "tough on crime" rhetoric meant to attract votes rather than to address underlying ills.

The racism theory is based on the contention that more black males are under some form of correctional supervision than are on college campuses (Mauer, 1991). As Robert Powell, assistant academic affairs officer at Shaw University observes, "if you want to educate black men, if you want to reclaim that talent there, you have to go into the prison" (quoted in Worden, 1991). With this in mind, barring prisoners from Pell Grant eligibility is a clear example of racist policy making, as its results disproportionately impact black students. To exclude prisoners as a category from Pell Grant funding is to economically refuse and socially deprive minority youth from one of the few venues available to earn a higher education (Sullivan, 1991). Whatever the motivating factors behind the effort to bar inmates, an analysis of the economics, demographics, and as we shall see in the following section, the results of PSCE do not justify prisoners' exclusion from funding.

THE EFFECTS OF POSTSECONDARY CORRECTIONAL EDUCATION

In corrections over the past twenty years, as Wreford (1990:9) observes, "the most heated debates result from disputes concerning the efficacy of intervention strategies for the incarcerated." Perhaps even more so with PSCE, the controversy of whether college programming can bring about reductions in recidivism remains central to the debate. Opponents either claim that these programs do not reduce recidivism or if they do, they accomplish this task with "self-selected" elites of the penal population that would successfully reintegrate, whether college educated or not.[8]

The rehabilitative ideal was strongly challenged in the 1970s by liberals and conservatives alike. The liberals criticized the programs of the medical model as control mechanisms co-opted by the state and employed to abuse and manipulate offenders (Cullen and Gilbert, 1982), while conservatives claimed that "the programs are failures; there is no evidence that they rehabilitate" (Goredki, 1979:75). The foundation for the "nothing works" doctrine was Robert Martinson's (1974) study of 231 rehabilitative programs conducted between 1945 and 1967. As Martinson's widely cited conclusions held, "with few and isolated exceptions, the rehabilitative efforts that have been reported so far have had no appreciable effect on recidivism."[9] Five years later, the National Academy of Sciences (Sechrest, White, and Brown, 1979), after reviewing the Martinson data, concurred with his conclusions.[10]

From the beginning of the assault on the efficacy of rehabilitation, there have been rebuttals and reevaluations of the "nothing works" doctrine. Initially, Bindman (1973) and Quay (1973) commented that it was "erroneous to say corrections ha[d] failed. Corrections had not yet been tried." Proponents of the rehabilitative ethic noted that the programs had been severely underfunded,[11] and adequate longitudinal follow-up evaluations had not been made to determine the efficacy or lack thereof for the programs that had been conducted. Critiques critical of the negative evaluations of rehabilitative programming continued (Martinson, 1974; Palmer, 1975; Halleck and Witte, 1977; Gendreau, 1981), while more effective evaluations of on-going, better focused, and more well-designed treatment programs were reported (Gendreau and Ross, 1979; Gendreau and Ross, 1987; Gendreau and Andrews, 1990). DiIulio (1991:147), after extensive analysis of the accumulated research, has concluded that "the facile notion that 'nothing works' is ready for the garbage heap of correctional history."

Postsecondary correctional education studies have traditionally failed to yield a coherent body of knowledge about program effectiveness (Maltz, 1984:30). Much of the research to date has been methodologically flawed, thereby inhibiting the drawing of valid conclusions. Additionally, the structure and dynamics of the penal environment make it a prohibitively difficult society to research (Sechrest, White, and Brown, 1979; Taylor and Tewksbury, 1993). Critical problems associated with correctional research, especially PSCE evaluations, include small sample sizes (sample sizes of fewer than 100 are common), questionable methodologies (lack of randomly selected control and experimental groups), varying definitions of recidivism (revocation of parole, rearrest, reconvictions, or reincarceration), statistically insignificant findings (or no statistical tests), and exceedingly short (or an absence of) follow-up periods. Consequently, "virtually every college prison program recidivism study of the 1970s and the 1980s exhibited either inadequate sample, or follow-up period deficiency, or both" (Wreford, 1990).

Over the years, there have been numerous reports hinting at prison college programming successes. The reports point to the controversy surrounding determination of PSCE efficacy; they provide no scientifically acceptable design to support the validity of the outcomes reported. McWilliams (1971), reporting on the Texas Department of Corrections Junior College program, noted that although in-depth studies were underway, program recidivism rates were approximately 15 percent compared to the system average of 50 percent. Thomas (1974), writing the evaluation for the Burlington County (NJ) College prison extension program, cited a recidivism rate of only 10 percent compared with a national rate of 80 percent. In 1982, Holden noted that after more than 200 inmates had participated in the Indiana State Reformatory–Ball State University college extension program, "those who had earned their degrees, none have yet returned as inmates to the reformatory." This was followed in 1983 by a report in *Psychology Today* that noted only 15 percent of inmate-college students (averaging fifteen credit hours) in the New Mexico State Prison returned to custody, as compared with 68 percent from the general prison population. Assad (1986) reported that not one graduate of the Boston University program at MCI-Norfolk had returned to prison.

The federal government also examined the apparent relationship between educational attainment and recidivism. Beck and Shipley (1987) observed that of 11,000 young ex-offenders with "some college," the recidivism rate was 31 percent, while high school graduates and dropouts recidivated at rates of 43 and 51 percent, respectively. Two years later, Beck and Shipley (1989), after studying the return rate of 108,000 parolees, reported recidivism rates of 30 percent for those with some college, 35 percent for high school graduates, and 40 percent for dropouts.[12] The researchers concluded that "the amount of prior education the parolees had received was related to the likelihood of rearrest" (Beck and Shipley, 1987:3).

The problems with these reports, as already mentioned, include the lack of defined methodology (if one was used at all). No matched control groups were used; no definition of recidivism was used other than return to the specific prison[13]; and even if definitions of recidivism and adequate time spans were provided (as in the federal studies), there was no definition of the programming structure or delivery location ("some college" prior to parole leaves open the question of the amount, type, and timing of academic achievement, and whether educational attainment was earned prior to initial arrest, during incarceration, or after parole and before reincarceration). Finally, no statistical evaluations were completed analyzing cause-effect relationships. The value of these reports, other than their presentation of interesting phenomena, is scientifically muted in the debate regarding PSCE's role in reducing recidivism.

In the early reviews of PSCE evaluations (Lewis, 1973; Seashore, Haberfield, Irwin, and Baker, 1976), no relationship was found between postsecondary education and recidivism. However, Linden and Perry (1982) reviewed the data from Project NewGate and found that the five separate programs achieved most of their goals but did not influence recidivism rates. Yet when analyzed individually, the Pennsylvania program, which had the most extensive postrelease transition program,[14] did have a lower recidivism rate than those at other sites. This result supports Haviland's (1982:78–79) observation that

> Isolating the impact of postsecondary education on inmates alone without consideration of the configuration of the prison setting makes meaningful evaluation difficult. . . . College placement services, counseling, curriculum development and admission procedures must be integrated into the inmate's education experience in order for meaningful conclusions to be made.[15]

In quasi-scientific evaluations,[16] the results of the effect of PSCE ranged from no statistically discernible relationship to significantly positive relationships between higher education and reduced levels of recidivism, but all suggested that an influence did exist to some degree. Haviland (1982) evaluated 193 inmate associate degree graduates (ranging from vocational to liberal arts fields of study) from an entire midwestern correctional system's PSCE program, and after three years compared these men with others at similar risk of recidivism from the general prison population. The results revealed no substantial difference between the two groups' recidivism rates (new conviction and reincarceration after release). However, "if the study focused only on those inmates who were paroled for the first time, one would realize higher success rates than those experienced in this study."[17] Also, by analyzing specific risk categories, well over half of recidivists came from the high to very high assaultive risk categories (i.e., those most categorically likely to recidivate).

Craig (1983) also found no evidence in the recidivism relationship in a northeastern penitentiary between those who earned college credits as compared with those with only secondary educations (GEDs and high school diplomas). Yet, the college students were three times as likely to have a sentence of at least ten years, were three times as likely to be incarcerated before age eighteen, three times as likely to have less than eight years of formal education (because they went right into the PSCG program),[18] and twice as likely to have been unemployed at the time of their arrest. Although the two studies did not find a significant difference between the experimental (PSCE) and control groups,[19] the higher risk classifications of the experimental group members suggest an educationally induced mediating effect: Similar return rates for different classification groups suggest an intervention has affected the experimental group.

A series of other PSCE evaluations noted a relationship between postsecondary education and reduced recidivism. Thompson (1976) reviewed the recidivism rates from students in one Alabama junior college's PSCE and found that college students recidivated at a rate of 16 percent compared with a national average of 70 percent to 75 percent. Blackburn's (1979) examination of the Maryland Correctional Training Center's college program compared students and other offenders, reporting a positive effect in recidivism reductions. In 1980, the Texas Department of Corrections also stated its belief that junior college enrollment resulted in lower recidivism rates (Gaither, 1980). In Canada, Duguid (1981) reported that inmate-students in the University of Victoria's PSCE program showed a recidivism rate of 14 percent, while nonstudents recidivated at a rate of 52 percent. Perhaps most remarkably, California's college program at Folsom prison reported a recidivism rate of 0 percent for students earning baccalaureate degrees. This compares with California's recidivism rate of 21.9 percent within the first year and 55 percent in three years (Chase and Dickover, 1983).[20] Thorpe, MacDonald, and Bala (1984:87), utilizing a computer model to compare actual recidivism rates of PSCE graduates in New York to projected recidivism rates based on past departmental analysis, "found that a sample of offenders who earned college degrees while incarcerated had a substantially lower return rate than the projected rate based on departmental overall data."[21] A Federal Bureau of Prisons recidivism study reported an average recidivism rate of 40 percent, while those with college degrees returned at a 5 percent rate (Harer, 1993).

Most of the preceding evaluations suffer from a lack of carefully selected and matched control groups. Critics of these studies cite the "self-selection" bias that skews results. This suggests that simply enrolling in a college program distinguishes inmates as among an elite of the institutional population. This could suggest, according to Holloway and Moke (1986:15), that "perhaps they would have succeeded on parole without college participation." In other words, based on these evaluations we simply do not know if the lower rates of recidivism are due to education or if these inmates would have failed to recidivate no matter the conditions.

Perhaps the most methodologically rigorous PSCE evaluations have accounted for self-selection bias in their analysis. These studies are focused on individual institutional programs and when viewed as a body, present compelling evidence regarding the positive effects PSCE can have on recidivism. Four major evaluations have been conducted to date, evaluating prison college programs in Pennsylvania, Ohio, New York, and Michigan.

Blumstein and Cohen (1979) compared all PSCE participants at the State Correctional Institution at Pittsburgh, Pennsylvania, with a control group of randomly selected offenders with secondary educations. They identified postsecondary education as the single statistically significant factor on recidivism out of 108 possible variables, but only for those inmates at the highest risk of recidivating. In Ohio, Holloway and Moke's (1986) evaluation of the college program at the Lebanon Correctional

Institution employed a similar, though less sophisticated, methodology. These researchers worked with two groups of offenders: college students and secondary school graduates. The two groups were matched for key variables, allowing education's impact to be assessed. Holloway and Moke (1986:16) concluded that

> The only significant difference, then, between the two groups was what they were able to do with their time in prison. Group One earning college degrees and Group Two completing high school/GED then pursuing other institutional assignments. . . . [The conclusion] supports the hypothesis that even persons who have a high likelihood of recidivating, based on their criminal backgrounds and lack of employment and educational histories, derive substantial benefit from access to college while in prison.

In New York, a follow-up survey of all male offender participants (986) in the Inmate College Program during the 1986–1987 academic year (and released in 1990) examined recidivism rates for inmates who earned degrees (356) or had dropped out or been administratively removed (630) from the college program. The degree-earning students had a statistically significant lower rate of recidivism compared with others (26 percent versus 44 percent). This finding led to the following conclusion: "Earning a college degree while incarcerated is positively linked to successful post-release adjustment as measured by return to the Department's custody" (Clark, 1991:1).[22]

Finally, Wreford (1990) reviewed 907 graduates of the Michigan Department of Corrections–Jackson Community College program. The students were compared with the Michigan and national penal populations on twenty-seven variables. College students were slightly older (twenty-eight versus thirty-four) and more likely to be minorities, in terms of criminal history, current offense, and length of sentence, students were identified as "some of the most hardened criminals to be found in the United States" (Wreford, 1990:62).[23] However, even with these characteristics, examination of recidivism rates three years after release shows a statistically significant difference between college graduates (23.8 percent) and the state's inmate population in general (30 percent). College graduates were statistically significantly less likely to return for a new felony, meaning that "graduates not only returned to prison significantly less often than the norm, but when they did it was generally for less egregious violations and thus, presumably, for shorter periods of incarceration" (Wreford, 1990:109).

All told, it can still be debated whether PSCE opportunities actually have a cause-effect relationship in reducing recidivism. It remains to be shown whether offenders who participate are somehow elite or special in ways that make their subsequent successful reintegration more likely than for the average inmate. Effectively determining this issue may be impossible; selection of true control and experimental groups for a PSCE evaluation raises difficult ethical considerations.[24] Ross and McKay (1978:290), the Canadian researchers who spent over two decades studying offender rehabilitation, have concluded that "nowhere else in the literature [of correctional programming] can one find such impressive results with the recidivistic adult offender." It is reasonable to suggest, as Palmer (1984:254) comments, that "studies need not be nearly perfect in order to yield valuable results or strong clues" that prison college programs produce significantly lower rates of recidivism. This means PSCE not only can make society safer, but as we shall see in the following sections, is also economically efficient.

INSTITUTIONAL IMPACT OF PSCE

Reducing recidivism is the *socially centered* goal of rehabilitative efforts; this, as we have seen, can be achieved through postsecondary correctional education. The *offender-centered* goal of rehabilitation is a positive attitude change and the development of healthy coping skills. These also have been shown to be achievable through the development of cognitive abilities ingrained in PSCE programming.[25] These changes in attitudes and coping skills become evident long before the time of release and thus can have direct positive impacts on institutional environments.

In general, as Luttrell (1991:55) observes, "educational programming has long been recognized as an important management tool" for correctional administrators. Colvin (1992) explains that an institution with a full range of programs is more likely to have stable and peaceful inmate-staff relations than an institution that warehouses inmates or operates on a paramilitary model with few programming opportunities. Although not a guarantee of peace, DiIulio (1991) notes that programs increase interactions between staff and staff and inmates. Consequently, these contacts break down barriers that may contribute to stressful (or even hostile and violent) relations. The direct impacts of PSCE, then, focus on both the achievement of individual-level goals and the structured operations of a prison. On the individual level, PSCE students have fewer misconduct incidents, improved relations with other inmates and staff, greater acceptance of responsibilities, and increased levels of self-esteem. On an institutional level, benefits are gained when the presence of a PSCE program offers an additional tool for staff recruitment and retention.

Participation in correctional programming is sometimes similar to a privilege, linked to institutional behavior. Violent or chronic rule violators are often denied participation opportunities (DiIulio, 1991). Evidence suggests that those who participate in prison college programs are perceived and documented as better behaved than the general inmate population. However, it has not been determined whether this is a cause-and-effect relationship or whether the phenomenon is actually a function of unique characteristics of those likely to seek out such opportunities.

Gendreau, Ross, and Izzo (1985), in their evaluation of a Canadian maximum security PSCE program, found no statistically significant effects on students' institutional conduct. However, while no documented impact was found, staff impressions of students known as "trouble makers" were noticeably improved as a result of enrollment. A similar evaluation compared inmate-students' behavior with offenders participating in a conjugal visitation program and found that conjugal visitation enhanced institutional control only when participants were not college educated (Davis, 1988). The level of an offender's education provided the best predictor of positive behavior. Taylor (1993a) surveyed inmates who retained full-time institutional employment along with full-time academic enrollment and reported that worker/students incurred only one fourth as many conduct violations as other inmates, with the PSCE students displaying almost no violent behavior.[26]

With cognitive-moral development suggested as the mediating influence of PSCE, evidence of such psychological change can be seen in several studies of such influence on offenders. A 1982 national survey of correctional education directors noted that 88 percent believed that college programming had a positive influence on the relationship between inmates and staff; 77 percent reported an increase in acceptance of personal responsibility for actions taken; and 94 percent reported positive impacts on inmate-students' self-esteem (Peak, 1983). Additionally, 70 percent of the directors observed improved relationships among offenders. Duguid (1987:5) reported a similar result in Canadian PSCE programs and found that "some administrators credit university students with creating a 'calmer' atmosphere in the prison and with 'defusing' potentially violent eruptions."[27] Pass (1988), working in the same prison as Davis, explains the Peak and Duguid observations as being a result of higher levels of education creating less social distance between inmates and staff.[28] Numerous researchers have noted that ethnic and racial divisions are a leading cause of tension and violence in prisons (Reasons, 1974; Carroll, 1974, 1982; Kruttschnitt, 1983). These divisions can be bridged by higher education that may enhance social interactions and harmony, rather than exasperate the consequences of overcrowding and anomic racial and ethnic interactions.

Another, perhaps complementary, explanation for reduced conflict and improved relations among PSCE students and graduates is traced to increased levels of self-esteem. Benson (1991) argues that incarceration serves to break an inmate's sense of adequacy and promotes feelings of worthlessness. In turn, Roundtree, Edwards, and Dawson (1982) report that prisoner self-esteem increases with educational attainment.

Anklesaria and Lary (1992) note significant reductions in hostility and aggression with increased offender self-esteem. With nearly universal increases in inmate-student's self-esteem (Peak 1983), and the noted positive relationship between behavior and self-esteem, the impact of PSCE programming on correctional populations becomes an important management tool.

Inmate-college students provide positive peer role models in a setting commonly devoid of such characterizations. PSCE students have been cited as "inspirations" (Begovich, 1990) and "precedents" (Harrell, 1991) in the penal environment. This influence is gained not simply through the status of their educational attainment, but through positive involvement in the community. Duguid (1987:14) expands on the inmate-student's role in the culture of the institution, saying:

> The prisoner-student is expected to assume specific obligations toward his less fortunate or less able fellow prisoners. Thus this new academic elite is encouraged to attract other men to education programs, to work with men pursuing the GED certificates or re-engaged in Adult Basic Education programs, and their skills to identify and work with men with literacy problems. It is here in this realm of community involvement, more than with the success of individual university students, that the real value of the program to the prison is to be found.

While the overall impact of positive peer role models may be difficult to identify empirically, it is clear that such impacts are not hard to identify subjectively.

Finally, PSCE programs can bring benefits not only to inmates and the administration of institutions, but can also provide convenient educational opportunities for institutional staff. It is not uncommon for the occasional correctional officer or administrator to participate in college classrooms alongside inmate-students (Nelson, 1975; Kiser, 1987a). Another way that PSCE programs can provide direct benefits to institutional staff is to offer separate, but similar, courses on-site for staff enrollment (Yarborough, 1989). This option encourages staff education but removes the potential dilemmas involved in staff and inmates being "peers." In this way it is not only the inmate population that is being educated, but staff can also pursue personal and professional advancement.

In 1967, the Task Force Report on Corrections for the President's Commission on Law Enforcement and Administration of Justice cited the need for recruiting and retaining qualified personnel. These tasks were directly linked with the recruitment of college-educated staff. Not long afterward (1974), the American Correctional Association encouraged institutions to work with local colleges to develop associate degree programs for their personnel. The assumption here is that a more educated staff is a better staff. Education can also prepare personnel for the psychological, social, and technological challenges presented by a job in corrections. Ross (1989) argues that corrections today combines the task of a high-tech security guard with the abilities of a social worker. As corrections continues to evolve into a complex social service bureaucracy, "advancement with an agency will depend more on one's qualifications and education and less on seniority" (Ross, 1989:274). Therefore, by providing correctional staff opportunities to continue their educations in a convenient and low-cost fashion, PSCE programs can enhance all aspects of institutional management.

Thus, postsecondary correctional education programs can provide correctional institutions and systems with a valuable tool for staff recruitment, training, and retention while also working to rehabilitate inmates and positively influence the institution's social environment. Furthermore, the involvement of postsecondary institutions in prisons can provide unique research opportunities in a host of fields, including (but certainly not limited to) criminal justice (Taylor, 1993a), adult education (Gubar and Hedlin, 1981), and sociology (Kandal, 1981): "This research in turn enhances the educational programs and professional well-being of both university and correctional staff" (Duguid 1987:12).

Postsecondary correctional education programs benefit the institutional environment by helping to resocialize offenders through modified attitudes, improved coping skills, and enhanced self-esteem. These offenders positively influence the institutional environment by providing positive role models who do not return to prison as recidivists. These programs can also offer educational opportunities to correctional personnel that would not be available without the offender-centered program to support staff opportunities. As we shall see in the next section, these programs can be offered in a cost-effective manner and provide significant returns on society's investment.

THE ECONOMICS OF PSCE

For fiscal year 1993–1994, the United States spent nearly $22 billion on corrections (Lillis, 1993). This sum is $10 billion more than was spent only five years earlier. Morris Thigpen, commissioner of corrections in Alabama, has warned that "we're on a train that needs to be turned around. It doesn't make sense to pump millions into corrections and have no effect on the crime rate" (Ticer, 1989:80). With governments' demands exceeding their fiscal capabilities, "smart programs" that invest now to reduce greater demands later and even strengthen the economic base of the nation are more necessary than ever before. Postsecondary correctional education is a program opportunity that achieves these goals.

To begin with, much of the financing for PSCE programs originates in correctional department budgets. From a correctional administrator's viewpoint, this can be a highly advantageous position. Prison industries and maintenance work engage, at best, only one half of the penal population. When this is contrasted with the fact that 10 percent to 15 percent of inmates enroll in college classes (when they are available), PSCE is seen as a major programming option.

Littlefield and Wolford (1982) reported that the most common funding sources for such programs (in descending order of investment) are

1. Pell Grants
2. State-funded student aid grants
3. Veterans benefits[29]
4. Individual student payments
5. Correctional department's education budgets
6. Scholarships from the sponsoring college or university

Because funding formulas vary from state to state, it is difficult to show a holistic example of the PSCE funding structure. Some examples of common funding configurations can be found in selected programs from Indiana, Pennsylvania, and Texas. Ball State University's three PSCE programs in Indiana prisons are funded by Pell Grants, state student aid grants, veterans benefits, and payments from inmate-students (Chistensen, 1989). The Pennsylvania Business Institute—only one of many schools offering PSCE programming in Pennsylvania's prisons—funds its PSCE program through Pell Grants and school-funded scholarships (Berkey, 1993b). The Texas Department of Corrections' PSCE program gets funding through a formula whereby department dollars pay for an inmate's first class, and then a combination of offenders' personal funds, Pell Grants, and veterans benefits covers subsequent costs (Texas Department of Criminal Justice, 1989).

At an average annual cost of $25,000 to incarcerate an individual (Zedlewski, 1987), with a substantial number of those incarcerated being recidivists (Greenfeld, 1985; Beck and Shipley, 1987), the possible savings from reducing the numbers of recidivists is great. Even with the average expense of $2500 per year in tuition, texts, and fee costs (Taylor, 1989), the return on the investment can be substantial. For 10 percent ($2500) of the cost of one year of incarceration ($25,000), one year of PSCE programming can be funded. If such programming is continued over two to four years, the demonstrated recidivism rate for participants can be drastically reduced. Even figuring the provision of baccalaureate level education, the cost is only 40 percent of *one* year of incarceration. And, as we have seen, this will most likely result in single (rather than high double) digit return rates for graduates.

The possible cost savings that PSCE programs can provide through reduced recidivism have been well documented (Greenwood and Turner, 1985; Wreford, 1990; Chancellor, 1991). Haber (1983) argued that if the

Lorton (D.C.) Prison college program did indeed achieve a near-zero recidivism rate for its participants (approximately 10 percent of the institutional population), approximately 10 percent of the District of Columbia's prison budget would be saved: "This amount of money is no doubt between several thousand and a million dollars" (Haber, 1983:54).

On a national scale, Taylor (1992a) developed a model for analyzing the potential cost savings of PSCE programming. This argument holds that if PSCE programming were expanded so that 15 percent of the offenders released annually had earned at least an associates degree,[30] with an annual recidivism rate of 15 percent compared with the standard return rate of 50 percent, this would result in a savings of $120 million annually in nonincurred incarceration costs. Taking this model a step further, the savings this outcome would produce in crimes not committed would range from $2 to $20 billion in nonincurred victimizations. Taylor (1992a:137) concludes by observing that

> By either measure presented, and these are only the crudest of projections, the return on investment that postsecondary education provides the nation is substantial, thus lending credibility to the notion that the most cost-effective way to control crime is through prevention rather than through retaliation.

In general, the financial benefit society realizes for its investment in public and private higher education exceeds a 12 percent rate of return (Bernstein and Magnusson, 1993), and the total return from its investment in PSCE is far greater.

Furthermore, as Gail Hughes, deputy director of Missouri's Department of Correction, has observed, the purpose of corrections is not to spend money but, rather, "to produce a good product at a reasonable cost to society" (*Financial World,* 1991:55). The "product" produced at a reasonable cost by PSCE programming is most likely a law-abiding individual who remains free, gains employment at a livable wage, pays taxes, and becomes what many of us would simply call "a better citizen." From a social investment viewpoint, the observation by Chase and Dickover (1983:94) of the Folsom Prison college program speaks for the PSCE opportunity as a whole: "It seems evident that the public, whose tax dollars on both the state and federal level support the[se] program[s], have realized a high return on their investment."

THE CURRENT STATE OF PSCE

As Kiser (1987b:102) has observed, "one of the most dramatic twentieth century developments in American penitentiaries has been the widespread introduction of college programs for inmates." However, as has been noted throughout this chapter, this "dramatic development" has not been without criticism. These criticisms have in turn led to reductions in these opportunities. In 1987, Ryan and Woodard noted that 92 percent of the states reported some form of PSCE programming. By 1992, Sarri noted that this had dropped to 84 percent of states reporting "some type of postsecondary educational programming" (1993:2). Since that time five states[31] have retracted their PSCE programs because of Pell Grant ineligibility.[32]

The most comprehensive analysis of the scope of PSCE opportunities available today (Sarri, 1993) reports the following current conditions:

1. Approximately one third of the programs are for vocational training and one third lead to associate degrees. Only 15 percent are for baccalaureate degrees and 15 percent are nondegree granting programs.

2. Universities are the most common type of educational institution involved in the delivery of higher education in prisons, accounting for 42 percent of programs. Community colleges rank a close second, providing nearly 40 percent of programs. Vocational/technical schools account for the remaining 19 percent of these programs.

3. More than one half of the students are enrolled in associate degree programs, less than 6 percent in baccalaureate degree programs, and nearly 40 percent in vocational certification programs.

4. The large majority (85 percent) of PSCE programs are provided on-site at prisons. Less than 2 percent of programs bring inmate-students to campus, and 10 percent of programs rely on correspondence courses.

5. Pell Grants are the most common source of program financing, nearly twice as common as correctional budgets. Less frequently, higher education is financed by individual offenders, and least common are funds provided by colleges and foundations.

Sarri goes on to note various problems that impact both programs and student offenders in postsecondary correctional education in the 1990s. It is interesting to note that many of these issues are the same as those cited by Adams (1968) as problems more than twenty-five years earlier. Obviously, not much has changed in the implementation of PSCE over the past several decades. Among the problems facing PSCE are

1. Limited number and variety of courses. This is attributed to the lack of equipment as well as to the fact that curriculums are often determined by corrections, not educational, administrators.

2. Prison library resources are extremely inadequate, and offenders have numerous difficulties receiving appropriate resources in a timely manner.

3. Special educational and language needs are not being met.

4. Explicit goals for educational programs are often lacking. Very few states have qualified educational coordinators in charge of programs.

5. Transfers of offenders between institutions are given little or no consideration regarding participation in educational programs. Often this interrupts the educational process and leads an inmate to end his or her educational pursuits.

6. Many states' educational programs are the lowest paid of institutional work assignments and thus provide a built-in *dis*incentive for enrollment.

7. Most states' correctional facilities are overcrowded and thus do not provide students space, privacy, or an environment (i.e., relative quiet, desks and chairs, adequate access to libraries) conducive to study.

Concluding her report, Sarri (1993:7) correlated state incarceration rates with offender enrollments in educational programs, the results of which revealed that "states with the highest rates of incarceration [had] the lowest percentages of their prisoners in educational programs." It appears that in those locations with the most need, there is the least opportunity.

Postsecondary correctional education involves a program structure that "promotes civility, develops cognition and encourages confidence. These three Cs should guide the thinking of our approach to criminal rehabilitation" (Pendleton, 1988:83). Without an effective rehabilitation strategy, our current correctional policies will eventually deplete society's resources, thereby draining the funds allocated for education, health care, and investments for the future. PSCE is an effective and cost-efficient means by which to offer offenders opportunities to break the costly cycle of crime perpetuation, victimization, and reincarceration. We believe that by implementing short-run, cost-saving strategies of reducing or eliminating educational opportunities, in the long run crime will be perpetuated. This, in turn, will produce yet higher levels of victimization, pain, and expense to us all.

In one of the original evaluations of a prison college program, Lockard (1974:22) poignantly suggested a policy prescription that carries as much, if not more, wisdom today than it did then: "Simply, and aside from humanitarian concerns—it is cheaper in the not-so-long run to pay (adequately) for effective anti-recidivism measures, than to finance law enforcement, justice administration, and penal services and apparatus."

NOTES

1. Correctional education had its foundation in the late 1700s when the Quakers employed religious teachings at the Walnut Street Jail. In 1825, Louis Dwight, who believed that criminality was spawned in the lack of familiarization with the Scriptures, sponsored the

Sabbath Prison schools, which utilized chaplains, theology students, and volunteers to teach literacy through Bible readings (McKelvey, 1936).

2. However, this growth has not been continuous or smooth. For example, Wolford and Littlefield (1985) report that fifty-eight prison college programs were discontinued between 1976 and 1982.

3. Andrews and associates (1990) point out that effective correctional treatment depends on the type of programming provided to which type of offenders in which type of setting. Orsagh and Marsden (1985) suggest that by employing the rational-choice theory of crime causation, treatment programs aimed at "economically motivated offenders" who place a high value on income and work should prove effective when they enhance work and income-generating skills. Ross, Fabiano, and Ewles (1988:30) focus more on the irrational behaviors of offenders caused or at least influenced by cognitive deficits and do note that white collar criminals (economically motivated offenders) "are less likely to have such cognitive deficits." Thus, even though PSCE obviously can impart strong employment and income-generating skills, the "treatment" aspect lies in the cognitive development area of the programming. As such, neither theory conflicts with the other; rather, they serve to complement one another.

4. Coleman's co-sponsor of Amendment 1168 was Representative Bart Gordon (D-TN). In 1993, Gordon reintroduced 1168 (without Coleman's sponsorship) after the original motion had been defeated in committee hearings. As of November 1993, 1168 had thirteen co-sponsors, and as of that session, all of the exclusionary proposals have been stricken from bills passed during committee hearings.

5. No one knows how many inmates receive Pell Grants each year. The application form has no specific designation that would declare that an individual is incarcerated, and the lack of income, although suggestive of incarceration, by no means assures such a situation. In 1982, the Department of Education reported that 37 percent of inmate-students relied on Pell Grants for their primary source of funding a college education (O'Hayre and Coffey, 1982). In 1994, Senator Pell's staff calculated that only 27,771 inmates received grants during the 1993–1994 academic year.

6. In 1992, the Higher Education Reauthorization Act was signed into law. It increased the program's appropriation, raising the family income ceiling to $42,000 (90 percent coming from below $39,000), and increased the number of grant recipients by nearly 1 million. Ironically, Senator Helms, who initiated the movement against inmates' Pell Grants because of a stated concern about traditional students not receiving aid, cast the only dissenting vote against the Reauthorization Act (Krauss, 1992).

7. Emphasis added by authors. However, since the Senate had debated the Helms amendments the previous fall, the senators' expansive statements do seem quite telling.

8. Ross (1978) calls this the YAVIS syndrome accusation. He defines this as the charge that only young, attractive, verbal, intelligent, and successful candidates are selected for treatment programming.

9. The issue that rehabilitative programming was not achieving reductions in recidivism had been known more than fifteen years preceding the publication of Martinson's findings (Wootan, 1959; Bailey, 1966; Robison, 1971). The reason Martinson's article had such a profound impact was not necessarily its intellectual argument, but rather following the turmoil of the 1960s, it was published in the midst of a conservative campaign to provide "objective data" to advance a particular vision of criminal justice (Cullen and Gendreau, 1989).

10. The same year the National Academy of Sciences issued its affirmation of Martinson's 1974 findings, Martinson (1979:243), upon continuing evaluations of correctional treatment, stated that "on the basis of the evidence in our current study I withdraw this conclusion" that nothing works. Additionally, the conclusions of both Martinson and the Academy of Sciences studies were misinterpreted by those seeking to discredit the rehabilitative ethic. What was reported was that based on the available data, the relationship between treatment and rehabilitation efficacy measured by recidivism rates was *ambiguous.*

11. Chaneles (1976) reported that, on average, less than $100 per year was spent per inmate for social services and extended rehabilitation programming. Furthermore, this was for only 5 percent of the penal population. A decade later, Ryan and Woodard (1987) noted that, on average, the amount devoted to education in correctional budgets barely exceeded 3 percent.

12. Recidivism was defined in three ways: rearrest, reconviction, and reincarceration for a new offense. Primarily, however, recidivism in the Beck and Shipley studies refers to rearrest.

13. This means a parolee on a technical violation could return to another prison in the state or a reconvicted offender could be sent to another prison system entirely, and both situations could be counted as program successes.

14. A 1972 study identified eleven needs of ex-offenders (i.e., financial help, counseling, living arrangements, medical care, substance abuse treatment) that if unmet tend to correlate with higher levels of recidivism. The U.S. Department of Labor (1977) and Mallar and Thornton (1978) each reported that providing temporary financial assistance was quite successful in reducing recidivism rates of parolees.

15. Complicating the evaluations of PSCE effectiveness, Peak (1983:82) observed that many consider recidivism an unreliable "method of assessing correctional effectiveness. . . . The common opinion is that there are simply too many other variables impacting on recidivism that should be taken into account." Others (Martinson, 1974) have identified recidivism as the quantifiable measure of the efficacy of treatment programs, and (Taylor, 1992) notes that virtually all PSCE evaluations have employed recidivism barometers as their measure of efficacy. If return rates (treatment failures) are not utilized, then what standards are to be employed to evaluate program effectiveness?

16. Quasi-scientific studies are defined by the following methodology: (1) defined experimental and control groups, (2) evaluation periods of at least one year, with most analyzing at least three years of postrelease behavior, and (3) a percentage comparison between groups, with most but not all determining statistical significance.

17. Several researchers (Wallerstedt, 1984; Greenfeld, 1985; Beck and Shipley, 1987) have noted that a relationship generally exists between the number of incarcerations and the propensity to recidivate.

18. The control group had a "significantly higher percent of inmates with a high school diploma than the college (experimental) group" (Craig, 1983:76). This is noteworthy for the ongoing debate over the actual educational value between a high school diploma and general equivalency degree (GED).

19. The Haviland (1982) study revealed a lower recidivism rate for the experimental group as compared with the control group, while Craig's (1983) study revealed a higher recidivism rate for the experimental group. However, both results failed to achieve statistical significance.

20. The evaluation period for the college graduates was for only six months after release, which tends to dilute the results. This is especially true in light of Glaser's (1964) and Gottfredson and Ball's (1965) observation that at least 75 percent of recidivism occurs within three years after release. Consequently, it is suggested that three years should serve as the minimum period of study in determining programming effectiveness.

21. None of these studies determined statistical significance of a relationship between postsecondary education and reductions in recidivism. However, the substantial differences in return rates are suggestive of a possible true relationship.

22. This result coincides with Glaser's (1964) findings twenty-five years earlier, that prison education was related to lower recidivism rates only when the education was extensive and occurred over prolonged periods of confinement.

23. All of these factors are commonly associated with a high likelihood of recidivism (Kitchener, Schmidt, and Glaser, 1977; Harer, 1993).

24. The central ethical question in a truly scientific design is how to select control and experimental groups, which must (to eliminate the self-selection bias) come from a common pool desiring enrollment. The question that blocks such assignment is who has the authority to grant and deny access to those who desire a college education? Even if such a study were set up, legal challenges could well be raised, with a strong possibility of such an experimental design being voided by the courts.

25. The terms *socially centered* and *offender-centered* were originally proposed by Palmer (1983).

26. These results mirror Petersilia and Honig's (1980) observation that offenders involved in treatment programs and work assignments experienced significantly lower infraction rates.

The significance of this finding is that Gottfredson and Adams (1982) found that institutional behavior is correlated to postrelease success, a fact validated by Harer (1993).

27. Similarly, Taylor witnessed such an influence in 1991 at a midwestern maximum security prison when the inmates protested institutional conditions. The initial form of that protest was to be a violent eruption; however, many college students (who were respected among the population) suggested a tactic based on Gandhi and King (whom the inmate-students had studied in the prison's PSCE program) that entailed peaceful demonstrations over four days during recreation periods. This tactic did not violate institutional rules and allowed the entire population an opportunity to participate. This strategy was successfully implemented, avoiding what could have been a violent altercation (Taylor, 1992b).

28. *Social distance* is defined as "the degree of closeness or remoteness one desires in interaction with members of a particular group" (Parrillo, 1985:491).

29. McCollum (1994) explains that prison college funding received an unexpected boost in the 1960s and 1970s when an increased number of those incarcerated were also military veterans who utilized their G.I. Bill educational benefits to enroll in prison college programs.

30. Taylor based the choice of 15 percent of the released population achieving PSCE graduation on a theorized 60 percent parity of the 25 percent of the adult U.S. population with postsecondary educations. This parity is chosen because of the associated educational learning disabilities and pathologies concentrated in penal populations, leaving Taylor to believe true parity to be unrealistic.

31. California, Michigan, Missouri, Nebraska, and New Jersey.

32. The 1992 Higher Education Reauthorization Act placed a number of restrictions on prisoner's eligibility for Pell Grants (including prohibitions on grants for death row and life without parole inmates). One of these limitations was that the grants must only supplement, not replace, state funding for PSCE programs. The formula established to make this determination was a comparison of states' 1988 PSCE funding with that in 1992. The five states cited previously did not meet this formula, and thus their inmates are no longer eligible to receive Pell Grants.

REFERENCES

Adams, S. (1968). *The San Quentin Prison College Project.* Berkeley, CA: University of California Press.

Andrews, D., Bonta, J., and Hoge, R. (1990). "Classification for Effective Rehabilitation: Rediscovering Psychology." *Criminal Justice and Behavior,* 17:19–52.

Andrews, D., Zinger, I., Hoge, R., Bonta, J., Gendreau, P., and Cullen, F. (1990). "Does Correctional Treatment Work? A Clinically Relevant and Psychologically Informed Meta-Analysis." *Criminology,* 28(3):369–404.

Anklesaria, F. and Lary, S. (1992). "A New Approach to Offender Rehabilitation: Maharishi's Integrated System of Rehabilitation." *Journal of Correctional Education,* 43(1):6–13.

Arbuthnot, J. (1984). "Moral Reasoning Development Programs in Prisons: Cognitive Development and Critical Reasoning Approaches." *Journal of Moral Education,* 34(2):112–123.

Assad, G. (1986, August). "A Beacon of Light: Exemplary Education at MCI-Norfolk." *Corrections Today:* 150–154.

Bailey, W. (1966). "Correctional Outcome: An Evaluation of 100 Reports." *Journal of Criminal Law, Criminology and Police Science,* 57:153–160.

Baker, K., Irwin, J., Haberfeld, S., Seashore, M., and Leonard, D. (1973). *Summary Report: Project NewGate and Other Prison College Education Programs.* Washington, D.C.: Office of Economic Opportunity.

Beck, A. and Shipley, B. (1987). *Recidivism of Young Parolees.* Washington, D.C.: Bureau of Justice Statistics.

Beck, A. and Shipley, B. (1989). *Recidivism of Prisoners Released in 1983.* Washington, D.C.: Bureau of Justice Statistics.

Begovich, R. (1990, May 31). "Pendleton Inmates Earn Degrees." *Muncie Evening Press.*

Bell, R., Conrad, E., Laffey, T., Lutz, J., Miller, P., Simon, C., Stakelon, A., and Wilson, N. (1979). *Correctional Education Programs for Inmates.* Washington, D.C.: U.S. Department of Justice.

Bell, R., Conrad, E., and Suppa, R. (1984). "Findings and Recommendations of the National Study on Learning Deficiencies in Adult Inmates." *Journal of Correctional Education,* 35(4):29–37.

Benson, I. (1991). "Prison Education, and Prison Education in the UK." *Yearbook of Correctional Education.* Burnaby, BC: Institute for the Humanities, Simon Fraser University: 3–10.

Berkey, K. (1993a, October 25). "PBI: Pottstown, Prison Business Institute." *The Mercury,* Pottstown, PA:A1, A5.

Berkey, K. (1993b, October 27). "Commit Murder, Go to College." *The Mercury,* Pottstown, PA:A1, A5.

Bernstein, A. and Magnusson, P. (1993, February 22). "How Much Good Will Training Do?" *BW:* 76–77.

Bindman, A. (1973). "Why Does Rehabilitation Fail?" *International Journal of Offender Therapy and Comparative Criminology,* 17(3):309–324.

Blackburn, F. (1979). "The Relationship Between Recidivism and Participation in Community College Associate of Arts Degree Program for Incarcerated Offenders." (Unpublished doctoral dissertation, Virginia Polytechnic Institute and State University.)

Blumenstyk, G. (1991, June 8). "Use of Pell Grants to Educate Prisoners Provokes Criticism." *The Chronicle of Higher Education.*

Blumstein, A. and Cohen, J. (1979). "Control of Selection Effects in the Evaluation of Social Problems." *Evaluation Quarterly,* 3(4):583–608.

Boyte, H. (1991). "Democratica Engagement: Bringing Populism and Liberalism Together." *American Prospect,* (Summer):55–63.

Burns Indiana Statutes Annotated, Constitution. (1990). "Article 1, Section 18." Charlottesville, VA: Michie Company.

Carroll, L. (1974). *Hacks, Blacks and Cons: Race Relations in a Maximum Security Prison* (reissued 1988). Prospect Heights, IL: Waveland Press.

Carroll, L. (1982). "Race, Ethnicity, and the Social Order of the Prison." In Johnson and Toch (eds.), *The Pain of Imprisonment.* Beverly Hills, CA: Sage.

Chancelor, F. (1992). *A Study of Alabama Prison Recidivism Rates of Those Inmates Having Completed Vocational and Academic Programs While Incarcerated Between the Years of 1987 thru 1991.* A Special Report by the Department of Post-Secondary Education, Alabama Department of Corrections.

Chaneles, S. (1976). "Prisoners Can Be Rehabilitated Now." *Psychology Today,* 10(5):129–133.

Chase, L. and Dickover, R. (1983). "University Education at Folsom Prison: An Evaluation." *Journal of Correctional Education,* 34(3):92–5.

Chistensen, J. (1989, February 6). "Penitentiary Program Offers Inmates Chance for College Education." *Ball State Daily News.*

Clark, P. (1985). *Perceptions of Criminal Justice Surveys, Executive Summary.* Michigan Prison and Jail Overcrowding Project.

Clark, P. (1991). *Analysis of Return Rates of the Inmate College Program Participants.* Albany, NY: New York Department of Correctional Services.

Clark, R. (1970). *Crime in America.* New York: Simon and Schuster.

Cohen, M. (1972). *A Study of Community Based Needs in Massachusetts.* Springfield, MA: Massachusetts Department of Corrections.

Colvin, M. (1992). *The Penitentiary in Crisis: From Accomodation to Riot in New Mexico.* Albany, NY: State University of New York Press.

The Congressional Record–Senate. (1991). "Amendment No. 938." (July 30):11329–34.

The Congressional Record–House. (1992). "Amendment Offered by Mr. Coleman of Missouri." (March 26):1892–98.

The Congressional Record–Senate. (1992). "Higher Education Amendments." (February 21):1946–1969.

The Congressional Record–Senate. (1993). "Crime Bill." (November 16):15746.

Corrections Digest. (1986, January 29). "Ruling on Free College Educations for Inmates" :6.

Craig, J. (1983). "A Study of Inmate Participation in College-Level Academic Programs and Recidivism." (Unpublished Ed.D. disseration, Teachers College, Columbia University.)

Cressey, D. (1955). "Changing Criminals: The Application of the Theory of Differential Association." *American Journal of Sociology,* 61(5):116–120.

Cullen, F. and Gendreau, P. (1989). "The Effectiveness of Correctional Rehabilitation: Reconsidering the 'Nothing Works' Debate." In L. Goodstein and D.L. MacKenzie (eds.), *The American Prison: Issues in Research Policy.* New York: Plenum Publishing.

Cullen, F. and Gilbert, K. (1982). *Reaffirming Rehabilitation.* Cincinnati: Anderson Publishing Co.

Cullen, F., Skovron, S., Scott, J., and Burton, V. (1990). "Public Support for Correctional Treatment: The Tenacity of Rehabilitative Ideology." *Criminal Justice and Behavior,* 17(1): 6–18.

Davis, R. (1988). "Education and the Impact of the Family Reunion Program in a Maximum Security Prison." *Journal of Offender Counseling, Services and Rehabilitation,* 12(2):153–159.

DiIulio, J. (1991). *No Escape: The Failure of American Corrections.* New York: Basic Books.

Doble, J. (1987). *Crime and Punishment: The Public's View.* New York: Public Agenda Foundation.

Duguid, S. (1981). "Rehabilitation Through Education: A Canadian Model." In L. Morian (ed.), *On Prison Education.* Ottawa, Canada: Canadian Publishing Centre.

Duguid, S. (1987). *University Education in British Columbia,* Burnaby, BC: Prison Education Program, Simon Fraser University.

Englehardt, N. (1939). "Fundamental Factors Governing Success of a Correctional Education Program." *Correctional Education Today,* American Prison Association.

Financial World. (1991, May). "The Costly Penal System": 54–55.

Gaither, C. (1980). "An Evaluation of the Texas Department of Corrections' Junior College Program." Huntsville, TX: Department of Correction Treatment Directorate, Research and Development Division.

Gendreau, P. (1981). "Treatment in Corrections: Martinson Was Wrong." *Canadian Psychology,* 22(4):332–338.

Gendreau, P. and Andrews, D. (1990, January). "Tertiary Prevention: What the Meta-Analyses of Offender Treatment Literature Tells Us About 'What Works.'" *Canadian Journal of Criminology:* 173–184.

Gendreau, P. and Ross, R. (1979). "Effective Correctional Treatment: Bibliotherapy for Cynics." *Crime and Delinquency,* 25:463–489.

Gendreau, P. and Ross, R. (1987). "Revivification of Rehabilitation: Evidence from the 1980s." *Justice Quarterly,* 4(3):349–407.

Gendreau, P., Ross, R., and Izzo, R. (1985). "Institutional Misconduct: The Effects of the UVIC Program at Matsqui Penitentiary." *Canadian Journal of Criminology,* 27(2):209–217.

Glaser, D. (1964). *The Effectiveness of a Prison and Parole System.* Indianapolis: Bobbs-Merrill.

Goredki, J. (1979). *A Theory of Criminal Justice.* New York: Columbia University Press.

Gottfredson, D. and Ballard, K. (1965). *The Validity of Two Parole Prediction Scales: An Eight Year Follow-up Study.* Vacaville, CA: Institute for the Study of Crime and Delinquency.

Gottfredson, M. and Adams, K. (1982). "Prison Behavior and Release Performance." *Law and Policy Quarterly,* 4(3):373–391.

Gottfredson, S. and Taylor, R. (1984). "Public Policy and Prison Populations: Measuring Opinions about Reforms." *Judicature,* 68(4–5):190–201.

Greenfeld, L. (1985). "Examining Recidivism." Washington, D.C.: Bureau of Justice Statistics, U.S. Department of Justice, NCJ-96501.

Greenfeld, L. and Minor-Harper, S. (1991). *Women in Prison.* Washington, D.C.: U.S. Department of Justice.

Greenwood, D. and Turner, S. (1985). *The Vision Quest Program: An Evaluation.* Santa Monica, CA: Rand Corporation.

Greider, W. (1991, September 5). "The Politics of Diversion: Blame It on the Blacks." *Rolling Stone:* 32, 33, 96.

Gubar, S. and Hedlin, A. (1981). "A Jury of Our Peers: Teaching and Learning in the Indiana Womens Prison." *College English:*779–89.

Haber, G. (1983). "The Realization of Potential by Lorton, D.C. Inmates with UDC Education Compared to Those without UDC Education." *Journal of Offender Services, Counseling and Rehabilitation,* 7:37–55.

Hallack, S. and Witte, A. (1977). "Is Rehabilitation Dead?" *Crime and Delinquency,* 23:372–382.

Harer, M. (1993). *Recidivism Among Federal Prison Releases in 1987: A Preliminary Report.* Washington, D.C.: Federal Bureau of Prisons, Office of Research and Evaluation.

Harrell, G. (1991, January). "Bar Exam: Prisoners Finding Rehabilitation from Ball State's School of Hard Knocks." *The Indianapolis New Times:* 8–9.

Haviland, J. (1982). "A Study of the Differences Between Prison College Graduates and the Total Released Inmate Population on Recidivism by Risk Category." (Unpublished doctoral dissertation, Western Michigan University.)

Herron, R., Muir, J., and Williams, D. (1984). *National Survey of Post-Secondary Education Programs for Incarcerated Offenders.* Hackensack, NJ: National Council on Crime and Delinquency.

Holden, A. (1982, July 9). "MEMO: Indiana State Reformatory—RE: Ball State University Program." Indianapolis: Indiana Department of Correction.

Holloway, J. and Moke, P. (1986). "Post-Secondary Correctional Education: An Evaluation of Parole Performance." Wilmington, OH: Wilmington College.

Homant, R. (1984). "On the Role of Values in Correctional Education." *Journal of Correctional Education,* 35(1):8–12.

Humphreys, T. (1972, April 24). "Inside Prison and on Study Release Plans, More Convicts Are Given College Training." *The Chronicle of Higher Education:*3.

Hutchinson, K. (1993, November 15). "Dear Colleagues: (CORRESPONDENCE)." Washington, D.C.: U.S. Senate.

Innes, C. (1988) "Profile of Inmates, 1986, Special Report." Washington, D.C.: Bureau of Justice Statistics, U.S. Department of Justice, NCJ-109926.

"Judge Says Indiana Can't Deny College Aid Inmate Students." *Indianapolis Star.* (1987, April 18).

Kandal, T. (1981). "Behind Closed Doors: Teaching Sociology in Prison." *Social Policy,* 11:53.

Kiser, G. (1987a). "Disciplinary Problems Among Inmate College Students." *Federal Probation,* 51(2):42–48.

Kiser, G. (1987b). "Teaching College Courses to Inmates." *Journal of Correctional Education,* 38(3):102–107.

Kitchener, H., Schmidt, A., and Glaser, D. (1977). "How Persistent Is Post-Prison Success?" *Federal Probation,* 41(1):9–15.

Kohlberg, L. (1970). "The Just Community Approach to Corrections: A Theory." *Journal of Moral Education,* 4(3).

Krauss, C. (1992, February 21). "Senate Votes to Expand Aid to College Students." *The New York Times:*6.

Kruttschnitt, C. (1983). "Race Relations and the Female Inmate." *Crime and Delinquency,* 29:578–592.

Lawyer, H. and Dertinger, T. (1993). "Back to School or Back to Jail?" *Criminal Justice,* 8:16–21, 51, 52.

Lewis, M. (1973). "Prison Education and Rehabilitation: Illusion or Reality?" College Station, PA: Institute for Research on Human Resources, Pennsylvania State University.

Lillis, J. (1993). "DOC Budget Nearly $22 Billion." *Corrections Compendium,* 18(9):7, 10.

Linden, R. and Perry, L. (1982). "The Effectiveness of Prison Education Programs." *Journal of Offender Counseling, Services and Rehabilitation,* 6:43–57.

Littlefield, J. and Wolford, B. (1982). "A Survey of Higher Education in U.S. Correctional Institutions." *Journal of Correctional Education,* 33(1):14–18.

Lockard, R. (1974). "Outside Evaluation of the Educational Media Technology Technician Program." Burlington County College, NJ:1–21.

Luttrell, M. (1991). "The Impact of Sentencing Reform on Prison Management." *Federal Probation,* 55(4):54–57.

Mallar, C. and Thornton, C. (1978). "Transitional Aid for Released Prisoners: Evidence from the Life Experiment." *The Journal of Human Resources,* 13(2):208–236.

Maltz, M. (1984). *Recidivism.* Orlando, FL: Academic Press.

Marsh, J. (1973, March). "Higher Education in American Prisons." *Crime and Delinquency Literature:* 139–144.

Martinson, R. (1974). "New Findings, New Views: A Note of Caution Regarding Sentencing Reform." *Hofstra Law Review,* 7:243–58.

Mauer, M. (1991). "Sentencing Project Receives National Attention." *The Sentencing Project,* (Summer):2.

McCollum, S. (1994). "Prison College Programs." *The Prison Journal,* 73(1):51–61.

McKelvey, B. (1936). *American Prison.* Chicago: University of Chicago Press.

McWilliams, J. (1971). "Rehabilitation versus Recidivism." *Junior College Journal,* 41:88–89.

Nelson, T. (1975). "Prisons and Colleges." *Adult Leadership,* 23(12):372–373, 383.

New Encyclopaedia Britannica. (1983). 15th ed., Vol. 5. Chicago: Helen Hemingway Benton: 268.

Niederpruem, K. (1987, January 31). "Senate Passes Bill Denying Jailed Felons State Education Funds." *Indianapolis Star.*

O'Hayre, B. and Coffey, C. (1982). *The Current Utilization of Pell Grants by Men and Women Incarcerated in State Correctional Facilities.* Washington, D.C.: U.S. Department of Education.

Orsagh, T. and Marsden, M. (1985). "What Works When: Rational-Choice Theory and Offender Rehabilitation." *Journal of Criminal Justice,* 13:269–277.

Palmer, T. (1975). "Martinson Revisited." *Journal of Research in Crime and Delinquency,* 12:180–191.

Palmer, T. (1983). "The Effectiveness Issue Today: An Overview." *Federal Probation,* 47:3–10.

Palmer, T. (1984). "Treatment and the Role of Classification: A Review of Basics." *Crime and Delinquency,* 30:245–267.

Parrillo, U. (1985). *Strangers to These Shores* (2d ed.). New York: John Wiley and Sons.

Pass, M. (1988). "Race Relations and the Implications of Education Within Prison." *Journal of Offender Counseling, Services and Rehabilitation,* 13:145–151.

Peak, K. (1983). "Directors of Correctional Education Programs: A Demographic and Attitudinal Profile." *Journal of Correctional Education,* 34:79–83.

Pendleton, E. (1988). "Student-Centered Instruction: A Prison Model for Building Self-Esteem." *Journal of Correctional Education,* 39(3):82–84.

Petersilia, J. and Honig, P. (1980). *The Prison Experience of Career Criminals.* Santa Monica, CA: Rand Corporation.

The President's Commission on Law Enforcement and Administration of Justice. (1967). *Task Force Report: Corrections.* Washington, D.C.: Author.

Psychology Today. (1983, April). "Learning Maketh the Honest Man":77.

Quay, H. (1973, May 24). "What Corrections Can Correct and How." *Federal Tribune-Star.*

Quinney, D. (1979). *Criminology* (2d ed.). Boston: Little, Brown and Co.

Reagen, M. and Stoughton, D. (1976). *School Behind Bars: A Descriptive Overview of Correctional Education in the American Prison System.* Metuchen, NJ: The Scarecrow Press.

Reasons, C. (1974). "Racism, Prison and Prisoners' Rights." *Issues in Criminology,* 9:3–20.

Roberts, A. (1972). *Sourcebook on Prison Education.* Springfield, IL: Charles C Thomas.

Roberts, J. (1992, April). "American Attitudes About Punishment: Myth and Reality." *Overcrowded Times:*1, 8–10, 13.

Robison, T. and Smith, G. (1971). "The Effectiveness of Correctional Programs." *Crime and Delinquency,* 17(1):67–80.

Ross, D. (1989). "Educational Requirements for Correctional Officers: Standards for Entry Level and Promotion." In *Yearbook of Correctional Education.* Burnaby, BC: Institute for the Humanities, Simon Fraser University:263–277.

Ross, R. and McKay, H. (1978). "Behavioral Approaches to Treatment in Corrections: Requiem for a Panacea." *Canadian Journal of Criminology,* 20(2):279–95.

Ross, R. and Fabiano, E. (1980). *Time to Think: Cognition and Crime Link and Remediation.* Ottawa: Ministry of the Solicitor General.

Ross, R., Fabiano, E., and Ewles, C. (1988). "Reasoning and Rehabilitation." *International Journal of Offender Therapy and Comparative Criminology,* 32:29–35.

Rotman, E. (1986). "Do Criminal Offenders Have a Constitutional Right to Rehabilitation?" *International Journal of Offender Therapy and Comparative Criminology,* 32:29–35.

Roundtree, G., Edwards, D., and Dawson, S. (1982). "The Effects of Education on Self-Esteem of Male Prison Inmates." *Journal of Correctional Education,* 32(4):12–17.

Ryan, T. and Woodard, J. (1987). *Correctional Education: A State of the Art Analysis.* Washington, D.C.: National Institute of Corrections.

Sagan, C. and Drayan, A. (1991, September 8). "Real Patriots Question." *Parade Magazine.*

Samenow, S. (1986). "Making Moral Education in Prison Living Reality." *Journal of Correctional Education,* 37(2):44–46.

Sarri, R. (1983). "Educational Programs in State Departments of Corrections: A Survey of the States." (Paper presented at the annual meetings of the American Society of Criminology, Phoenix, AZ.)

Scharf, P. and Hickey, J. (1976). "The Prison and Inmates Conception of Legal Justice: An Experiment in Democratic Education." *Criminal Justice and Behavior,* 3(2):107–122.

Seashore, M., Haberfield, S., Irwin, J., and Baker, K. (1976). *Prison Education Project NewGate and Other College Programs.* New York: Praeger.

Sechrest, L., White, S., and Brown, E. (1979). "Report on the Panel." In *The Rehabilitation of Criminal Offenders: Problems and Prospects.* Washington, D.C.: Academy of Sciences.

"60 Minutes." (1991, May 5). "Prison U."

Stephan, J. (1992). *Census of State and Federal Correctional Facilities, 1990.* Washington, D.C.: Bureau of Justice Statistics.

Sullivan, C. (1991). "Dear Board Members (CORRESPONDENCE)." Citizens United for the Rehabilitation of Errants, Washington, D.C.

Taylor, J. (1989). "The Economics of Educational Rehabilitation." *Journal of Prisoners on Prison,* (Fall):57–63.

Taylor, J. (1992a). "Post-Secondary Correctional Education: An Evaluation of Effectiveness and Efficiency." *Journal of Correctional Education,* 43(3):132–141.

Taylor, J. (1992b, June). "Where's a Reporter When You Need One?" *Indiana Defender:* 16.

Taylor, J. (1993a). "Quierer Es Poder: A Call for Criminal Justice Educators to Teach in the Penal Setting." *The Criminologist,* 18(4):1, 6–8.

Taylor, J. (1993b). "College Student/Worker Survey: Indiana State Reformatory." (Unpublished manuscript.)

Taylor, J. (1994). "Should Prisoners Have Access to Collegiate Educations: Questions & Answers." *Educational Policy.*

Taylor, J. and Tewksbury, R. (1993). "From the Inside Out and Outside In: Team Research in the Correctional Setting." (Paper presented at the annual meetings of the Southern Criminal Justice Association, Charleston, SC.)

Texas Department of Criminal Justice. (1989). *Overview.* Austin: Author.

Thomas, F. (1974). "Narrative Evaluation Report on the Institute for Educational Media Technology." Burlington County College, NJ.

Thomas, J. (1983). "Teaching Sociology in Unconventional Settings: The Irony of Maximum Security Prisons." *Teaching Sociology,* 10:231–250.

Thompson, J. (1976). "Report on Follow-up Evaluation Survey of Former Inmate Students of Alexander City State Junior College." Alexander City, AL: Alexander City State Junior College.

Thorpe, T., MacDonald, D., and Bala, G. (1984). "Follow-Up Study of Offenders Who Earn College Degrees While Incarcerated in New York State." *Journal of Correctional Education,* 35(2):86–88.

Ticer, S. (1989, May). "The Search for Ways to Break Out of the Prison Crisis." *Business Week*:80–81.

Toch, H. (1987). "Regenerating Prisoners through Education." *Federal Probation,* 51(3):61–66.

U.S. Department of Justice. (1992a). "Bureau of Justice Statistics: National Update," 1(3).

U.S. Department of Justice. (1992b). *Correctional Populations in the United States, 1990.* Washington, D.C.: Bureau of Justice Statistics.

U.S. Department of Labor. (1977). *Unlocking the Second Gate: The Role of Financial Assistance in Reducing Recidivism among Ex-Prisoners.* Washington, D.C.: Employment and Training Administration.

Volpe, R., Waksman, M., and Kearney, C. (1985). "Cognitive Education in Four Canadian Prisons." *Journal of Correctional Education,* 36(2):66–74.

Wallerstedt, J. (1984). *Returning to Prison.* Washington, D.C.: Bureau of Justice Statistics.

The Washington Spectator. (1992). "FYI Items of Interest from Spectator Files." *The Washington Spectator,* 18(2):4.

Wolford, B. and Littlefield, J. (1985). "Correctional Post-Secondary Education: The Expanding Role of Community Colleges." *Community / Junior College Quarterly,* 9:257–272.

Wootan, B. (1959). *Social Science and Social Pathology.* London: George Allen & Unwin.

Worden, B. (1991, July 14). "Inmates Get Student Aid for College Classes." *Raleigh News & Observer.*

Wreford, P. (1990). "Community College Prison Program Graduation and Recidivism." (Unpublished doctoral dissertation, University of Michigan.)

Yarborough, T. (1989). "An Analysis of Why Inmates Drop Out of Higher Education Programs." *Journal of Correctional Education,* 40:130–135.

Zedlewski, E. (1987). *Making Confinement Decisions.* Washington, D.C.: U.S. Department of Education.

Zyble, J. (1990, November–December). "Financial Aid Not Meeting College Costs." *National College Newspaper.*

NINE

Treatment Needs of Women in Prison

BARBARA H. ZAITZOW
Appalachian State University

INTRODUCTION

Ideally, jailing or imprisoning women is meant to exact retribution for their crimes and rehabilitation of their character; the majority of these women eventually return to society. In practice, however, the problems prevalent in most women's correctional facilities negate any real effectiveness in their stated goals. On the contrary, the one thing incarcerated women can look forward to once the door closes behind them is being transformed from offenders into victims. This chapter focuses on the paradox of incarcerated women as criminals and victims. Issues related to the programmatic needs and availability of treatment programs for women offenders are discussed. Recommendations for change are put forth in which treatment is advocated as a viable option for offenders who are interested in positive change in their lives.

Sykes (1958) described the pains of imprisonment for men as the deprivation of liberty, the deprivation of goods and services, the deprivation of heterosexual relationships, the deprivation of autonomy, and the deprivation of security. All these deprivations apply equally to female prisoners, and some may be more severe for women (Carlen, 1994). An obvious example is separation from one's family. Women may also suffer from receiving fewer leisure, work, and educational opportunities and closer surveillance than men.

Women's prisons increase women's dependency, stress women's domestic rather than employment role, aggravate women's emotional and physical isolation, jeopardize family and other relationships, engender a sense of injustice (because women are denied many of the opportunities available to male prisoners), and may indirectly intensify the pains of imprisonment. The irony of this situation is that the majority of women currently housed in institutions throughout the United States will be released from confinement and expected to fit in to mainstream society. Without providing these women the necessary social skills with which they may become viable contributors to society, their chances for successful assimilation as well as day-to-day survival will be impeded. Thus, a reevaluation of the purpose(s) of imprisonment as well as consideration of the unique needs of women offenders is long overdue.

HISTORICAL OVERVIEW OF THE TREATMENT OF WOMEN IN PRISON

The history of penology in this country presents a dismal picture of the treatment of all criminal offenders. Until penal reforms were instituted in the mid-nineteenth century, men, women, children, mentally ill persons, and every form of degenerate were frequently locked up together. No consideration was given to age, type of offense, or circumstance (Pollock-Byrne, 1990). Since women's crimes were predominantly restricted to sex offenses and drunkenness, a criminal woman was considered disgraced, dishonored, and pathetic (Giallombardo, 1966:7). Women involved in criminal offenses were not considered dangerous, and often their male partners took the total blame, thus precluding their imprisonment (Chandler, 1973:3). Prisons were seen as places to exact retribution or restitution for misdeeds. The concept of rehabilitation—making positive changes in offenders in order to restore them to society as useful members—was late in coming.

This notion of rehabilitation has undoubtedly been the single most damaging influence on female corrections, largely because the idea of "treatment" for women entailed the fostering of sexual morality, the imposition of sobriety, the instilling of obedience, and the prescribing of the sex-role stereotype of mother and homemaker, rather than addressing treatment needs (Chandler, 1973:7; Freedman, 1981).

Social-Sexual Environment

The reformists demonstrated their philosophy in the architecture of prisons for women. Instead of the massive fortress-like penitentiary housing used for men that had high concrete walls, armed personnel, and gun towers, the "domestic model" for women provided each woman her own room in "the home":

> "The home" planned for women was a cottage that was built to house twenty to thirty women, who could cook their own food in a "cottage kitchen." Several similar cottages would be arranged in quadrangles on green, tree-filled lawns. The cottages in most states were built to contain a living room, dining room and one or two small reading rooms. The idea was that a domestic atmosphere would help the women learn the essential skills of running a home and family. (Burkhart, 1973:367)

This was the first "cottage" penal facility for women. Since that time three additional types of women's prisons have developed. The "campus" plan is designed to resemble a college campus. Grass and trees surround numerous buildings, each with separate functions and separated by grassy court areas. In the "complex" model, several buildings that may contain one or more functions such as living areas, dining halls, vocational training facilities, or classrooms cluster around the central administration building. The "single-building" style consists of one major facility that houses all of the prison functions (Glick and Neto, 1977:20).

DECEPTION IN PRISON APPEARANCE

On the surface, most women's prisons are more attractive than men's. Some have been converted from country mansions or children's homes, and the obvious aspects of security (such as gun towers) are often lacking. Indeed, prison departments have recognized that for women, security considerations do not loom so large because there is less public anxiety and fear when women escape from custody. Most women's institutions retain the traditional categories of minimum, medium, and maximum security differentiated by the degree of surveillance, the number of security-check body counts, the frequency of room searches or "shake downs," freedom of movement, and architectural design. The most desirable type of incarceration, minimum security, allows freedom for a number of activities within the prison schedule and rules. However, most women's prisons are medium security, which are more restrictive than minimum security institutions but permit more freedom than close custody or maximum security facilities (Stephan, 1992). Close custody means that inmates must be escorted at all times by a custody officer for daytime activities such as meals, group sessions, and counseling, and they are barred from participation in night activities. The small proportion of dangerous women, estimated at 5 percent to 8 percent, is found in strict custody under the highly controlled environment known as maximum security. In addition to the more danger-ous inmates, women under death sentences are also confined to maximum security. Temporary maximum security may be imposed on women who are dangerous to themselves or others because of emotional disturbance. This status is also used to punish rule breaking.

Although women can wear their own clothes and decorate their rooms, facades are deceptive. In many ways female prisoners are worse off than their male counterparts. As the inmates point out, there is only the appearance of a campus. Repression is every bit as strong as in men's pris-ons; it is simply more subtle. In fact, inmates have referred to the social control in women's prisons as "pastel fascism," control glossed over and concealed by a superficial facade of false benevolence and concern for the lives of inmates. What few possessions they have are often confiscated or destroyed, and they are subject to arbitrary body searches at any time (Velimesis, 1972; personal communications with women inmates housed in a maximum security prison in the southeast, 1994 and 1995). When women in prison fail to conform to expectations, physical control is quickly instituted. For example, on Christmas day, 1975, all 700 women inside the California Institute for Women were locked in their cottages and not al-lowed on the grounds. The majority were denied holiday visits from family and friends. All tours of the institution were also canceled. A rebellion had occurred a week earlier in response to the cancelation of prison holiday plans and a special Woman's Day. So-called instigators of the rebellion were put in solitary confinement ("An Inside View," 1976:2).

In recent years, women inmates have begun to use litigation to rem-edy the institutional abuses that they have been subjected to. For example, indictments were filed against ten male and four female employees at the Georgia Women's Prison in 1992 after ninety inmates alleged that they had been victims of a variety of forms of sexual abuse (including rape, ex-change of sex for favors and/or retaliation for refusal to participate, coerced into prostitution as well as forced to have abortions when sexual activity between officers and women inmates resulted in pregnancy). The Georgia case is not uncommon, and serious cases have been brought to the atten-tion of the media and the courts in a number of states (Wilson, 1992).

ENTRY INTO PRISON

The objectives of the correctional system and the crimes of female offend-ers notwithstanding, once women enter institutions they often go from be-ing victims of justice to victims of injustice. Cruel and unusual punishment is not supposed to exist today; however, one would never know it by ob-serving life in a women's penal facility.

After arriving at her assigned correctional home, the new female pris-oner must go through a series of orientation or "get-acquainted" procedures. She may come in handcuffed and be refingerprinted and photographed for institutional records. She soon loses all remaining dignity when she is stripped and searched for contraband, showered, and issued prison attire and bedding. Over the next two to six weeks the incarcerated woman, who is segregated during this period, goes through medical and psychiatric examinations for everything from venereal disease to mental illness.

By the time she joins the general prison population, she has been instilled with the extensive rules and regulations of her confinement, including her new status of "institutional dependency." Although women's prisons are usually not the maximum security fortresses that men's prisons are, some suggest that the rules women must abide by are stricter (Carlen, 1994). These rules and regulations, as well as disciplinary actions for infractions, vary from one institution to another.

Many female inmates view the rules and regulations of prisons as willful efforts to "diminish their maturity" by "treating them like children and fostering dependency" (Mann, 1984:210). An example of such a rule is found at the Pennsylvania State Correctional Institution for Women, where inmates are required to "recite the Lord's Prayer in unison at bedtime" (Deming, 1977:159). The reality of women's prisons is that they create just as much frustration and pain as men's prisons (Giallombardo, 1966:Ch. 7; Freedman, 1981; Rafter, 1990).

THE PERPETUATION OF DEPENDENCY AMONG WOMEN INMATES

Much of the treatment and control of women in prison is premised on the individualization of women's problems. The women are typically characterized as having in some way "failed" to meet their adult responsibilities. While the prison administrators and staff recognize that many of the problems experienced by the women are endemic to their social situation outside prison, they argue, perhaps quite reasonably, that there is little they can do about the wider social problems of poverty, inadequate housing, and unemployment. On the other hand, many stress that a number of the problems presented by the women reflect personal limitations that could be effected by staff intervention, either by means of education and training or by personal interaction and informal counseling. Here, a shared objective of staff is to encourage a degree of self-confidence among the women and to help them cope with the difficult decisions they face in their outside lives.

There is, however, an inevitable contradiction here, in that the ordered regimes governing prison life inevitably deny women choice over even the most trivial aspects of day-to-day living. They are told what time they will get out of bed; what time they will take their meals; when they will read, write letters, or watch television; and at what time they will again be in bed with their lights out. Indeed, there are few areas of prison life in which the women are encouraged, or indeed able, to take responsibility for making decisions (Clark, 1995:312). Regardless of their age, women prisoners have the status of schoolgirls. This is powerfully brought home by the practice in some establishments of calling all women "girls," irrespective of their age, and of addressing female staff members as "miss." Many inmates are not allowed to see their children or families and, in fact, often lose custody of their children. At some places, children under eighteen are not allowed to visit at all. Furthermore, just as in male prisons, the arbitrary and capricious nature of parole boards wears down inmates' ability to be self-reliant and to plan a constructive program for themselves that would lead to their release.

Historically, the dominant model of training was domestic: the socialization of women to their traditionally accepted roles. The emphasis, therefore, was on gardening and housework, and instruction was provided in needlework, cookery, child care, and dressmaking. Rafter (1985:174) makes an interesting point in this context. She refers to the work of such writers as Foucault (1977), who argue that imprisonment was economically useful to capitalism. But whereas imprisoned men did provide a source of cheap labor, the institutions for women functioned to keep women *out* of the industrial labor force. When training was given to women, it paralleled as nearly as possible the work that the women would do on release—namely, domestic work. The prison commissioners, in their report for 1945, summed up this objective well: Training should be directed toward "better housewives rather than better housemaids. Every aspect of domestic work, whether in shops or in the service of prison, should be made to serve one idea—that of instilling into the women the ideas of a good home and how they may best be achieved" (Commissioners of Prisons, 1947:73). The objective was to turn female inmates into decent housewives and good mothers. This emphasis continues today (Fletcher, Shaver, and Moon, 1993).

PROGRAMS

Since there are so few women's prisons, women of all ages and all crimes are thrown together. The population is also much more heterogeneous than in men's prisons, where there is the opportunity for some degree of classification. Classification systems serve two purposes: to provide the type of security arrangements necessary to protect society, and to consider the personal characteristics of the individual insofar as these may reflect possibilities for training. But most jurisdictions have few institutions for women, and so in effect women remain unclassified. In contrast, an effort is made to separate experienced male offenders from the less dangerous.

Hence the majority of women experience the rules and restrictions necessary only for the minority (Feinman, 1994).

In women's prisons there is little provision for work or education, primarily because of the domestic ideology that permeates the regimes. In the words of Dobash, Dobash, and Gutteridge, "the emphasis which predominates implies that the failure of women prisoners is their failure as wives, mothers and housekeepers" (1986:182). In practice, work is geared to the maintenance of the institution and seems to have little positive purpose. This is not to say that work is good in men's prisons, but there are clear differences in emphasis.

Vocational Programs

Vocational education and training for women in many women's institutions or women's divisions of men's prisons are very limited (Moyer, 1992). Female inmates who already have advanced education have little use for the educational programs that may be offered, and there is no avenue for them to make use of their academic skills (for example, as teachers). Conversely, no special programs or incentives are available for female prisoners who are educationally handicapped, mentally retarded, or simply uninterested, assuming such women could be identified.

Vocational training programs that do exist usually are in such traditionally female areas as sewing, clerical skills, food services, and cosmetology. Even in the larger women's institutions, no more than two or three programs are offered, and these are virtually always geared toward preparing women in a domestic or otherwise "women's" capacity. While such training may result in the cost-efficient maintenance of the prison, it does not address or prepare women inmates' need to be self-supporting upon release (Durham, 1994).

The scarcity of vocational and rehabilitation programs for female prisoners can usually be attributed to one of the following:

- Such programs are not cost-effective as there are so few female prisoners.
- Financial expenditures are unwarranted for female inmates who pose less of a threat to society than their male counterparts.
- There is a low rate of women's participation in such programs.
- Many female correctional facilities are inaccessible.
- Women are still regarded foremost in the traditional roles of housewife and mother.

Consequently, legislators and corrections officials continue to give full priority to men's vocational programs while teaching women merely to cook, sew, and clean (Haft, 1974; Feinman, 1994). Unfortunately, this gives women, especially those serving long sentences, few or no opportunities to learn new skills or earn enough money to aid their families on the outside.

Vocational programs in correctional institutions are not impressive in overall quality. For the most part, the instructors are poorly trained, use out-of-date equipment, and teach nonmarketable skills. Several factors deter the development of more effective vocational programs: The equipment necessary for many of the programs is considered too costly in most correctional systems; the inmate's average term of two or three years is too short for the completion of apprenticeship requirements for most trades; overcrowded conditions often result in waiting lists for training programs; and the debilitating conditions of prison life discourage offenders from participating in training until it is too late for them to learn enough to make participation worthwhile (Conrad, 1983). But even with up-to-date equipment and good instructors, inmates often have difficulty in gaining admission into labor unions in the free community and in persuading private industry to hire them.

Educational Programs

Academic education is offered in most women's prisons. Remedial education is prevalent, and basic courses leading to an elementary education or a high school diploma are commonly provided. Some prisons offer college curricula leading to the associate of arts degree or, more rarely, to the bachelor of arts. Most states offer college courses to women inmates either through correspondence courses or in conjunction with nearby colleges (Pollock-Byrne, 1990).

Adult education courses that are offered include subjects such as consumer education, family life education, child development, and personal grooming. While such courses are undoubtedly useful, they also indicate sexual stereotyping. Evidence that such courses are associated with the traditional roles of housewife and mother is seen when these educational courses for women are compared with the social education programs common to men's educational curriculum. These recent trends in correctional education for men are "specifically geared to reorienting the incarcerated or community treated offender with the normative and socially acceptable attitudes and values of free society" and include major areas such as "improving communication skills, personal management, personality development, social and family relationships, laws, and economic issues" (Roberts, 1971:131). Social values are instilled with a goal of restructuring an inmate's attitudes, values, and orientations to societal institutions and undoing years of "negative acculturation."

However, no mention is made of efforts toward these ends in the studies of women's prisons. Instead, the roles of mother, homemaker, and successful shopper are perpetuated in the few adult education courses available in women's institutions.

DEFINING CORRECTIONAL TREATMENT

When correctional treatment is discussed, terms such as *humanitarian reform, corrections, rehabilitation,* and *treatment* are often used interchangeably, creating some confusion as to exactly what correctional treatment involves. Also at issue is the part played by incarceration and mandatory supervision in the correctional treatment process. However, for the sake of simplicity, correctional treatment may be defined as any planned and monitored program of activity that has the goal of rehabilitating or "habilitating" the offender so that she or he will avoid criminal activity in the future. Unfortunately, the implementation of various rehabilitative programs has typically involved only the male population; women offender's unique needs have been ignored.

REHABILITATION OF OFFENDERS

Perhaps more studies have been directed toward determining the effect of prison rehabilitation programs than any of the other justifications for imprisonment. The accumulated empirical evaluations of these programs have proved disappointing for advocates of rehabilitation. The widely circulated assessment by Martinson and his colleagues (1974) has been verified in large measure by a subsequent Panel on Research on Rehabilitation Techniques organized by the National Research Council of the National Academy of Sciences (Lipton, Martinson, and Wilkes, 1975; Sechrest, White, and Brown, 1979). The panel drew the following conclusions:

> The current state of knowledge about rehabilitation of criminal offenders is cause for grave concern, particularly in view of the obvious importance of the problem. After 40 years of research and literally hundreds of studies, almost all the conclusions that can be reached have to be formulated in terms of what we do not know. The one positive conclusion is discouraging: the research methodology that has been brought to bear on the problem of finding ways to rehabilitate criminal offenders has been generally so inadequate that only a relatively few studies warrant any unequivocal interpretations. The entire body of research appears to justify only the conclusion that we do not know of any program or method of rehabilitation that could be guaranteed to reduce the criminal activity of released offenders. Although a generous reviewer of the literature might discern some glimmers of hope, those glimmers are so few, so scattered, and so inconsistent

that they do not serve as a basis for any recommendation other than continued research.

Furthermore, a more penetrating inquiry into the nature of the problem of rehabilitation and the programs and methods that have been tried leads to the conclusion that there is even less in the research than meets the eye. The techniques that have been tested seem rarely to have been devised to be strong enough to offer realistic hope that they would rehabilitate offenders, especially imprisoned felons. In general, techniques have been tested as isolated treatments rather than as complex combinations, which would seem more suited to the task. And even when techniques have been tested in good designs, insufficient attention has been paid to maintaining their integrity, so that often the treatment to be tested was delivered in a substantially weakened form. It is also not clear that all the theoretical power and the individual imagination that could be invoked in the planning of rehabilitative efforts have ever been capitalized on. Thus, the recommendation in this report that has the strongest support is that more and better thinking and research should be invested in efforts to devise programs for offender rehabilitation. (Sechrest et al., 1979:3–4)

Faced with such discouraging assessments, many policy analysts urged abandonment of rehabilitation as an organizing objective of the prison system. In most maximum security prisons, of course, the small number of programs designed to deal with the rehabilitative needs of the inmates often served as show-piece programs that cast a rhetorical gloss of rehabilitation over a basically punitive custodial system. A national survey of correctional administrators, however, indicates that the vast majority are not prepared to give up rehabilitative programs altogether (Cullen, Latessa, Burton, and Lombardo, 1993). They appear convinced that such programs will work for subgroups of offenders with both the need and motivation to take advantage of them. Furthermore, such programs offer some relief from the personally destructive features of prison life: the debilitating idleness; loss of autonomy and ability to exercise initiative; the latent and overt threats of force and violence; and the routinization, monotony, and regimentation of activities and relationships.

The efforts to create academic and vocational training opportunities, self-help programs for drug abusers, individual and group therapy and counseling possibilities, and paid work in prison industries also serve an important symbolic function. They express confidence and hope in the ability of people to change when they become motivated to seek new directions in their lives. They embody a continuing faith that such directions are never fully determined by the past. Prison administrators now appear more inclined to make participation in such programs voluntary rather than mandatory as a condition for release on parole. It appears that in the prison world, the rehabilitative ideal is not dead so much as reduced in expectation to accord more fully with the realities and limitations of the prison experience.

We are left then with many questions about such programs: What types of programs are likely to be most successful? What types of inmates respond effectively to the different types of programs that can be made available? What types of measures best reveal the changes attributable to the programs? What effect do such changes have on recidivism rates or other indicators of postprison adjustment? What kinds of continuing support during the postrelease period are needed to sustain the changes achieved and their effect on future criminality? What types of research procedures must be instituted to determine what works and what does not?

Individual Counseling

There have been two studies of the effects of individual psychotherapy on young incarcerated female offenders, and both of them (Adams, 1959; Adams, 1961) report no significant effects from the therapy. But one of the Adams studies (1959) does contain a suggestive, although not clearly interpretable, finding: If this individual therapy was administered by a psychiatrist or a psychologist, the resulting parole suspension rate was almost two-and-a-half times *higher* than if it was administered by a social worker without this specialized training. Thus, social workers were significant contributors to the administration of individual psychotherapy.

Group Counseling

Group counseling has indeed been attempted in correctional institutions, both with and without a specifically psychotherapeutic orientation. Most research on the use of psychotherapy within a correctional setting has been conducted with male samples. The few and dated studies with females, however, are worth noting.

Adams's (1959) research on individualized treatment for women inmates found that there was nothing gained from treating females by group rather than individual methods. A study by Taylor of borstal (reformatory) inmates in New Zealand (1967) found a similar lack of any great improvement for group therapy as opposed to individual therapy or even to no therapy at all. But the Taylor study does offer one positive finding: When the "group therapy" participants *did* commit new offenses, these offenses were less serious than the ones for which they had originally been incarcerated.

There is a third study that does report an overall positive finding as opposed to a partial one. Truax, Wargo, and Silber (1966) found that females subjected to group psychotherapy and then released were likely to spend less time reincarcerated in the future. But what is most interesting about this improvement is the very special and important circumstance under which it occurred. The therapists chosen for this program did not merely have to have the proper analytic training; they were specially chosen for their "empathy" and "nonpossessive warmth." In other words, it may well have been the therapists' special personal gifts rather than the fact of treatment itself that produced the favorable result.

Common Elements of Effective Programs

The most effective treatment programs appear to have a number of common elements. First, many of these programs are set up by inspired and dedicated leaders. Second, the programs commonly transmit a philosophy of life that generates a sense of mission or purpose among offenders. Third, they usually have a unified treatment team. Fourth, they generally entrust offenders with some decision-making responsibilities. Fifth, they usually help offenders develop skills that make them believe they can do something or that they have mastered some important insights about themselves or life. Sixth, the most effective programs are often unique. Seventh, successful community-based institutional programs avoid alienating formal decision makers. Resistance to administrators is usually costly to institutional programs, and good public relations is a critical factor in the survival and development of community-based programs. Finally, effective programs have adequate community support networks.

Sometimes the basic element in an effective program is thought to be the charismatic and inspired leader who can persuade others to accept whatever he or she has to offer, regardless of the program structure. This viewpoint reflects a psychological reductionism that claims that effective programs are established and sustained only through the initiative and commitment of such inspired persons. Effective programs, however, depend on a variety of interrelated factors in addition to effective leaders, such as receptive clients, adequate funding, compliant organizational-environmental structures, and acceptance within the larger political and correctional community.

The task of correctional research today is to determine the effect of the interrelationship between leadership and program structure in various types of settings, to ascertain whether different styles of leadership are needed to implement and conduct effective programs in community-based and institutional settings, to identify the components that are intrinsic to effective programs, and to weigh the effect of the interrelationships among the common elements of effective programs.

Recommendations for Correctional Treatment

To expand the role of, and to improve the services of, correctional treatment in the future, several recommendations are in order:

1. Involvement in treatment should be entirely voluntary. Participation, or the lack of participation, in these programs should not be related to

the length of institutional stay or to the length of supervision in community programs.

2. Adult inmates should have the opportunity to become involved in meaningful and adequately paid work during incarceration.

3. Both juvenile and adult inmates should have the opportunity for some degree of self-governance during confinement.

4. Safe environments must be provided for institutionalized offenders. Only when inmates feel safe can they be concerned about much more than personal survival.

5. A variety of programs should be offered in correctional institutions. These interventions should be grounded on good program design, implemented with program integrity, and evaluated on an ongoing basis with sophisticated research methods.

6. More care must be taken to ensure that common elements of effective programs thrive in correctional environments.

7. A progressive array of services must be established for offenders in the community. Such a network of support services, as therapeutic communities have demonstrated, is imperative to improve the positive impact of correctional treatment.

8. Career and economic incentives must be made available for persons who have the motivation and skills to become effective treatment agents so that they will be persuaded to seek out such employment and to stay involved in correctional service.

9. Only through well-planned and soundly executed research can further development of treatment concepts and practices take place; therefore, research on correctional treatment must be given a much higher priority than it is presently accorded.

The future of correctional treatment ultimately depends on three factors: funding research, so that more effective technologies can be developed for the treatment process; the identification of what works for which group of offenders, so that offenders interested in treatment can be given the interventions most compatible with their needs and interests; and the creation of more humane correctional contexts, so that the environment will not interfere with the treatment process.

The United States is not a pacesetter for corrections and has not been for a long time; contentment with warehousing offenders will put our nation back in the Dark Ages of corrections. Considerable fanfare went into the burial of treatment in the mid-1970s, although treatment programs continue to exist in community and institutional settings. We need to put the same burst of energy into reemphasizing treatment, not as a panacea or as a condition of release, but as a viable option for those who are interested in change, growth, and positive movement in their lives. Anything less will be cruel and unusual punishment.

TOWARD CHANGE

Changes in women's prisons are more apparent in the United States than in other countries. In 1964, the Supreme Court ruled that state prisoners could sue state officials in federal courts for the denial of their constitutional rights. Since then, the courts have upheld prisoners' rights in such areas as the need to maintain a law library, limits on censorship of mail, and procedural fairness in prison discipline. Most of the litigation has been based on two constitutional amendments: the Fourteenth, which guarantees equal protection of the law, and the Eighth, which prohibits cruel and unusual punishment. For example, the court held that prisoners in a women's jail in San Francisco must be allowed to participate in a work furlough program from which they had been excluded. Other cases have given reasonable parity with male prisoners in vocational training, apprenticeship programs, medical care, educational programs, work-release opportunities, and access to legal materials. A class action suit by women in a New York county jail resulted in a judgment that it was unconstitutional for the conditions of imprisonment for women to be inferior to those of male prisoners.

It is questionable, however, that achieving parity with men's prisons is the best solution. These institutions are themselves in considerable need of reform. Nor would complete equality be entirely beneficial for women. To attempt to eradicate gender differences within prisons while they persist in the outside world makes little sense. For example, the fact that women continue to be responsible for child care means that prison programs should be designed to take this into account (see Baunach, 1985, for examples of programs that are geared toward female prisoners increasing contact with their children).

An alternative approach in the United States was the establishment of co-correctional institutions. In the mid-1970s, there were over twenty co-correctional state and federal institutions, but, since then, more than half have reverted to one-sex institutions. Co-correctional institutions have a variety of objectives: to reduce the dehumanizing and destructive aspects of confinement, to reduce institutional control problems (that is, to reduce assaultive homosexuality and violent behavior), to provide a more normal atmosphere, to aid the prisoner's adjustment on release, to obtain economies in staffing and in the provision of training programs for both male and female prisoners, and to expand the career opportunities for female correctional officers. Although coed prisons increase social opportunities for male prisoners, they have yet to generate similar advantages for female inmates because they offer no additional program resources or operational adaptations (Smykla and Williams, 1995).

Co-correctional institutions are not without their critics. Crawford (1980), for example, draws attention to the fact that they still have a disproportionately male population. This has two consequences: It destroys any separate programming for women and forces them into programs designed to meet the needs of male prisoners, and the atmosphere in co-correctional prisons continues the exploitation by men that many of the women in institutions previously experienced in the outside world. According to Crawford, the real reasons behind the move to co-corrections are money, overcrowding, and the need to smooth out the operation of *men's* institutions. They do not meet the unique and special needs of female offenders. Instead, she proposes mother-child institutions. Another critic (Schweber, 1984) makes much the same point. She believes that men continue to dominate higher status positions and occupational courses in the institutions and proposes instead what she calls the "co-ordinate" prison. This means that the women's prison is separate but shares programs and services with a nearby male facility.

Heidensohn (1985) has argued that the prison system was designed to deal with men, but discussions of, for example, the merits of the "classic" silent versus the separate system were not geared toward one particular sex. Rather, their adoption resulted from beliefs about the best way to mold the *human* spirit. Also the domestic and psychiatric ideologies that have permeated the regimes of women's prisons indicate that special account was taken of female prisoners. The real difficulty is that stereotypical assumptions have been made about the characteristics of female prisoners and hence about their "needs." We clearly need to know much more about who these women are. Only then can we design a coherent policy for dealing with them.

No one can argue with the necessity of prisons and jails for people who commit crimes, even women. However, although incarceration is not a picnic for anyone (nor, some argue, should it be), clearly on a collective basis female inmates are a great deal worse off than male inmates. For one thing, it is arguable that many of these women should be in prison at all. Often their biggest crime seems to be trying to feed their families or having the misfortune to be pregnant or nonwhite. Outdated rules and regulations, poor diet, neglectful health care, degradation, lack of vocational training and recreational facilities, exploitation, abuse, and unsanitary conditions typify the conditions in many prisons and jails that house women. Reform is needed both within the correctional system and in a society that condones inhumane treatment of women prisoners.

REFERENCES

Adams, S. (1959, March 6). "Effectiveness of the Youth Authority Special Treatment Program: First Interim Report." *Research Report No. 5.* California Youth Authority.

Adams, S. (1961, January 31). "Assessment of the Psychiatric Treatment Program, Phase I: Third Interim Report." *Research Report No. 21.* California Youth Authority.

Baunach, P. (1985). *Mothers in Prison.* New Brunswick, NJ: Transaction Books.

Burkhart, K. (1973). *Women in Prison.* Garden City, NY: Doubleday.

Carlen, P. (1994). "Why Study Women's Imprisonment? Or Anyone Else's?" *British Journal of Criminology,* 34:131–139.

Chandler, E.W. (1973). *Women in Prison.* Indianapolis: Bobbs Merrill.

Clark, J. (1995). "The Impact of the Prison Environment on Mothers." *Prison Journal,* 75:306–329.

Commissioners of Prisons. (1947). *Report for the Year 1945.* London: HMSO.

Conrad, J. (1983). "Correctional Treatment." *Encyclopedia of Crime and Justice.* New York: Macmillan.

Crawford, J. (1980). "Two Losers Don't Make a Winner: The Case Against the Co-Correctional Institution." In J. Smykla (ed.), *Co-ed Prison.* New York: Human Sciences Press.

Cullen, F.T., Latessa, E.J., Burton, V.S., and Lombardo, L.X. (1993). "The Correctional Orientation of Prison Wardens: Is the Rehabilitative Ideal Supported?" *Criminology,* 31:85.

Deming, R. (1977). *Women: The New Criminals.* Nashville, TN: Thomas Nelson.

Dobash, R., Dobash, R., and Gutteridge S. (1986). *The Imprisonment of Women.* Oxford: Basil Blackwell.

Durham, A.M. (1994). *Crisis and Reform: Current Issues in American Punishment.* Boston: Little, Brown and Co.

Feinman, C. (1994). *Women in the Criminal Justice System.* Westport, CT: Praeger Publishers.

Fletcher, B.R., Shaver, L.D., and Moon, D.G. (1993). *Women Prisoners: A Forgotten Population.* Westport, CT: Praeger Publishers.

Foucault, M. (1977). *Discipline and Punish: The Birth of the Prison.* London: Penguin Press.

Freedman, E. (1981). *Their Sister's Keepers: Women's Prison Reform in America, 1830–1930.* Ann Arbor: University of Michigan Press.

Giallombardo, R. (1966). *Society of Women: A Study of a Women's Prison.* New York: Wiley.

Glick, R. and Neto, V. (1977). *National Study of Women's Correctional Programs.* Washington, D.C.: U.S. Government Printing Office.

Haft, M. (1974). "Women in Prison: Discriminatory Practices and Some Legal Solutions." *Clearinghouse Review,* 8:1–3.

Heidensohn, F. (1985). *Women and Crime: The Life of the Female Offender.* New York: New York University Press.

"An Inside View of CIW." (1976, February). *Sister Newspaper.* Venice, CA: The Women's Center.

Leonard, E. (1983). "Judicial Decisions and Prison Reform: The Impact of Litigation on Women Prisoners." *Social Problems,* 31:1, 45.

Lipton, D., Martinson, R.M., and Wilkes, J. (1975). *The Effectiveness of Correctional Treatment: A Survey of Treatment Evaluation Studies.* New York: Praeger.

Mann, C.R. (1984). *Female Crime and Delinquency.* University, AL: University of Alabama Press.

Martinson, R. (1974). "What Works: Questions and Answers About Prison Reform." *Public Interest,* 35:22–54.

Moyer, I.L. (1992). *The Changing Roles of Women in the Criminal Justice System* (2d. ed.). Prospect Heights, IL: Waveland Press.

Pollock-Byrne, J.M. (1990). *Women, Prison, and Crime.* Belmont, CA: Wadsworth.

Rafter, N. (1985). *Partial Justice: Women in State Prisons 1800–1935.* Boston: Northeastern University Press.

Rafter, N. (1990). *Partial Justice: Women, Prisons and Social Control* (2d. ed.). New Brunswick, NJ: Transaction.

Roberts, A.S. (1971). *Sourcebook on Prison Education.* Springfield, IL: Charles C. Thomas.

Schweber, C. (1984). "Beauty Marks and Blemishes: The Co-Ed Prison as a Microcosm of Integrated Society." *The Prison Journal,* 46:1, 3.

Sechrest, L., White, S., and Brown E. (1979). *The Rehabilitation of Criminal Offenders: Problems and Prospects.* Washington, D.C.: The National Academy of Sciences.

Smykla, J., and Williams, J. (1995). "Co-Corrections in the United States of America, 1970–1990." In J. Smykla and J. Williams (eds.), *Women and Criminal Justice.*

Stephan, J. (1992). "Census of State and Federal Correctional Facilities, 1990." Washington, D.C.: Bureau of Justice Statistics:8.

Sykes, G. (1958). *The Society of Captives.* Princeton, NJ: Princeton University Press.

Taylor, A.J.W. (1967). "An Evaluation of Group Psychotherapy in a Girls' Borstal." *International Journal of Group Psychotherapy,* 2:168–177.

Truax, C.B., Wargo, D.G., and Silber, L.D. (1966). "Effects of Group Psychotherapy with High Adequate Empathy and Nonpossessive Warmth upon Female Institutionalized Delinquents." *Journal of Abnormal Psychology,* 4:267–274.

Velimesis, M. (1972). *Women in County Jails and Prisons.* Philadelphia: Pennsylvania Program for Women and Girl Offenders.

Wilson, T. (1992, November 16). "Ga. Indictments Charge Abuse of Female Inmates." *USA Today:*3A.

TEN

Health Care for Women Offenders

Challenge for the New Century

PHYLLIS HARRISON ROSS, M.D.
New York Medical College at Metropolitan Hospital

JAMES E. LAWRENCE
New York State Commission of Correction

INTRODUCTION

Based on the unprecedented increase in the number of incarcerated women, particularly poor and minority women, in the last fifteen years, this chapter addresses the specific health care needs of women in U.S. prisons. Prisons have been notorious for their neglect of women and their treatment needs, and the influx of women who have abused drugs has created critical care needs for HIV/AIDS, tuberculosis, and related respiratory and reproductive tract diseases. A model of improved care to address this new prison crisis is presented.

The population of incarcerated women underwent profound change in the 1980s, as did the impact of women offenders on jail and prison systems. Some of this is related to the fact that U.S. jail and prison populations became the world's largest during the past decade (Butterfield, 1992). However, the real change in focus on women is associated with the impact on correctional systems of increasing and intensified demand for specialized health care services hitherto not delivered on a large scale in prisons and jails. The combined effect of high rates of incarceration employed as the social sanction of choice and the increased involvement of poor and minority women in behaviors regarded as criminal has been to concentrate unprecedented numbers of women with serious medical problems in state and local correctional institutions. The forces driving this change are unlikely to abate as the new century approaches.

The largest U.S. prison and jail systems, such as those in New York and California, have not traditionally been called on to respond to the special health care needs of large populations of women or even to provide basic parity of the quality and availability of primary care afforded men. Jail and prison health care systems have largely been defined and operated by men for a nearly exclusive male clientele. In New York, for example, eighteen county jails (35 percent) had no services for women in 1990; in fact, they were even unable to detain them. Women were boarded out to the relatively few facilities that would accept them, leaving incarcerated women far from home, family supports, and legal counsel (New York State Commission of Correction, 1993). The closed and punitive nature of prison life amplifies impediments to primary care access widely experienced by poor women in the community at large, as does the episodic, discontinuous approach to ambulatory health care encounters within prison and jail settings.

The medical problems of urban women of color who most often find themselves incarcerated are usually more severe and intractable than those of their male counterparts. Often these needs have been ignored or given low priority outside of prison in favor of meeting the needs of male domestic partners and children. Including the unique reproductive health problems of women, 28 percent of women admitted to state prison in New York in 1993 had medical problems requiring immediate and ongoing intervention (New York State Department of Correctional Services, 1994). In most large correctional systems, women offenders, particularly women of color, have the highest rates of HIV infection and associated tuberculosis, far exceeding rates for male offenders. In New York, mortality among incarcerated women remains more than twice that of women in the same age group in the community (New York State Executive Chamber, 1994). High-risk pregnancies that come to term or premature delivery can be expected to increase annually with the growth in offender census. The growing population of incarcerated women has also evidenced high rates of mental health problems. A California study found more than 40 percent of incarcerated women with a *DSM-III-R* (IV) diagnosis (Fogel and Martin, 1992). Anxiety disorders predominated among incarcerated mothers and grew proportionately over time. Among both mothers and nonmothers a high prevalence of depression was found (Fogel and Martin, 1992).

As both the volume and intensity of demand for services rise in coming years, prison and jail administrators will be required to critically examine their traditional male-centered health care delivery models and refocus on the needs of women. An emphasis on managed primary care, on planning parity of services for women into new systems, and on changing attitudes and beliefs antithetical to quality care for women must come about as women offenders become a larger part of the criminal justice clientele.

In this chapter we examine the changing demographics of women offenders that drive health care service demand, the scope and prevalence of women's health problems, and the current impediments to adequate services. Some recommendations for positive change are discussed.

WOMEN IN CUSTODY

The last half of the 1980s saw a dramatic increase in the number of women committed to local jails. Nationally, the census of women in jail increased an average 6.5 percent annually between 1990 and 1994, a rate nearly two thirds greater than that of men over the same period (U.S. Department of Justice, 1996).

In New York, the second largest American jail system, women represented 5 percent of jail admissions in 1984. By 1994, 10 percent of the jail census were women. Moreover, women no longer went to jail for criminal court processing and expedited release; they remained as detainees and local sentence servers. In upstate New York and Long Island in 1984, 13,000 women were sent to jail, but the average daily census was only 550. In 1992, there were 19,600 total admissions of women and a daily census of 1160, a proportional increase of 50 percent.

Women were sent to state prisons at a rate that increased faster than jail admissions. In 1984, New York's prison system incarcerated about 1000 women on an average day in only two facilities.

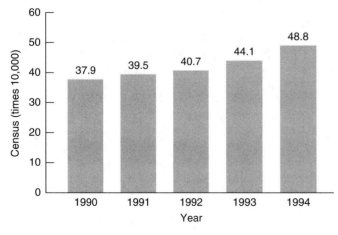

FIGURE 10.1
Women in U.S. jails: 1990–1994.
(*Source:* Bureau of Justice Statistics.)

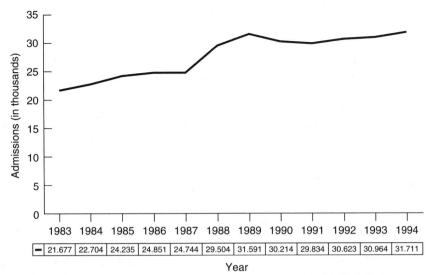

FIGURE 10.2 Admissions of women to jail in New York: 1983–1994.
(*Source:* 1994 Crime and Justice Annual Report.)

	1983	1984	1985	1986	1987	1988	1989	1990	1991	1992	1993	1994
—	21.677	22.704	24.235	24.851	24.744	29.504	31.591	30.214	29.834	30.623	30.964	31.711

By 1994, New York's average daily prison census of women was 3575 in eight facilities. The mean annual increase in New York's population of imprisoned women was 14 percent over that period as was California's, compared to an annual growth of male prisoner populations of 8 percent and 12.5 percent, respectively. In 1994, this growth levelled off at 10.6

FIGURE 10.3 New York prisons: Women in custody—November 1981–1994. (*Source:* 1994 Crime and Justice Annual Report.)

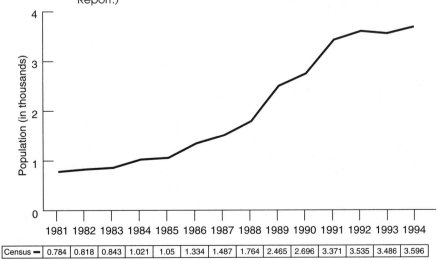

Census —	0.784	0.818	0.843	1.021	1.05	1.334	1.487	1.764	2.465	2.696	3.371	3.535	3.486	3.596

Year

percent, a figure still higher than the increase in male inmates (8.5 percent). Much of this extraordinary change is a function of the war on drugs plus the involvement of women in the substance-use culture. Between 1980 and 1984, admissions to New York jails for drug-related charges increased at an annual rate of 13 percent. Beginning in 1985, the annual rate of increase tripled to 39 percent; commitments of women for these charges increased accordingly. In 1984, only 640 women were admitted to jail for drug possession or sale. By 1990, 2468 women were charged with drug crimes and sent to jails in upstate New York and Long Island.

MORTALITY AMONG WOMEN OFFENDERS

Figure 10.4 illustrates mortality among women offenders in New York and in the five other largest correctional jurisdictions in the nation, compared with women ages fifteen to forty-four in the nation's general population. While mortality rates for young women in the community have remained static, rates for women in large penal systems around the country now exceed those of the general population. New York's mortality rate for incarcerated women was more than twice that of the population-at-large in 1991; a reflection in part of the disproportionate prevalence of HIV/AIDS in New York and the increasing concentrations of HIV-infected women in that state's correctional system. It is evident that incarcerated women experience higher morbidity and mortality than young American women generally and may be considered less healthy as a group, HIV notwithstanding.

FIGURE 10.4 Mortality—women in prison (with U.S. general rates): 1986–1991. (*Sources:* NYS Commission of Correction, National Center On Health Statistics, Bureau of Justice Statistics.)

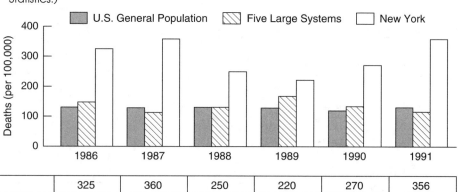

	1986	1987	1988	1989	1990	1991
New York	325	360	250	220	270	356
Five Large Systems	150	112	130	169	133	117
U.S. General Population	130	130	130	130	120	128

Year

It is clear that women have changed the demographics of prison and jail populations in the United States and with it the picture of prisoner morbidity and health care delivery imperatives.

HEALTH CARE NEEDS OF WOMEN OFFENDERS

The social histories of women prisoners are instructive in exploring their health problems as a group. The vast majority of women prisoners are poor people of color with substandard housing, legitimate incomes of less than $500 per month, and dependent children. Thirty-two percent head broken homes, 53 percent come from broken homes, and 41 percent report a history of sexual or physical abuse (U.S. Department of Justice, 1992). These women have limited access to the community-based health care system and limited experience in negotiating its complexities. To an increasing extent, women as a group are immersed in the illicit drug culture as alcoholics, addicts, or the domestic partners of alcoholics or addicts. Recent studies of syphilis reveal that its incidence follows that of cocaine use in a manner that suggests an increasing prevalence of sex-for-drugs exchange not explained by prostitution alone (Farley, Hadler, and Gunn, 1990; Forney, Inciardi, and Lockwood, 1991).

The medical problems of women are associated with these conditions and behaviors. They most often include asthma; diabetes; HIV/AIDS; tuberculosis; hypertension; unintended, interrupted, or lost pregnancy; dysmenorrhea; chlamydia infection; papillomavirus (HPV) infection; herpes simplex II infection; cystic and myomatic conditions; chronic pelvic inflammatory disease; anxiety neurosis; and depression.

Mental Disorder

Wherever women prisoners have been available in numbers sufficient for reliable study, their mental health service needs have been shown to exceed those of men. Anxiety and depression are the most important mental health problems among women prisoners, with some recent evidence that many women suffer from posttraumatic stress disorder while in jail. Mothers and nonmothers typically show similarly high levels of depression. The mean depression level shown by a sample of incarcerated women assessed with the Center for Epidemiologic Studies' Perceived Depression Scale was more than twice that found in general population samples of women using the same instrument. Moreover, these patterns did not abate over the period of incarceration, as might be expected if they were purely situational (Forney, Inciardi, and Lockwood, 1991). There is also a growing suspicion that manic and depressive states in women are underdiagnosed in prison populations (Good, 1978). Maternal incarceration was most responsible for high prevalence rates of anxiety among incarcerated women (Sobel, 1980). At the North Carolina Correctional Center for Women, 51 percent of mothers had high anxiety levels when first studied, and 54 percent of the same group had high anxiety levels six months later (Fogel and Martin, 1992). Among the 41 percent of women inmates who report histories of physical and sexual abuse, the phenomenon of being locked up in a small space by intimidating male authority figures can be a potent stressor. A woman's first symptoms of posttraumatic stress syndrome may be encountered in prison, something not considered for either sex until recently, and then mistakenly thought to be confined to combat veterans. Women victims of abuse and other crimes may become floridly ill when subjected to confinement, separation from children, strip searches, and other stressors reminiscent of abuse (Dvoskin, 1990). Abused women inmates often exhibit histories of long duration involving multiple episodes at the hands of fathers, husbands, boyfriends, and strangers, and this abuse is often directly linked to the offense for which they find themselves in jail (Browne, 1987).

In Great Britain, a study of 638 women in prison revealed that 20 percent of the women detained for trial were mentally ill, as were 15 percent of the sentenced offenders and 16 percent of those in prison only for failure to pay a fine. Similar proportions of the same group reported a history of psychiatric hospitalization. An average 25 percent of detainees and sentenced women reported past suicide attempts (Gibbens, 1975).

It is also increasingly apparent that deinstitutionalization has begun to show its effects in populations of women offenders, effects long seen only among men. Mentally ill women who, before deinstitutionalization, would have been lifetime residents of psychiatric institutions now find themselves in jail. A California study explored the nearly systematic diversion of women from psychiatric institutions to jails through a failure to address problems such as homelessness, prostitution, violent acting-out behaviors, inability to care for children, and impediments to access to psychiatric treatment (Lamb and Grant, 1983; Bachrach, 1984).

Figure 10.5 is based on medical problems elicited from a random sample of 5 percent of the women offenders entering New York's prison system in 1993–1994. It is immediately apparent that 29 percent of women who were admitted to prison in New York had health problems requiring intervention. What is less apparent but nonetheless likely is that diagnoses of HIV and tuberculosis are less frequent than their actual incidence in the population, a grim indication that a significant pool of serious illness may escape detection at entry to prison.

HIV/AIDS and Tuberculosis

Women, along with adolescents, have been identified as the fastest growing group of HIV-infected people in the United States (New York State Executive Chamber, 1994). The rate of HIV infection among women prison inmates now exceeds that of men in nearly every large correctional jurisdiction in the United States. AIDS was the leading cause of death for women

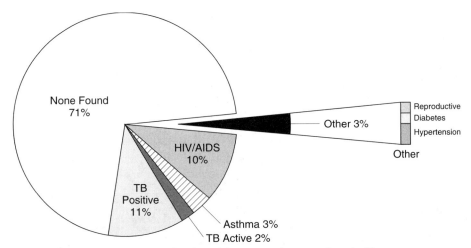

FIGURE 10.5 Women's medical problems upon reception to New York state prisons: 1993–1994. (*Source:* NYSDOCS FPMS; *n* = 130.)

aged twenty-five to thirty-four in New York City as long ago as 1987 (Nobles, 1987). In the Texas Department of Correction, the female HIV seroprevalence rate is 7 percent compared to 3 percent for men; in Maryland 15.5 percent of women inmates are seropositive compared to 8.7 percent of men. North Carolina found its HIV infection rate for women prisoners to be nearly twice that (6.1 percent) of men (3.1 percent) (Sutton, 1992). In New York, 20 percent of women prison entrants are HIV positive in contrast to an 11.5 percent rate for men (New York State Department of Health, 1992), with cumulative AIDS case rates 6 percent higher than male inmates and equivalent mortality rates of 70 percent (Morse, Truman, Hanrahan et al., 1990).

The incidence of tuberculosis (TB) among women inmates is following that of HIV/AIDS. Nine percent of the sample of women admitted to New York State prisons (Figure 10.3) were PPD positive for TB and 2 percent had evidence of active disease. Contrasted with an overall reported rate of TB of 271 cases per 100,000 in 1991 for New York's prison system, it becomes apparent that occult HIV cases among women prison entrants are correlative with TB. The TB rate for men in New York prisons actually fell from 202 cases per 100,000 in 1991 to 143 in 1992 (−29 percent). Rates for women, however, increased from 200 cases per 100,000 in 1991 to 228 in 1992, an increase of 14 percent and a rate 59 percent higher than men (Greifinger, 1992).

Asthma

Respiratory asthma has been more prevalent in the United States and Europe since the early 1970s, but its incidence among women has accelerated since 1980. Mortality from asthma increased 31 percent among all groups between 1980 and 1987, but mortality among women increased 50 percent over this period, as compared with a 23 percent increase for men. The rates are also consistently higher for blacks. The black-white ratio for mortality among females was 2.2 over this period. The greatest increase in newly detected asthma cases occurred among young women, an increase of 69 percent in this group over the period, but rates were higher for females in all age groups (Asthma–United States, 1990).

Reproductive Tract Disease

The relationship between reproductive tract disease and the general health of poor and minority women has not been thoroughly studied. Interviews and focus groups conducted with poor women and with their health care providers throughout New York in 1991 elicited a widespread complaint that the medical community discounts the importance of reproductive health to the overall wellness of women (New York State Executive Chamber, 1994). Yet many women, including physicians, argued that a particular emphasis on the reproductive tract misdirects the approach to women patients and inflates the cost of their care, particularly in view of the fact that the leading causes of morbidity and mortality among women lie outside the reproductive tract. Women's health care reform advocates point to an almost total discontinuity of clinical interest and diagnostic approach between gynecologists and other clinicians when dealing with women patients. This often forces women to act as their own primary care coordinators, evaluating and referring themselves for subspecialty care needs (New York State Executive Chamber, 1994).

With the emergence of women as a statistically relevant aspect of the HIV pandemic, interest has begun to focus on reproductive tract disease as a cofactor and/or marker in HIV/AIDS and in associated drug use behaviors (Quinn, Glasser, Cannon, and Matuszak, 1988; Forney, Inciardi, and Lockwood, 1991). A significant fraction of women in the New York study of women's health who found themselves with HIV infection reported long-standing untreated pelvic inflammatory disease, papillomavirus infection, consistently mutagenic Pap smears, and chronic dysmenorrhea (New York State Executive Chamber, 1994). Recent studies summarized in a New York State AIDS Institute paper implicated repeated and chronic sexually transmitted disease, including chancroid, syphilis, and HSV II, as a co/risk factor in HIV infection (New York State Department of Health, 1992). Vaginal candidiasis is a frequently overlooked early symptom of HIV-induced immune deficiency (Minkoff, 1987). Increasing drug abuse in women has increased their rates of STDs as well as of HIV infection and is aggravated by the phenomenon of exchange of sex for crack-cocaine by women who are not sex workers (Forney, Inciardi, and Lockwood, 1991). In the United States, 24.9 percent of women admitted to jail in 1989 were under the influence of cocaine at the time of their offense, compared to 7.4 percent in 1983. Percentages of women intoxicated with opiates or depressants decreased over the same period (U.S. Department of Justice, 1995). In the Connecticut correctional system, 7 percent of women admitted for drug offenses were infected with an STD. Women cocaine users, especially crack smokers, had the highest rate of syphilis. Interestingly, STD rates did not correlate with parenteral drug use (Farley, Hadler, and Gunn, 1990).

The most visible, growing, and problematic health care issue for incarcerated women is pregnancy and childbirth. The incidence of admission of pregnant women to Alameda County, California, jails doubled during the 1980s (Ryan and Grassano, 1992). In New York, about 7 percent of women admitted to state prison in 1991 were pregnant. This influx becomes more problematic when one considers that New York State law allows pregnant women prisoners to live with their infants at the prison for up to eighteen months postpartum (New York State Correction Law, 1996). Further complicating this picture are well-founded suspicions that pregnancy can mask the symptoms of HIV disease or misdirect clinicians in cases where HIV symptoms mimic those of a high-risk or even normal pregnancy (Minkoff, 1987).

Care of newborns of HIV-infected mothers is a complex and daunting task, particularly if complicated by drug dependance in the infant. Studies of HIV seroconversion in neonates from seropositive mothers ranged from 20 percent to 50 percent and were often complicated by concomitant infection with STDs, hepatitis B or C, tuberculosis, and congenital opportunistic infection (Minkoff, 1987).

IMPEDIMENTS TO HEALTH CARE FOR WOMEN

At a series of public hearings and focus groups in New York's major metropolitan areas in 1991, women's health care providers, advocates, and patients testified that the health care problems and concerns of women, particularly poor women and those incarcerated, have been largely marginalized by the medical community. A common refrain was that health care delivery systems designed to meet the needs of men misrepresent or altogether miss female-specific manifestations of illness. Problems are trivialized as benign or functional complaints peculiar to women and are therefore thought to be of no importance. Another common perception was that physician-patient relationships are inadequate from the woman patient's point of view, characterized by poor communication, lack of insight, impatience, insensitivity, and occasional outright abuse from providers (New York State Executive Chamber, 1994). Another recent study points out that issues relevant to women's health receive attention only as they affect the bearing of healthy children. This has resulted in a dearth of scientific data on their health care needs. Classism, sexism, and racism have a profoundly negative impact on the health of women as a group, something not seen with men regardless of class or race (Mitchell, Tucker, Loftman et al., 1992).

These perceptions and realities are exaggerated in penal institutions where "bad women" are kept. Most health care providers adhere to a middle-class ethic regardless of ethnicity, so their judgment may come down hardest on women offenders. Women attempting to access care in correctional facilities are often regarded as a complicating nuisance, and those who displease authority figure providers by demanding attention will, more often than not, see their care suffer (Mitchell, 1988).

There has been a traditional reluctance to invest in the services and support mechanisms necessary to adequately address the primary care needs of women prisoners that is only now being addressed in large prison systems. At New York's largest prison exclusively for women, a court-appointed physician found in 1988 that women were treated by five per diem physicians who never saw each other and never consulted. These physicians did not record diagnoses or plan for necessary diagnostic tests. The diagnostic studies and subspecialty consultations that were done were rarely reviewed or followed up at the facility. Tuberculosis incidence had been rising at an alarming rate since 1986, yet no surveillance program had been contemplated (Rundle, 1988). The appointment of a full-time medical director in 1989 resulted in significantly improved continuity of care and coordination of support services at this facility designated expressly for management of women offenders, which has been under a federal court order to improve health care for women since 1978 (*Todaro* v. *Ward,* 1977). Support for health care providers, most notably in-service training in detection, diagnosis, and management of HIV, has improved dramatically.

Jails in large jurisdictions have not fared as well. In 1990, the New York State Commission of Correction evaluated the care of a young woman who died several days after childbirth. She had received no antepartum care in jail and no postpartum evaluation, and she died from complications of undiagnosed and untreated sepsis with sickle cell crisis in the most sophisticated contracted jail health care delivery system in the United States (New York State Commission of Correction Medical Review Board, 1991). In upstate New York in the same year, a woman inmate delivered an infant at twenty-six weeks gestation two hours after transfer from jail, never having seen an obstetrician during two separate incarcerations and despite three days of complaints of pain, spotting, and amniotic leakage (New York State Commission of Correction, 1991).

Reproductive health care access notwithstanding, the systematic denial to women of parity of services readily and routinely available to incarcerated men is the most widespread and invidious impediment to adequate health care for women offenders. Alternate levels of care, such as skilled nursing care, chronic and rehabilitative care for the physically disabled, services for geriatric inmates, sheltered communities for the retarded and developmentally disabled, renal dialysis, reconstructive surgery, investigational therapies, and cardiovascular surgery are all routinely available to men in federal and large state correctional systems. They are generally unavailable, restricted, or provided on an ad hoc basis to women (Resnick and Shaw, 1980; Pennsylvania Prison Society, 1983; Anno, 1991).

The available research characterizes mental health treatment for women offenders as "conspicuous by its absence," almost entirely focused on the needs of men (Moss, 1986). Current widely accepted standards for prison health care proceed on the assumption that when standards are met, women have the same access to quality primary and specialty care as men, in addition to the services unique to them as women (Moss, 1986). This assumption is by no means validated by experience. This issue will likely become a central theme supporting a tide of equal protection litigation that will seek to compel rapid and comprehensive improvements in many jurisdictions, something Eighth Amendment litigation has hitherto been unable to accomplish for women (Dale, 1990; Rafter, 1990).

A MODEL OF IMPROVED CARE

Although the reflex defense mechanisms of state and local governments when confronted with prison reform litigation often become impediments to improved care, the courts have prodded some jurisdictions into developing and implementing improved women's services. In California, Santa Rita County officials implemented a consent decree in 1989 in settlement of *Jones* v. *Dyer* that established a comprehensive OB/GYN and prenatal service for incarcerated women (Ryan and Grassano, 1992). It features a new $174 million facility that is staffed according to a specially tailored $21 million provider contract. The discrete OB/GYN unit is staffed by a multidisciplinary medical team composed of a perinatal case manager, a nurse practitioner, a physician, and a nursing staff. All women admitted to the facility are afforded a comprehensive reception health appraisal and are screened for pregnancy. Pregnant substance users are immediately sent to the outpatient OB service of the hospital, evaluated, and enrolled in a substance abuse treatment program.

All pregnant women receive relevant prenatal laboratory studies, ruling out diabetes, HIV, Hepatitis (B) (C-D), tuberculosis, herpes simplex virus, and so on. A Pap smear and STD serologies are obtained, and therapeutic abortion is available on request. Counseling with credentialed mental health professionals is immediately available. Women are placed on a therapeutic prenatal diet with appropriate supplements. Ultrasonography is done at sixteen to twenty weeks. Pregnancies complicated by risk factors or illness result in admission to a thirty-two-bed inpatient unit with twenty-four-hour nursing. A structured exercise program conducted by qualified staff is afforded. Social services that include information and assistance on adoption, resources and coping skills for single-parent mothers, options and skills for child care, and family planning are afforded.

FUTURE DIRECTIONS: TOWARD DECENT CARE

Santa Rita's experience shows that there is little mystery regarding the operational components required for establishing a credible, comprehensive primary care service for women. Poor correctional health care for women is not a function of staff or equipment, but rather a manifestation of pervasive and insidious attitudes, behaviors, and beliefs that influence government policy. State and local government policy makers who elect to improve the quality and availability of health care for incarcerated women in advance of a court order to do so should focus on education and training, installation of modern managed primary care models, health care finance strategies, and emphasis on diversion and aftercare.

Women offenders need to develop living skills that raise self-esteem and build confidence necessary to avoid high-risk behaviors, to negotiate the complexities of the health care system as consumers, and to adopt wellness as a primary personal value. This would seem a more worthwhile activity than, for example, insisting that women inmates learn cosmetology. Health care providers should be required to demonstrate satisfactory skills for delivery of respectful and considerate care in a sexually and culturally diverse society while in medical and postgraduate school and on a mandatory continuing medical education basis. Many medical professionals would do well to learn and adopt a less judgmental approach to their patients and trouble themselves less over whether offenders deserve their skill and effort.

Given the high proportion of mothers and nonmothers who suffer from mental and emotional disorders while incarcerated, several studies have recommended formation of self-help groups, enhancement of family-oriented group counseling, stress management training, and strategies to enhance self-esteem (Fogel and Martin, 1992).

Managed primary care for women seeks not, as the third party payors might have it, to keep the access gate to the health care system shut, but to draw all clients into promotion and maintenance of health. This requires that correctional medical departments implement aggressive protocols for identification of and intervention in medical problems, that they manage patients within diagnostic cohorts, emphasize wellness, promote continuity, and place a premium on care that is respectful and considerate. The present demand-for-service and episodic style of ambulatory care in jails and prisons treats each encounter as unprecedented, each complaint as isolated; it is the single greatest impediment to quality of care.

As the enormous growth of health care costs imperils our world economic position even as we ration health care to the poor, the United States is now compelled, however unwillingly, to adopt a universal health care access and finance system. Medicaid, the primary health finance guarantor for the poor, is summarily denied to prison and jail inmates under federal Title 42 CFR while they are incarcerated, even to those participating prior to incarceration. A great deal of preventive health care while in custody is deferred for lack of Medicaid reimbursement. There is no justifiable rationale for such an anomaly. Deferral of care benefits no one; it inflates the cost of care that inevitably must be delivered later at higher levels of acuity. Planners of universal care systems for the new century would be well advised to revisit health care financing for the incarcerated.

Incarceration as the sanction of choice for criminal behaviors is no longer socially or economically sustainable in the United States. In 1994, 1.36 million persons, about one in every 189 adults, were in jail or prison. Of these, about 83,000 were women (U.S. Department of Justice, 1995). Prison operating costs per inmate in New York have been increasing at a mean rate of 5.44 percent per year (State of New York, Office of the Comptroller, 1990). None of this appears to have any appreciable impact on crime rates. Criminal justice systems will be increasingly compelled to expand alternative and diversion programs, and the population of women offenders offers attractive opportunities in this regard. Reduction in unnecessary incarceration of women will reduce demand for scarce specialized services. For those women who must be incarcerated, planned referrals to postincarceration services with emphasis on Medicaid eligibility, family planning, drug abuse services, and coordinated health maintenance for mothers and their children should be emphasized.

The irony of Santa Rita County Jail as quite possibly the highest quality comprehensive health service provider for poor women in its community is an instructive one. The subpopulation of women offenders comes from the growing pool of poor and often victimized women in our urban centers who are quickly returned there. Their health problems and needs do not arise in prison, rather they are brought to prison with them. Informed commentators now discuss jail as the social net of last resort, providing neither punishment nor deterrence; rather respite from hopelessly untenable life situations and access to health and human service programs unavailable in their home communities (Butterfield, 1992). If this is indeed the case, then the correctional institution has, for better or worse, become integral to the community. The line between the prisoner "others" and the rest of us is no longer so clear, and the right to decent health care is no longer exclusive.

REFERENCES

Anno, J. (1991). *Prison Health Care: Guidelines for Management of an Adequate Delivery System.* Washington, D.C.: U.S. Department of Justice, National Institute of Corrections.

Asthma–United States, 1980–1987. (1990). *MMWR.* 39:493–497.

Bachrach, L.L. (1984). "Deinstitutionalization and Women: Assessing the Consequences of Public Policy." *American Psychologist,* 39(10):1171–1177.

Browne, A. (1987). *When Battered Women Kill.* New York: Free Press:23.

Butterfield, F. (1992, July 19). "Are American Jails Becoming Shelters from the Storm?" *The New York Times.*

Dale, M.J. (1990). "The Female Inmate: An Introduction to Rights and Issues." *American Jails,* 4:56–58.

Dvoskin, J.A. (1990). "Jail-Based Mental Health Services." In H.J. Steadman (ed.), *Jail Diversion for the Mentally Ill: Breaking Through the Barriers.* Boulder, CO: National Institute of Corrections.

Farley, T.A., Hadler, J.L., and Gunn, R.A. (1990). "The Syphilis Epidemic in Connecticut: Relationship to Drug Use and Prostitution." *Journal of Sexually Transmitted Diseases,* 17(4):16–18.

Fogel, C.I. and Martin, S.L. (1992). "The Mental Health of Incarcerated Women." *Western Journal of Nursing Research,* 14(1):30–47.

Forney, M.A., Inciardi, J.A., and Lockwood, D. (1991). "Exchanging Sex for Crack-Cocaine: A Comparison of Women from Rural and Urban Communities." *Journal of Community Health,* 17(2):73–85.

Gibbens, T.C.N. (1975). "Female Offenders." *British Journal of Psychiatry.* Spec. 9:326–333.

Good, M.I. (1978). "Primary Affective Disorder, Aggression and Criminality: A Review and Clinical Study." *Archives of General Psychiatry,* 35(8):954–960.

Greifinger, R., M.D. (1992, December). Chief Medical Officer, NYS Department of Correctional Services. Interagency communication.

Lamb, H.R. and Grant, R.W. (1983). "Mentally Ill Women in County Jail." *Archives of General Psychiatry,* 40:463–468.

Minkoff, H.L. (1987). "Care of Pregnant Women Infected with Human Immunodeficiency Virus." *JAMA,* 258:2714–2717.

Mitchell, J.L. (1988). "Women, AIDS and Public Policy." *Law and Public Policy Journal,* 3:50–51.

Mitchell, J.L., Tucker, J., Loftman, P.O., et al. (1992). "HIV and Women: Current Controversies and Clinical Relevance." *Journal of Women's Health,* 1:35–39.

Morse, D.L., Truman, D.I., Hanrahan, J.P., et al. (1990). "AIDS Behind Bars: Epidemiology of New York State Prison Cases, 1980–1988." *New York State Journal of Medicine,* 90:133–138.

Moss, S.R. (1986). "Women in Prison: A Case of Pervasive Neglect." *Women and Therapy,* 5(2–3):177–185.

New York State Commission of Correction. "In the Matter of Tammy M." (91LG026).

New York State Commission of Correction (SCOCa). (1993). *Statewide Data Compilation from Sheriff's Annual Reports: 1984–1993.* Albany, NY: Author.

New York State Commission of Correction Medical Review Board. (1991). "In the Matter of the Death of Jowana G." Albany, NY: Author.

New York State Correction Law. (1996). Section 611.

New York State Department of Correctional Services (DOCS). (1994, October). *FPMS Online Offender-Based Data Report.* Albany, NY: Author.

New York State Department of Health. (1992, May). "HIV Seroprevalence: Semi-Annual Report." Albany, NY: Author.

New York State Department of Health. (1992, September). "Role of Barrier Methods in HIV Prevention." Albany, NY: Author.

New York State Executive Chamber. (1994). *Women's Health. Report of the Interagency Work Group on Women's Health.* Albany, NY: Author.

Nobles, M. (1987, October 1). Testimony to the New York State Governor's Advisory Committee for Black Affairs. *Women in Crisis.* New York.

Pennsylvania Prison Society. (1983). "Women in Prison." The Prison Journal, 63(2).

Quinn, T.C., Glasser, D., Cannon, R.O., and Matuszak, D.L. (1988). "Human Immunodeficiency Virus Infection Among Patients Attending Clinics for Sexually Transmitted Diseases." *New England Journal of Medicine,* 318:197–203.

Rafter, N.H. (1990). "Equal Protection Forcing Changes in Women's Prisons." *Correctional Law Reporter,* 2(4):49–52.

Resnick, J. and Shaw, N. (1980). "Prisoners of Their Sex: Health Problems of Incarcerated Women." In I. Robbins (ed.), *Prisoner's Rights Sourcebook: Theory, Litigation and Practice,* Vol. II. New York: Clark Boardman Co.

Rundle, F.L., M.D. (1988). "Report of Audit of Medical Services at the New York State Correctional Facility for Women, Bedford Hills, NY." (Unpublished manuscript.)

Ryan, T.A. and Grassano, J.B. (1992). "Taking a Progressive Approach to Pregnant Offenders." *Corrections Today,* 54(6).

Sobel, S.B. (1980). "Women in Prison: Sexism Behind Bars." Professional Psychology, 11:2.

State of New York, Office of the Comptroller. (1990). "Staff Study on the High Cost of Imprisonment in New York vs. Other States." Albany, NY: Author.

Sutton, G. (moderator). (1992). "Management of the Seropositive Prisoner: Medical, Ethical and Economic Perspectives. A Roundtable Discussion Among Professionals in Correctional Health Care Focusing on HIV/AIDS." *Correct Care,* 6:4. New York: World Health Communications, Inc.

Todaro v. *Ward.* 565 F.2d 48 (1977).

U.S. Department of Justice. Bureau of Justice Statistics (BJSc). (1992). *Sourcebook of Criminal Justice Statistics–1991.* Washington, D.C.: Author. See also: (BJSd). *Women in Prison–1991.*

U.S. Department of Justice. (1996, June). Bureau of Justice Statistics (BJSa). *Correctional Populations in the United States: 1994.* Washington, D.C.: Author.

U.S. Department of Justice. Bureau of Justice Statistics. (1995). *Prisoners in 1994.* Washington, D.C.: Author.

ELEVEN

Problems Facing Immigration and Naturalization Service Detention Centers

Policies, Procedures, and Allegations

MICHAEL WELCH
Rutgers University

INTRODUCTION

In the absence of systematic inspections and routine monitoring of Immigration and Naturalization Service (INS) detention centers, questions persist about institutional conditions and services. This chapter relies on recent investigations of these detention facilities and includes reports of numerous institutional problems, including allegations of human rights violations. Policy recommendations regarding procedures and institutional reform are offered.

Although corrections experts confront numerous problems facing various types of correctional institutions, including prisons and jails at the federal, state, and local levels, they tend to restrict their investigations to facilities located within the traditional criminal justice system. Each year, however, thousands of persons are detained in facilities existing outside the traditional criminal justice system; namely, in detention centers operated by the Immigration and Naturalization Service (INS).

INS detention centers are exceedingly neglected facilities. Apathy and resentment by government and citizens alike toward undocumented immigrants, commonly known as "illegal aliens," fuel this neglect. Over the last decade of shrinking government resources, growing antagonism has focused on those perceived as threatening viable employment; most notably, undocumented immigrants. Indeed, the immigration issue has become a lightning rod for mounting anger over undocumented immigrants. Both the public and criminal justice experts lack an understanding of the specific problems related to the detention of thousands of undocumented persons. Expectedly, massive warehousing, a prevailing practice in the traditional criminal justice system, is widely supported as a rational and justified response to illegal immigration.

As a result of massive warehousing, INS detention facilities face numerous institutional problems that are compounded by the lack of systematic inspections and routine monitoring. Recent investigations of these detention facilities report serious institutional problems (poor staffing, obstructed access to counsel and the courts, inhumane living conditions, inadequate medical care, etc.). Moreover, allegations of human rights violations, such as physical and sexual assault, are also reported (Welch, 1996a, 1996b, 1997).

Whereas it is the responsibility of legislators to establish fair procedures by which undocumented immigrants are processed, it is the task of human rights advocates to ensure that the INS provides humane confinement conditions for its detainees. Similarly, it is important that correctional expertise be applied to detention facilities existing outside the traditional criminal justice system—in particular, to INS detention centers. Corrections experts can contribute to institutional reform by participating in inspecting, monitoring, and formulating fair detention policy and practice.

Because detention interferes with detainees' ability to pursue their legal claims, it is recommended that current INS detention policy be reexamined. In addition to inhumane conditions at the detention facilities, INS detention practices are costly, unnecessary, and unjust for most undocumented immigrants. This chapter explores the problems plaguing INS detention centers and offers policy recommendations for institutional reform.

THE EMERGENCE OF THE CURRENT PROBLEM

Efforts to warehouse large numbers of undocumented immigrants are a relatively recent development. According to the American Civil Liberties Union Immigrants' Rights Project (1993), the INS's use of detention grew significantly during the 1980s: "In 1981, the average stay in an INS detention facility was less than four days. By 1990, it had grown to 23 days, with many individuals detained for more than a year" (ACLU, 1993:1; see General Accounting Office, 1992). The U.S. General Accounting Office (GAO, 1992) reports that during the 1980s, the INS's detention budget grew from $15.7 million to more than $149 million, thereby expanding the detention capacity to hold more than 6000 persons. In terms of expenses, the estimated daily cost to taxpayers is approximately $50 per detainee.

Since the 1980s, more than twenty-six INS detention centers have opened; currently, more than 6000 undocumented persons are detained, most of whom are people of color. Critics argue that whites seeking asylum in the United States are met with much less resistance and are generally not detained for indefinite periods of time. However, persons of color are usually detained by INS officials while they apply for residency. Among the most unpopular detainees are those from Cuba, Haiti, and Central America, who seek asylum in the United States because they fear persecution in their homelands (Arp, Dantico, and Zatz, 1990; Welch, 1991).

Policy shifts during the Reagan and Bush administrations account for the increase in the length of detention. With the arrival of the Cuban and Haitian boat people in the early 1980s, policy was reformulated to use detention to serve as a deterrent to illegal immigration. In 1986, the Immigration Reform and Control Act (IRCA), also known as the Simpson-Rodino law, was passed, requiring all workers to prove their citizenship. The major consequence of these developments was the employment of repressive measures against undocumented immigrants. Before 1980, INS detention was the exception. During the 1980s, however, "INS policy changed significantly. As a result many individuals previously eligible for release are now subject to mandatory detention" (ACLU, 1993:3). Other detainees, although not subjected to mandatory detention, are also held because they cannot meet the excessively high bonds.

THE VARICK STREET INVESTIGATION, NEW YORK CITY

Among the major barriers to revealing institutional problems in INS detention centers is the lack of systematic inspections and routine monitoring. However, one of the few comprehensive investigations of an INS detention facility was organized and coordinated by Judy Rabinovitz, staff counsel with the American Civil Liberties Union (ACLU) Immigrants' Rights Project. The ACLU Immigrants' Rights Project engages in litigation, public education, and advocacy and professional training to protect immigrants against discrimination and exploitation and to enforce the fundamental safeguards of due process and equal protection (ACLU Immigrants' Rights Project, 1993).

In its report *Justice Detained,* the ACLU Immigrants' Rights Project summarizes a two-year investigation of the INS's Varick Street detention facility in New York City (ACLU Immigrant's Rights Project, 1993; also see Sontag, 1993a, 1993b). In addition to documenting the conditions at Varick Street, the investigation exposed egregious errors by the INS. For example, U.S. citizens have occasionally been mistakenly detained by the INS. During the ACLU study, researchers assisted in the release of a detainee who had been held for fourteen months, long beyond the statutory release period. In this case, the detainee was held despite uncontroverted evidence of U.S. citizenship. Also during the investigation, two other detainees were in the process of verifying their U.S. citizenship.

The report confirms that many detainees at Varick Street are legal permanent residents with longstanding ties to this country, with family members who are U.S. citizens, and with bona fide legal claims to remain in this country. Moreover, the report reveals that INS detention policies and practices subject detainees to lengthy periods of confinement in a facility that was designed solely for short-term detention. At Varick Street, detention has averaged six months, sometimes extending to three years.

According to Lucas Guttentag, director of the ACLU Immigrants' Rights Project, "Immigrants awaiting administrative hearings are being detained in conditions that would be unacceptable at prisons for criminal offenders" (Sontag, 1993a:B8). Even when detainees are ruled deportable, often they are held for several more months or years, because the INS fails to promptly arrange travel and execute their departures (ACLU Immigrants' Rights Project, 1993).

Complaints over conditions at INS facilities in New York are not new: During the 1980s, the INS was sued twice. In fact, the facility at Varick Street was opened following one of these lawsuits, yet the problems followed. In 1986, the U.S. General Accounting Office (GAO, 1986) issued a report criticizing the Varick Street facility for, among other things, the lack of outdoor exercise facilities and poor quality staffing.

The results of the most recent investigation of the Varick Street facility are summarized in the following items (ACLU Immigrants' Rights Project, 1993):

1. Detention at Varick Street interferes with detainees' ability to pursue their legal rights and to protect themselves from unlawful detention and deportation. While the mere fact of detention makes it more difficult for detainees to pursue their legal rights, specific conditions at Varick Street exacerbate the problem. These include an inadequate law library, insufficient access to telephones, and lack of confidentiality in attorney/client communication. During our investigation we identified a number of individuals who were improperly detained by INS at Varick Street, including several U.S. citizens. Of particular concern to the ACLU are the obstacles these and other detainees faced obtaining documentation and legal assistance to prove their cases.

2. Living conditions at Varick Street fall well short of acceptable standards of detention. Varick Street provides no access to the outdoors,

affords minimal educational or program activities, and imposes an extremely restrictive visiting policy. In addition, detainees routinely complain about poor sanitation, inadequate food, delays in receiving medical care, and arbitrary and punitive use of segregation.

3. Many of the problems at Varick Street are directly linked to the increased length of detention. Varick Street was initially intended for short-term stays of less than one week; the average Varick Street detainee now spends approximately six months at the facility.

Among the principal findings, the report also cites the following problems:

1. *Staffing problems.* The staff has often been cited for misconduct, and in 1990 a report revealed that as many as 30 Detention Enforcement Officers were under investigation for either personnel, criminal, or civil rights violations. Indeed, many of the officers were found to be unqualified and unsuited for the job. Incidents of physical abuse and verbal harassment by officers also have been cited.

2. *Inadequate access to counsel and the courts.* Undocumented immigrants have no right to paid counsel in immigration hearings since proceedings are deemed civil, not criminal. Because few detainees can afford private counsel, most go unrepresented—recently, a GAO report found that 60 percent of the detainees at Varick Street were unrepresented.

   Other problems cited at Varick Street include an inadequate law library, an inaccurate legal services list, and lack of confidentiality in attorney/client visiting. Moreover, there are additional obstacles that make access to counsel and the courts difficult, such as a collect-call-only telephone policy (no incoming calls) which prevents attorneys from contacting clients. Finally, many detainees report being pressured to "sign out," which means that they waive their legal rights and simply agree to deportation.

3. *Inhumane living conditions.* The following are problems related to living conditions at the Varick Street facility: overcrowding; poor sanitation and hygiene; lack of fresh air and sunlight; inadequate exercise, recreation, and activities (no outdoor exercise, no educational programs, or significant work opportunities); arbitrary and punitive use of segregation; lack of commissary; delays in medical care; unnecessary restrictions on social visiting; lack of effective grievance mechanisms; and processing delays.

Recommendations

The ACLU Immigrants' Rights Project recommends the following improvements for the INS detention facility at Varick Street:

Access to Courts

INS must provide Varick Street detainees with

- An accurate and regularly updated legal services list
- The ability to make noncollect local telephone calls
- Private attorney-client visitation areas
- A complete and up-to-date law library
- A paralegal to assist detainees with their cases and ensure that legal materials are regularly updated
- Access to a copying machine, writing materials, and notary

Living Conditions

- Program space should not be used for housing except on a very limited basis.
- All living quarters must meet accepted space requirements.
- Bathroom facilities must be adequately maintained.
- Outdoor exercise must be provided for all detainees held at Varick Street more than two weeks.
- Recreational and program activities must be expanded.
- All detainees placed in segregation must be provided notice within twenty-four hours of the reason for the placement and a hearing.
- Detainees placed in segregation must not be deprived of basic necessities.
- A commissary should be provided.
- Medical care should not be delayed for reasons unrelated to health.
- Visiting houses should be expanded.
- Detainees must be provided with detailed and specific information regarding grievance procedures.
- When an order of deportation cannot be effectuated, detainees should be released from detention under orders of supervision.

The investigation of the conditions at the Varick Street facility also revealed an important characteristic of the detainee population: "Virtually all of the detainees we spoke with had close family members who were either U.S. citizens or legal permanent residents" (ACLU Immigrants' Rights Project, 1993:10):

- Mr. D had lived in the United States for twenty-seven years, twenty-five as a legal permanent resident. Almost all of his relatives reside in the United States.
- Mr. C had lived in the United States almost ten years after fleeing from Bangladesh as a political refugee. His wife is a legal

permanent resident of the United States and his three children are
U.S. citizens.

- Ms. A had lived in the United States for twenty-two years, seventeen
  as a legal permanent resident. Her two children are U.S. citizens.
- Ms. M had been a legal permanent resident for eighteen years, immi-
  grating from Haiti with her family at the age of seven. All of her immediate family members live in the United States, including her nine-
  month-old U.S. citizen daughter.

In light of these cases, serious questions are raised about the usefulness and fairness of current INS detention policies. Clearly, these detainees do not meet the most basic justification for mandatory detention,
since they do not pose a security risk and their chances of absconding are
quite low because they have family and relatives in the United States.

PROBLEMS AT OTHER INS DETENTION FACILITIES

It should be noted that the problems at the Varick Street facility are generally representative of several other INS detention centers. In fact, similar problems exist with INS detention practices nearby in Queens, New
York. At Kennedy Airport, INS officials must deal with travelers without
visas (TWOV); however, the detention practice features a double standard:

> INS has forced airlines to act as jailers for the TWOVs, even though
> the agency lets most political asylum applicants enter the country
> without much fuss. Applicants are simply told to show up months
> later when their case is called. But the INS has decided any TWOV
> who requests asylum should get different treatment. All TWOVs must
> be detained by the air carrier that ferried them into the country—at
> the airline's expense. ("Motel Kafka," 1993:3)

The INS detention policy costs the airline industry $8 million per
year, including the expense of detaining TWOVs in neighboring motels—
sometimes known as "Motel Kafkas." Indeed, such detention is quite
Kafkaesque. For example, private guards are hired by the airlines to serve
as detention officers, but these officers do not answer to the government.
Moreover, while being held in a motel room for months, detainees are deprived of fresh air, telephones, and in some cases, are shackled and sexually abused. The following cases further illuminate problems with current
INS detention policy:

> In August [1993], three teenagers—two boys and a girl—from Sri
> Lanka arrived at Kennedy Airport on a Northwest Airlines flight and

requested asylum. Northwest detained them for about two months, footing the motel and security guard bills until the airline persuaded the city to arrange for foster care. During those two months, the teenagers' lawyer never knew where they were being held. And the young people weren't allowed to call him. They told him that they only were fed twice a day because the guard said there wasn't enough money for three meals. ("Motel Kafka," 1993:3)

In May 1992, Delta Airlines found itself with 13 TWOV passengers from China who requested asylum. Two escaped, a pregnant woman was paroled and Delta ended up housing, feeding and guarding the remaining 10 until August when INS arranged for them to get an asylum hearing. Delta shelled out $181,000 which included $9,800 in medical bills for a woman who broke her arm when she leapt from her hotel room in an attempt to escape. ("Motel Kafka," 1993:3; also see Hartocollis, 1990)

Major problems at INS detention centers are not confined to New York. For instance, during the past several years, the Krome Detention Center in Miami has been plagued with numerous institutional problems, including complaints of sexual harassment and physical abuse. Moreover, the controversy heightened in 1990 when three people working at the Krome Detention Center were dismissed: Each of them was a whistleblower who had complained of the mistreatment of the detainees (mostly Haitians). INS officials concede that there are institutional problems at Krome, but point to understaffing as a major source of their difficulties (LeMoyne, 1990).

At Krome, detainees "wear orange uniforms, and the guards on the grounds are armed, and the intimidating sound of gunfire can echo through the camp from a nearby target range where INS officers practice" (Rohter, 1992:E-18). Richard Smith, the immigration service regional director, has been asked why Krome looks so much like a jail. "That's because it is a jail, albeit a minimum security jail. The sign outside may say that it's a processing center, but that's just semantics" (Rohter, 1992:E-18).

Although Krome was designed for short-term detention, many detainees spend more than ninety days there. Another point of controversy is the detention of minors, who by INS regulations are not to be held in the same facility as adults. According to Joan Friedland, an immigration lawyer at Krome, "The basic problem is that there are no rules . . . Everything is discretionary" (Rohter, 1992:E-18).

INS officials at Krome deny allegations of violence and human rights abuses. Constance K. Weiss, an INS administrator at Krome, argued, "Why would we want to run a place where we beat the hell out of people?" Refugee advocates reply to this with a two-part answer: "to discourage other potential refugees and because it is easy to get away with. Detained immigrants are a powerless group . . . without recourse to normal political or legal channels" (Rohter, 1992:E-18; also see DePalma, 1992).

Problems have surfaced at other INS detention facilities as well. In June 1993, a federal class-action suit was filed against the INS alleging substandard conditions at the INS detention center in Los Angeles (San Pedro, Terminal Island). Additionally, the suit addresses problems with access to counsel, including the following: (1) The conditions for visitation for lawyers and their clients are inadequate; (2) the law library and legal materials also are inadequate; and (3) the need exists for more interpreters. Attorneys cite other problems at the detention center in Los Angeles: (1) There have been numerous complaints about inadequate medical care; (2) several detainees have been "lost" in the system; and (3) INS officials resort to frequent transfers that result in the "housing" of detainees on buses (Welch, 1993).

Years earlier, the INS was sued for an alleged pattern of beatings of detainees by guards at the facility in El Centro, California. The INS detention center in Chicago also was sued for inhumane conditions of confinement and denial of access to counsel. Currently, attorneys representing clients in INS detention centers acknowledge numerous problems, particularly with regard to access to counsel. At the INS detention center in Denver (holding approximately 300 detainees), for instance, attorneys report difficulty in efforts to visit their clients. More specifically, internal policies regarding attorney/client visitation change daily. Compounding this problem is the requirement that attorneys submit a G-28 form (indicating that they legally represent a particular detainee), even if lawyers have not determined whether they will represent a particular detainee. Further, law students, who provide a valuable service to detainees, are subjected to FBI background investigations. Critics of this policy argue that in-depth background investigations are lengthy, unnecessary, and unreasonable and make access to counsel elusive. Attorneys also report lack of privacy in meeting with detainees, and that access to telephones is unreasonably restricted (detainees are allowed only one phone call per day) (Welch, 1993).

At the Denver detention facility, there do not appear to be other major institutional problems; however, without adequate access to counsel, it is difficult for complaints to surface. Indeed, one of the advantages of greater access to counsel is that it gives detainees a better opportunity to report problems about inhumane conditions and abuse. Access to counsel is similarly a problem at the INS detention facility at Seattle (holding approximately 140 detainees) (Welch, 1993).

It must be emphasized that not all INS detention centers feature inadequate access to counsel (as well as other problems). A case in point is the INS detention facility at Florence, Arizona, where attorneys and staff enjoy adequate access to detainees. Attorneys there report a friendly, cooperative, and accommodating rapport with the INS staff. However, it should be pointed out that the cordial relationship that exists between INS staff and attorneys is probably attributable to the presence of the Florence Immigrants' Rights Project (funded by IOLTA and the Arizona State Bar Association). The presence of a nonprofit detainee representation project benefits everyone involved in the detention process: clients, attorneys, and INS officials and staff as well. Perhaps because of the presence of the Immigrants' Rights Project, adequate medical care and exercise opportunities are also reported at the Florence facility, which holds about 400 detainees (Welch, 1993).

At this time, five INS detention centers are accredited by the American Correctional Association (ACA): Three of these facilities are operated by the INS, and two by private contractors. The ACA is a nationwide correctional organization that inspects institutional conditions, monitors procedures, and provides staff training for all types of correctional facilities. Since ACA accreditation requires systematic inspections, institutions that undergo such evaluation are assumed to have fewer problems than those facilities that are not monitored.

ACA ACCREDITED INS DETENTION FACILITIES

INS Operated Facilities
1. El Centro (California)
2. Florence (Arizona)
3. San Pedro (Terminal Island, Los Angeles, California)

Facilities Operated by Private Contractors
1. Denver (Colorado): operated by Wackenhut
2. Seattle (Washington): operated by Esmor

At first glance, one might assume that because these INS detention facilities are accredited by the ACA that they are free of institutional problems. This is certainly not the case. Although ACA accreditation offers numerous benefits for the facility, it is not without its imperfections. Numerous problems have been known to persist even after the inspection and accreditation process. In fact, among the ACA-accredited facilities, only Florence is currently exempt from complaints of inadequate access to counsel. As mentioned previously, this is because of the presence of the Florence Immigrants' Rights Project.

INS officials claim that they rely on several standards and manuals to determine institutional policy and operations, such as the INS Standards for Detention, the INS Operational Manual (1983), the INS Manual and Rules (developed for the Denver facility) (1990), and the ACA Standards for Adult Local Detention Facilities (3d ed., 1991). The publication of manuals for policies and procedures offers important benefits, including recognition of important issues related to detention, as well as establishment of uniformity among INS detention facilities. Overall, however, the sections devoted to access to counsel are exceedingly brief and vague (perhaps deliberately). Greater specificity concerning access to counsel and the courts is needed, so that the legal process is facilitated and not obstructed. Recently, Susan Douglas Taylor, an attorney who serves as an INS detention liaison to the Seattle facility, presented INS officials with specific recommendations for policy and practice concerning access to counsel, such as ensuring privacy for attorney/client meetings, providing more interpreters, free phone access by detainees to attorneys, and so on. Similar improvements are needed at other INS detention facilities because existing standards and manuals are limited in facilitating access to counsel and the courts.

Finally, another issue relating to INS policy that remains controversial is the detention of undocumented immigrant children. Whereas some undocumented adults are eligible for release to await their hearings, undocumented children are detained if they lack a close relative or legal guardian in the United States. In 1993, the U.S. Supreme Court upheld this INS detention policy (*Reno* v. *Flores,* No. 91-905). An earlier decision by the U.S. Court of Appeals for the Ninth Circuit, in San Francisco, however, held that the policy had violated the children's constitutional right to due process. The appeals court ruled that children are entitled to a hearing, including an inquiry into whether an unrelated adult was available to care for the child during the deportation hearing.

Each year, thousands of children are arrested on suspicion of being deportable aliens: Of the 8500 arrested in 1990, 70 percent were not accompanied by adults. Most of these youths were teenage boys from Mexico and Central America. Currently, the INS holds more than 2000 undocumented youth. INS reports that it has neither the resources nor the expertise to conduct thousands of hearings to approve suitable caretakers.

Justice Stevens, in a dissenting opinion of the 1993 decision, introduced the question of detention in broader constitutional terms as "the right to be free from Government confinement that is the very essence of the liberty protected by the Due Process Clause." Justice Stevens argued that the Constitution requires that the INS demonstrate in each case why detention was better than being released to an unrelated adult (Greenhouse, 1993:A-19). The conditions of confinement also have been challenged in several law suits concerning the detention of undocumented children. In 1987, a consent decree required that the INS improve such conditions (Johnson, 1992; Greenhouse, 1993).

CONCLUSION

The intent of this chapter is not to engage in unfair or groundless criticisms of INS detention policy; rather, the objective is to expose the problems inherent in INS detention practices. In doing so, it is useful to present INS detention in the larger context of immigration policy. For example, the INS has been historically underfunded and understaffed. Of the more than 140,000 immigration claims filed in 1993, the INS expects to process only 30,000. Currently, there is a backlog of 300,000 cases that probably will never be reviewed, since it takes months (sometimes years) to decide a case. Moreover, asylum seekers represent a significant portion of these cases. But while frivolous cases should be ferreted out, legitimate claims must be identified so that they can be fairly reviewed and not get lost in the bureaucratic morass ("Motel Kafka," 1993).

In the early 1980s, the House Immigration and Refugee Subcommittee sponsored the Mazzolli-Schumer-McCollum bill. This bill intended to offer meaningful reform to immigration policy and to improve the review process, allocate adequate resources for the INS, and create humane detention conditions. At this time, the review process often fails to identify the claims of legitimate refugees. Despite the volume of claims, the review process needs to become more precise so that legitimate cases are not overlooked. Additional funding and allocation of resources also are needed. In 1992, for instance, the INS had a staff of 297 to review all 103,447 asylum cases. Switzerland, by comparison, employed a staff of 500 to process 17,960 claims in 1992 ("Motel Kafka," 1993).

Finally, as emphasized throughout this chapter, the INS must assure humane detention conditions and discontinue the practice of requiring airlines to serve as jailers. Moreover, only those persons who pose a security risk or who are likely to abscond should be detained. Warehousing thousands of detainees is unnecessary, costly, and unjust: "When persons like those at Varick Street are detained by the INS without legal representation, they are deprived of an opportunity to pursue their legal claims, and the conditions of their confinement are allowed to continue, invisible to the outside world" (ACLU Immigrants' Rights Project, 1993:Acknowledgments).

In sum, the ACLU Immigrants' Rights Project recommends a national review of immigration detention policy, an upgrading of detention operations, and the adoption of alternatives to detention (such as a version of supervised parole) to ensure that immigrants appear at hearings. Moreover, routine inspections of all INS detention centers are desperately needed to expose inhumane and unjust institutional conditions. Such inspections would be the first step in correcting these problems.

REFERENCES

American Civil Liberties Union Immigrants' Rights Project. (1993). *Justice Detained: Conditions at the Varick Street Immigration Detention Center, A Report by the ACLU Immigrants' Rights Project.* New York: ACLU.

Arp, W., Dantico, M.K., and Zatz, M.S. (1990). "The Immigration Reform and Control Act of 1986: Differential Impacts on Women?" *Social Justice: A Journal of Crime, Conflict and World Order,* 17(2):23–39.

DePalma, A. (1992, September 21). "Winds Free 40 Aliens, Stirring Second Storm." *The New York Times:*A-10.

Greenhouse, L. (1993, March 24). "Detention Upheld on Alien Children: Justices Affirm a U.S. Policy on Deportation Hearings." *The New York Times:*A-19.

Hartocollis, A. (1990, July 25). "A Woman Without a Country." *New York Newsday:*Part II, 8–9.

Johnson, D. (1992, November 30). "Choice of Young Illegal Aliens: Long Detentions or Deportation." *The New York Times:*A-1, A-12.

LeMoyne, J. (1990, May 16). "Florida Center Holding Aliens Is Under Inquiry: Additional Complaints Made of Abuse." *The New York Times:*A-16.

"Motel Kafka." (1993, October 24). *New York Newsday* Editorial:2–3.

Rohter, L. (1992, June 21). "'Processing' for Haitians Is Time in a Rural Prison." *The New York Times:*E-18.

Sontag, D. (1993a, August 12). "Report Cites Mistreatment of Immigrants: ACLU Says Aliens Are Detained Too Long." *The New York Times:*B1, B8.

Sontag, D. (1993b, September 21). "New York City Rights Chief Investigating U.S. Immigration Centers." *The New York Times:*B3.

U.S. General Accounting Office. (1992). *Immigration Control: Immigration Policies Affect INS Detention Efforts.* Washington, D.C.: U.S. Government Printing Office.

U.S. General Accounting Office. (1986). *Criminal Aliens: INS Detention and Deportation Activities in the New York Area.* Washington, D.C.: U.S. Government Printing Office.

Welch, M. (1997). "Questioning the Utility and Fairness of Immigration and Naturalization Service Detention." *Journal of Contemporary Criminal Justice,* 13(1):36–46.

Welch, M. (1996a). "The Immigration Crisis: Detention as an Emerging Mechanism of Social Control. *Social Justice,* 23(3):169–184.

Welch, M. (1996b). *Corrections: A Critical Approach.* New York: McGraw-Hill.

Welch, M. (1993). *A Summary Report on INS Detention Practices.* Submitted to the ACLU Immigrants' Rights Project, New York.

Welch, M. (1991). "Social Class, Special Populations and Other Unpopular Issues: Setting the Jail Research Agenda for the 1990s." In G.L. Mays (ed.), *Setting the Jail Research Agenda for the 1990s: Proceedings from a Special Meeting.* Washington, D.C.: U.S. Department of Justice, National Institute of Corrections.

TWELVE

Boot Camps in Prisons, Jails, and Juvenile Detention Centers

MELISSA I. BAMBA
CSR, Inc., Washington, D.C.

DORIS LAYTON MACKENZIE
University of Maryland

INTRODUCTION

Boot camp prisons are a controversial new intermediate sanction. Since they were first developed in 1983, they have spread throughout the United States. The media, politicians, and the public appear to approve of sending youthful offenders to boot camps because the programs are viewed as tough on crime. Currently, there are programs in state and federal prisons, local jails, and juvenile detention centers. Although the programs differ greatly, all boot camps have a military atmosphere with drill and ceremony, physical training, and hard labor. Some programs also have extensive therapeutic programming such as drug treatment, academic education, and life skills training. Questions remain as to whether boot camps accomplish the desired goals of reducing prison crowding and changing offenders.

Boot camp prisons are an innovation in corrections that offer an alternative to a traditional prison sentence to convicted offenders. Boot camp prisons, often called shock incarceration, differ from other intermediate sanctions of the shock variety (i.e., shock probation, split sentencing, shock parole, or early release). What distinguishes boot camps from these other programs is the quasi-military atmosphere, resembling in many respects military basic training, and the separation of shock participants from the general prison population. Like other intermediate sanctions, however, boot camp prisons require a short period of incarceration and early release to supervision in the community.

The first boot camp programs were developed in Oklahoma and Georgia in 1983 (MacKenzie, 1993). These early boot camp programs emphasized the military atmosphere with drill and ceremony, physical training, and hard labor. While these components remain central to boot camps today, rehabilitative, educational, and drug treatment services now take an increasingly large share of the participants' time while in the program.

Since their beginning, the programs have continued to grow in size and number. By 1994, thirty states, ten local jurisdictions, the Federal Bureau of Prisons, and at least seven juvenile jurisdictions had boot camp programs (U.S. General Accounting Office, 1993). At the time there were almost 8000 beds dedicated to adult offenders. On the average, these offenders spend 107 days in boot camp prisons. Therefore, more than 27,000 offenders could complete the programs in a one-year period.

While correctional innovations rarely attract more than minimal media attention, boot camps have received a great deal of coverage by both local and national media. Why are boot camp programs attracting so much attention? In part, they are so popular with the media because they have such a strong visual impact. Video footage and photographs of drill sergeants yelling in the faces of boot camp participants present quite an evocative image.

Another reason why boot camps have received so much attention stems from the boot camp model itself. The model is part punitive and part rehabilitative. As such, it has wide appeal. For those who are concerned that punishments should be appropriately punitive, boot camps are seen as a "get tough" approach to crime and delinquency. For these advocates, individuals sentenced to boot camps are receiving their just deserts. Boot camps are one of the few intermediate sanctions that are accepted as being tough enough.

At the other end of the continuum are those who support boot camps because they believe that the educational, drug treatment, and counseling services that are a part of many boot camp programs will rehabilitate offenders. By addressing the "root" causes of criminal behavior and delinquency, these therapeutic programs and services may effect positive changes in offenders. Finally, the potential cost savings from a reduction in time served add to the appeal of the boot camp model.

However, support for boot camps is not universal. Critics of the boot camp model take issue with several of its central components (Morash and Rucker, 1990). For one, critics question whether the get tough approach to crime and delinquency is really communicated to boot camp participants. Participants often report as beneficial the opportunity boot camps provide for becoming physically fit. From the standpoint of altering offender attitudes and future behavior, physical fitness may be positive; however, we must question whether what offenders ultimately get out of boot camp programs has anything to do with the legitimate correctional goals of rehabilitation and punishment.

What then is the value of the quasi-military training boot camp participants receive? Some critics of boot camp programs believe that the military atmosphere, drill and ceremony, hard labor, and strict discipline communicate the wrong message to participating offenders. Morash and Rucker (1990) assert that these core components of boot camp programs may leave offenders more antisocial and alienated than when they entered the program. Further, even if the military aspects of boot camps do not have negative effects on offenders, it is not clear how the "skills" and new-found physical prowess developed in the boot camps will aid the participants once they are released. While graduates from military boot camps go on to become soldiers, boot camp prison graduates are seldom able to use their experience in the same way. Indeed, the core elements of boot camps may have little if any value in and of themselves (Morash and Rucker, 1990).

What of the treatment aspects of boot camp programs? Do substance abuse treatment and education programs, job training, and counseling effectively transform offenders? According to both proponents and critics of boot camps, offenders spend too little time in boot camps to affect more than minimal change. Any positive change that offenders may have achieved in boot camps is threatened once they are released from the program. Even with strict community supervision, ex-offenders might slip back into the same patterns of behavior that initially led to crime and delinquency.

Finally, critics cite the increased potential for abuse and injury associated with boot camps as reason for discontinuing these programs. Boot camps are in many respects safer than traditional prisons because the chances for inmate-on-inmate violence are reduced by strict staff oversight of program participants. However, the enhanced role of boot camp staff can lead to abuse of authority. This is an especially serious concern for boot camps, because the use of rigorous physical training, summary punishments, and strict discipline are core components of the model.

In this chapter, we evaluate the use of the boot camp model in prison, jails, and juvenile detention facilities. The chapter is divided into five sections. In the first section we outline the theoretical rationale of the boot camp model. Next, boot camp programs for adult felony offenders are discussed. The goals of boot camp programs generally and the success individual programs have had in reaching those goals are assessed in the next section. Then, jail-operated and juvenile boot camps are discussed as departures from the usual form of boot camp implementation.

THEORETICAL CONSIDERATIONS

The boot camp model includes elements of both rehabilitation and deterrence in its theoretical base. Boot camp programs are not solely punitive. In almost all cases, participants receive more treatment services in the boot camp than they would normally receive in a traditional prison setting. In a Multi-Site Study of Shock Incarceration (MacKenzie and Souryal, 1994) in eight states (Florida, Georgia, Illinois, Louisiana, New York, Oklahoma, South Carolina, and Texas), six of the program officials indicated that one goal of their boot camp program was to rehabilitate offenders. Rehabilitation strategies included teaching accountability and responsibility, developing self-worth and self-esteem, and providing academic education or drug treatment and education (Souryal and MacKenzie, 1994).

A majority of the states in the multisite study also indicated that specific deterrence (deterring offender recidivism) was a goal of their program. The core of boot camp programs, its military basic training aspects (drill, ceremony, strict discipline, and hard physical labor), was thought to deter future criminality in participating offenders. The idea behind the boot camp innovation is that offenders, especially young offenders, will be "jolted out" of criminality. By being placed in circumstances that (for a short period of time) are both physically and psychologically stressful, it is believed that the boot camp experience will cause offenders to rethink their past criminal conduct and be fearful of continuing such behavior in the future.

Research by Zamble and Porporino (1990) on inmate change during incarceration indicates that prison inmates are most receptive to individual change during the early periods of incarceration, when emotional stress is high. However, after several months of incarceration, the high stress level tapers off and the desire to change decreases. The implications of this research for boot camps are positive. The abbreviated sentence and military basic training components, in conjunction with mandatory participation in rehabilitation activities, may act as a catalyst for change in inmate attitudes and behavior.

Research on specific deterrence, however, has not been so promising. Finkenauer (1982), in a study of Scared Straight programs, failed to find any deterrent effect. This is somewhat sobering considering that, like boot camps, Scared Straight programs were developed as a "shock" variety program intended for young, at-risk offenders. MacKenzie and Souryal (1994) indicate in their summary of the Multi-Site Study that

> Realistically, it is unlikely that the "boot camp" experience will lead to increased perceptions of either the certainty or severity of punishment. Further, in terms of general deterrence, there is no reason to believe that individuals on the street will be deterred by the threat of serving time in boot camp prisons.

Arguably, however, the military basic training components of boot camp programs may encourage positive change (MacKenzie and Souryal, 1994). Participants have reported that boot camps helped them to get free of drugs and that the physical training and discipline they learned in the program made it a positive experience. In contrast, inmates who spend time in a traditional prison rarely speak so fondly of the experience.

In fact, the positive sentiments expressed by boot camp participants are, in part, the very same reasons why some politicians support boot camps. Highly structured and demanding boot camp programs are thought to inspire positive lifestyle changes, discipline, and a sense of accomplishment that may be generalized to offender activities and behavior outside of the boot camp (Osler, 1991).

Yet, both proponents and critics of boot camps question the efficacy of providing rehabilitation services in these programs with the incumbent military atmosphere. At issue is whether it is the rehabilitation or deterrence components of boot camp programs that produce positive change in participating offenders. Or is it possible that the combination of rehabilitation and punishment cancel each other out? From this discussion of the theoretical foundation of the boot camp model, it is clear that there is a degree of ideological tension that needs to be clarified if a fair assessment of the effectiveness of boot camps is to be made.

In the next section we discuss the characteristics of boot camp participants and several boot camp models for adult felony offenders.

BOOT CAMPS FOR ADULT FELONS

The majority of boot camp programs are designed for young, male, nonviolent, first-time felony offenders who are under the jurisdiction of state departments of corrections. In the Multi-Site Study, MacKenzie and Souryal (1994) found that, on the average, participants were twenty years old; they had eleven years of education; 49 percent were nonwhite; and most were serving time for drug, burglary, or theft convictions.

The Boot Camp Experience

Upon arriving at the boot camp site males are required to have their heads shaved; females may be permitted short haircuts. Inmates are then introduced to boot camp rules and regulations. This is usually a very intense experience, with correctional officers (called drill instructors) rapidly issuing commands to the new entrants. Summary punishments are meted out for even minor infractions and frequently involve push ups or other physical punishments. Major violations of the rules can result in dismissal from the program. Strict discipline and deference to authority require that participants address staff as "Sir" and "Ma'am" and refer to themselves as "this inmate."

The daily activity schedule of most boot camps involves inmates in activities from ten to sixteen hours a day. Inmates begin their day with an early workout period when they exercise for up to two hours. At breakfast participants line up in a military manner until they receive their food; they wait by their chairs until they are commanded to sit and eat. Meals are eaten in silence. Following breakfast, participants report to their work sites. Job assignments frequently involve community service such as picking up litter in state parks and on highways. After working from six to eight hours, participants return to the boot camp compound for more exercise and drill, and a quick dinner. Depending on the boot camp prison, they may receive counseling, life skills training, education, drug treatment, or educational services after dinner. Again, these rehabilitation services vary from boot camp to boot camp.

During the course of their sentence, inmates can, through positive progression through the program, earn special privileges and responsibilities. A special hat or uniform is issued as a reward for positive behavior and also serves as a sign of the inmate's new status in the program.

Upon successful completion of the program, boot camp graduates attend a graduation ceremony to which family, friends, and, many times, the media are invited. Awards are given during these ceremonies and inmates perform the military drills they have practiced during the boot camp program.

Beyond the core components of most boot camp programs there are a number of features that vary considerably both between and within jurisdictions. The following section outlines and describes these features.

Different Models

There is a common core of components that all boot camp programs share: short sentence length (three to six months) and a highly regimented military-style program that emphasizes drill and ceremony, physical exercise, and hard labor. Beyond these characteristics, boot camps vary widely.

Programs emphasize different rehabilitation, educational, vocational, and counseling services. These programmatic differences in boot camp programs may stem from the distinct correctional goals each program strives to achieve. The differences are not insignificant, because such programmatic features of a boot camp may have consequences for the camp's ability to successfully achieve its objectives.

Drug and Alcohol Treatment.   Many offenders sentenced to boot camps have drug problems. Correctional officials and legislators are not ignorant of this fact and have included programmatic provisions in boot

camp legislation that recognizes this problem. In a 1992 survey of boot camps, MacKenzie (1994) found that all camps incorporated some type of drug treatment or education into their program plans. In addition, four states reported that their programs are specifically designed for nonviolent drug-involved offenders. Nine states require, by law, that drug treatment and education be included in their boot camp's program design.

According to MacKenzie (1994), the implementation of drug and alcohol treatment and educational services in boot camps varies by program. For example, at the time of the survey, Florida participants were required to spend fifteen days in drug treatment; in comparison, New York required all boot camp participants to take part in drug treatment every day for the duration of their 180-day sentence.

Drug treatment and education also vary in the way each component is integrated into the schedule of activities of boot camp programs. For instance, New York uses a therapeutic community approach to drug treatment and education. In Illinois, counselors evaluate individual inmates, and the levels and durations of the required drug education and treatment are matched to the identified needs of the inmates. In contrast, Texas boot camp inmates receive five weeks of drug education. Additional treatment and individual counseling are provided only to those offenders who volunteer.

Selection Process.   One of the most important differences among boot camp programs is the selection of inmates. Generally there are two major differences in the selection procedures. In one, the sentencing judge places offenders in the boot camp program and retains decision-making authority over offenders until they exit the program. Failure to complete the sentence results in resentencing and a possible sentence to prison.

In the second type of decision-making model, officials in the Department of Corrections decide who will enter the boot camp. Offenders are sentenced to a term in prison by the judge. The department evaluates them for eligibility and suitability. Those who are admitted can reduce their term in prison by successfully completing the boot camp. If they are dismissed from the boot camp, they are automatically sent to prison to complete their sentence.

Eligibility.   Most boot camp programs for adult offenders restrict participation to offenders between the ages of seventeen and thirty (MacKenzie and Souryal, 1994). Some permit offenders up to the age of forty (i.e., Louisiana), and several have no upper age limit (i.e., Oklahoma). Participation is also frequently restricted to nonviolent, first-time felony offenders. While ten states report that violent and nonviolent offenders are eligible for their programs, most of their participants are in fact nonviolent offenders (U.S. General Accounting Office, 1994).

Like selection, eligibility requirements can undermine the success of a boot camp program. Restrictive eligibility requirements may mean that many of the boot camp beds will be empty, a serious problem in this era of prison crowding. This happened when Louisiana first opened its program; officials were forced to reduce their strict eligibility criteria in order to identify a sufficient number of offenders to fill the available beds (MacKenzie and Souryal, 1994).

Special Populations of Offenders

Female Offenders. Thirteen states and the Federal Bureau of Prisons have boot camp programs for women. In ten state camps, males and females are combined in one program where they live in separate quarters but are brought together for other boot camp activities. In other programs they are completely separated (MacKenzie, 1993).

In 1992, a focus group meeting comprised of correctional experts, feminist scholars, and criminologists was held at the University of Maryland to discuss the special concerns regarding females in boot camps. The issues identified included (1) equity and parity, (2) differential needs, (3) detrimental influences, (4) potential advantages for women, and (5) alternative correctional programs.

The focus group expressed concern about the impact of male correctional officers yelling at women offenders who may have been in abusive relationships prior to entering the boot camp. Such an environment might have a negative impact on the women participants. Furthermore, there was a question about how the programs address the specific issues of women offenders, such as parenting classes and the need for vocational training.

Additional concerns arose in regard to the programs that combined women and men. Frequently, there were only small numbers of women offenders participating, which was expected to result in higher levels of stress for these women. Furthermore, it was likely that such programs were not designed to address the specific needs of women offenders. There was a recognition that the female offenders' experiences in boot camp would be very different from the males' experiences because of the small number of participating women. As a result, the boot camp could have unintended negative consequences for women.

Conversely, since many of the boot camps were mechanisms for early release, women would be at a *disadvantage* if they were not able to obtain early release. This would mean that they would be required to spend more time away from their children. The nontraditional demands of the program may be *another possible advantage* for women. As a result of participating in the program, women may be willing to take advantage of new opportunities such as nontraditional employment or educational programs.

Disruptive Inmates. Boot camp-type models are also spreading to other parts of prisons. In Georgia, modified boot camp programs have been implemented for disruptive and mentally ill offenders. Through two separate programs, one designed for inmates who present special management problems, and the other designed for disruptive inmates who have been diagnosed as mentally ill, inmates are taught ways to channel aggression and use problem-solving skills to deal with feelings of fear, frustration, and anger (MacKenzie, 1993).

In the program designed for the mentally ill, inmates are followed by a caseworker after referral to the special boot camp program. In both programs, once offenders have successfully completed the program, they are allowed to return to the general prison population (MacKenzie, 1993).

Community Supervision

Offenders exit boot camps by being dismissed, voluntarily dropping out (in some jurisdictions), or through successful completion of the program. MacKenzie and Souryal (1994) found that some states had dismissal rate for offenders of 50 percent or more.

Offenders who successfully complete boot camp programs are placed on regular parole or intensive parole or their supervision varies according to their assessed risk. The importance of supervision cannot be underestimated. Not surprisingly, it is very difficult for many inmates to maintain the change initiated in the boot camp once released and returned to their homes in the community. Success in many cases is linked to postrelease support. New York recognized the difficulty offenders were having returning to the community and established an innovative "aftershock" program to help offenders during the community supervision phase of their sentence (MacKenzie, 1993). The program incorporates work programs, employment counseling, drug treatment, and a continuation of therapeutic community meetings.

Other state correctional jurisdictions are developing additional community release innovations (MacKenzie, 1993). For example, in Maryland, officials are developing transitional housing for boot camp graduates who do not have acceptable housing in the community. While in the program, boot camp inmates are renovating the housing that will be used for the transitional housing program.

In Illinois, boot camp graduates are electronically monitored for their first three months in the community (MacKenzie, 1993). In California's boot camp program at San Quentin, participants spend 120 days in the boot camp, after which they live at a nearby naval air station for sixty days (MacKenzie, 1993). Participants are allowed to leave the base if they have a job; unemployed participants work on the base while they look for employment. When participants do leave the base, they are intensively supervised in the community for an additional four months.

GOALS OF PROGRAMS

One survey of twenty-six boot camp programs conducted by MacKenzie and Souryal (1991) found that program officials at these camps considered rehabilitation and reducing offender rates of recidivism as their top priorities. Among the various services provided under the rubric of rehabilitation, officials considered drug education and the development of good work habits as being the most important services. The priorities next in importance were reducing prison overcrowding and providing a safe prison environment.

Program Evaluations

The Multi-Site study of boot camps examined the impact of the programs on inmate attitudes and recidivism, as well as the impact on the need for prison beds.

> ***Changing Inmate Attitudes.***   Critics of the boot camp model have theorized that because of the military atmosphere, drill, and hard physical labor (i.e., the stress-producing aspects of the model) components of boot camp programs, offenders would leave these programs more hostile, aggressive, and antisocial than when they entered (Morash and Rucker, 1990).

When researchers examined the attitudes of offenders in the eight different boot camps, they found that despite the differences between programs, boot camp participants were more positive about their experience in the program than were control groups of offenders in traditional prisons (MacKenzie and Souryal, 1994). Boot camp participants generally agreed that their experience in the program had taught them to be more self-disciplined and mature. These results were true of boot camp programs that emphasized treatment as well as those in which the military components of the boot camp model dominated. Thus, contrary to the assertions of boot camp critics, even in boot camp programs that emphasized strict discipline, drill, and hard physical labor, participants experienced positive attitudinal change.

When boot camp participants and the conventional prisoner groups were compared on antisocial attitudes, both groups became less antisocial while incarcerated. Researchers concluded from these findings that there was no evidence that boot camps had a negative effect on the attitudes of participating inmates.

Impact on Recidivism

The impact of boot camps on offender rates of recidivism is central to an assessment of boot camp success. In the Multi-Site study, the performance of community supervision on samples of boot camp graduates was compared to samples of prison parolees, probationers, and shock dropouts who were eligible but were not sent to the boot camp group (MacKenzie and Souryal, 1994). Offenders were followed in the community for a period of one or two years, beginning with the first day of community supervision. Recidivism data were collected either through an instrument administered to parole agents or through departmental official records.

The results indicated that boot camp programs had little impact on offender recidivism. In Texas and Oklahoma, there were no significant differences between the boot camp samples and the control groups on any of the measures of recidivism. In Georgia, boot camp graduates were more likely than the probation comparison sample to have their status revoked for the commission of a new crime, but there were no differences between the graduates and the parolees. In South Carolina and Florida, any differences among the samples were attributed to the effect of the selection of the comparison groups. In sum, five of the eight boot camps in the study did not have a positive impact on offender recidivism (MacKenzie and Souryal, 1994).

In the remaining three states—Illinois, Louisiana, and New York—boot camp graduates had lower rates of recidivism on some, but not all, of the measures of recidivism. All of these state programs devoted more than three hours each day to therapeutic programming, and the in-prison phase of the program was followed by intensive supervision. Thus, in these three states, the positive effect of the boot camp program may be due more to the treatment and intensive community supervision than to the in-prison phase of the boot camp sentence (MacKenzie and Souryal, 1994).

While boot camp graduates did no better than similarly situated offenders (i.e., those in prison or on probation) in most programs, they did not perform worse than these groups either. MacKenzie and Souryal (1994) conclude that offenders who spend time in boot camp programs do no worse than those who serve longer prison sentences, despite the fact that they serve less time incarcerated. Future research should examine whether the military atmosphere with hard labor and physical exercise increases the effect of the treatment and intensive community supervision in having a positive impact on offenders, or whether offenders released from programs incorporating only the treatment and intensive supervision do as well.

Reducing Prison Crowding

A major concern in many correctional jurisdictions is prison overcrowding. Many of the state correctional jurisdictions that instituted boot camp prisons did so specifically as a means to reduce prison overcrowding. By reducing the time an offender spends in prison, boot camp prisons can potentially reduce the demand for beds and reduce overcrowding. However, in order to do this, careful attention must be paid to program design (MacKenzie and Piquero, 1994).

As noted earlier in the discussion on selection, decisions regarding program entry have an impact on whether boot camps can in fact reduce crowding. In order to reduce crowding, boot camp participants must be selected from a group of offenders that would, without the boot camp program, go to prison. If boot camp participants are chosen from a group of offenders that would otherwise be put on probation, the boot camp program would be responsible for exacerbating the problem of prison overcrowding. Boot camp selection policies should thus maximize the probability that boot camp participants are chosen from prison-bound inmates.

When the sentencing judge has the responsibility for boot camp participant selection, the chances are greater that offenders will be chosen from a probation group, rather than a prison-bound group. This outcome is referred to as "widening-the-net" (Morris and Tonry, 1990). When the department of corrections has selection authority, the chance of net widening is minimized.

Another factor that affects the ability of boot camp programs to reduce overcrowding is the eligibility requirement. When eligibility criteria are set too high, potential participants do not qualify for boot camp programs and are thus sent to conventional prisons where they add to the crowding problem.

Further, when eligibility criteria restrict participation to offenders with a limited criminal history who have been convicted of nonserious offenses that carry short sentences, there is no incentive for this type of offender to participate in the boot camp. They will drop out and spend their time in a traditional prison rather than have to complete the difficult boot camp program.

The length of a boot camp program also affects its ability to reduce prison overcrowding. Program length operates in two ways, absolutely and relatively. Obviously, if the absolute sentence length of an offender was reduced by half, a greater number of offenders could graduate from a boot camp program during a year. In relative terms, when offenders decrease the amount of time they spend in prison by participating in a boot camp, there is a net reduction in time served that will have an impact on prison crowding. MacKenzie and Piquero (1994) indicate, however, that the reduction in time served must be more than negligible (i.e., greater than one or two months) to have an impact on prison crowding.

Program size is also important. The larger a boot camp program, the more offenders will graduate each year. It is essential that programs be large enough to have an impact on prison overcrowding. However, the effect could be canceled out if programs that have a large capacity also keep inmates in prison for long periods of time.

Finally, graduation rates must be worked into the equation in order to determine the real impact of the boot camp program on prison crowding. Programs must graduate a sufficient number of offenders to take advantage of the reduction in time served. If offenders are being dismissed at a high rate and sent to conventional prisons to serve their sentences, these offenders will add to prison overcrowding.

JAIL-OPERATED BOOT CAMPS

Most attention has focused on boot camps operated by state prison systems. More recently, there has been increased interest in the development of boot camps for jail populations. Jails increasingly house inmates who spend many months in confinement. Some of these offenders are state-sentenced; but because of the overcrowding in state prisons, they spend long periods of time in jails. In addition, significant numbers of adults violate probation or parole and must remain in jail waiting for the court's decision to revoke parole or release them. Thus, a boot camp could be used to reduce the length of stay of some of these offenders.

Austin, Jones, and Bolyard (1993) surveyed sheriffs, jail administrators, and state probation departments. They identified ten jurisdictions operating boot camp prisons, and an additional thirteen jurisdictions reported that they were planning to open boot camps in 1992 or 1993.

The earliest jail programs began in New Orleans in 1986 and in Travis County, Texas, in 1988. At the time of the survey, there were four jail boot camps in New York, four in Texas, and two in California. The size of the programs varied greatly from a low of twelve and fourteen beds in Brazos County, Texas, and Nassau County, New York, respectively, to highs of 210 beds for males in New York City (they had an additional 84 beds for women) and 348 in Harris County, Texas. However, most programs reported that they fail to operate at their designed capacity. The major reasons they do not operate at full capacity were attributed to several factors: (1) Many jail inmates spend only a short term in jail; (2) there may be a lack of coordination among criminal justice agencies; and (3) rigid selection procedures limit the number of eligible inmates.

Like the prison boot camp programs, the daily schedule for the inmates in jail boot camps involves military drill; physical training; work; and therapeutic programs such as education, vocational education, drug education, counseling, and life skills programs. After the in-jail phase of the boot camp, most programs also require participants to be supervised in the community for some period of time.

Los Angeles County's RID Program

The Los Angeles County Sheriff's Department developed a boot camp program for selected defendants who were likely to receive lengthy jail sentences. The program, called RID for *Regimented Inmate Discipline*, was funded primarily by money and sale of assets seized from convicted drug dealers. It consisted of a ninety-day stay in a military-style boot camp program followed by intensive aftercare supervision in the community. RID had a strong emphasis on programming. Inmates were required to participate in formal education, drug treatment, and counseling.

The program began in 1990 and lasted for only two years before funding was withdrawn. Austin, Jones, and Bolyard (1993), with funding from the National Institute of Justice, U.S. Department of Justice, completed a study of the program while it was in operation. The study examined the impact of the program on recidivism rates, jail management, and crowding and costs.

There was no evidence that the RID program reduced the recidivism rates of inmates who completed the program. Forty-seven percent were rearrested within twelve months of release from the boot camp. There were no differences in rearrest rates between the RID participants and a comparison group. Nor were there differences in recidivism between those who successfully completed RID and those who were terminated prior to completing the program.

The investigators did conclude that RID improved inmate control. The participants in RID behaved very differently from the other jail inmates. They also had fewer misconducts, and there were no serious acts of violence, weapons, or drug use during the term of the study.

There was no evidence that the program reduced jail crowding or saved money. This was due in part to the low utilization of the program. From its inception, the program was always underutilized. Additionally, when compared to the control group, the RID inmates spent significantly more time in jail. There were no cost savings because offenders were confined for longer periods of time and because the intense programming in RID was costly. This high cost, combined with the failure of the program to have any impact on recidivism, was the major reason the program was closed.

In conclusion, Austin et al. cautioned jurisdictions that were considering opening jail boot camps to carefully examine the goals of the program. Many jails could have problems similar to those faced by the RID program because the short length of stay and relatively rapid turnover of inmates may mean that the boot camp will increase the term of incarceration for many offenders. Prior to initiating a boot camp, jail administrators should perform a feasibility analysis to determine whether the identified goals can be achieved. This analysis should at the least ensure that there is a sufficient number of eligible offenders to approach the capacity of the planned program.

BOOT CAMPS FOR JUVENILES

Despite the popularity of boot camps for youthful adult offenders, the concept has not been as popular in the juvenile systems. A 1993 survey identified only nineteen juvenile boot camps: six in Florida, four in Texas, two in

California, and one each in Alabama, Colorado, Maryland, Mississippi, Ohio, Pennsylvania, and Tennessee.

Three of these boot camps had received funding from the Office of Juvenile Justice and Delinquency Prevention (OJJDP) to develop innovative programs that could be used as models by other jurisdictions. Most of the programs were relatively small (30 to 175 participants) and had eligibility criteria limiting participation. In all, there were fewer than 300 juveniles in the boot camps. Recently, however, there has been a renewed interest in developing more boot camps for juveniles.

There are some very different issues that arise in developing boot camps for juveniles. For one, the use of boot camps for adults has, although this is not always stated, a punitive aspect to it. The "tough" aspects of the programs can be thought of as achieving a sentencing goal of retribution. This may make the program acceptable as an exchange for a longer term in prison. Thus, the short intense program is a mechanism for offenders to earn their way out of prison earlier than they would otherwise be released. In a sense, they have paid their debt to society by being punished in a short-term but severe boot camp.

However, the primary mission of our juvenile justice system is treatment and rehabilitation, and not retribution and punishment. Furthermore, the daily hard physical labor required of adult offenders does not fit with the requirements for school and therapy for juvenile delinquents. Therefore, to fit within the mission of the juvenile justice system, boot camps for juveniles must be designed to address the needs of juvenile offenders. All of the juvenile programs in existence in 1992 devoted a significant amount of time to academic education, rehabilitative counseling, and physical training and drill. Instead of working all day like those in adult boot camps, juveniles spent most of the day in academic classes.

Another issue that has arisen in regard to juveniles in boot camps is a definition of the type of juvenile that should be placed in the programs. The target group for adult boot camps are most often nonviolent, youthful offenders who do not have an extensive past history of crime. In the last fifteen years, however, there has been a concentrated effort to use incarceration less frequently for juveniles who are not a danger to themselves or others. The dilemma for the boot camps is whether to admit juveniles convicted of more serious crimes or to potentially widen the net of control to include juveniles convicted of nonviolent crimes.

When Toby and Pearson (1992) surveyed juvenile boot camps, they found that the goals rated most important by the staff were providing safe custody for the youth in their charge, providing academic education, attempting to rehabilitate, and lowering recidivism. Punishment was relatively deemphasized—only two states rated it as "somewhat important," while the rest did not believe that it was an important goal.

SUMMARY

Boot camps in prisons, jails, and juvenile detention centers continue to grow in number and size. As yet there is little evidence that they accomplish their objectives. However, findings such as those discussed in this chapter have not diminished popular support for these "get tough" programs. Politicians, policy makers, and members of the public, generally, support the idea of boot camp prisons as a means of changing offenders and reducing the cost of imprisonment. The need for politically expedient responses to issues of prison crowding and public fear and agitation over what is perceived as increasing levels of crime add to the attractiveness of boot camp programs.

Some might suggest that we have nothing to lose by shifting already scarce correctional dollars to boot camps. This is not entirely true. Not only are taxpayer dollars squandered on hasty implementation strategies, but the belief that nothing works is given additional credence when popular, yet flawed, programs fall by the wayside.

The boot camp model should be examined as an experimental correctional "treatment." We would never permit a new medical procedure to be marketed without careful clinical trials, and yet we are willing to risk the health and well-being of correctional officers and inmates on correctional programs for which there is little available data demonstrating their impact. There are many unresolved questions regarding boot camps and the boot camp model. Before we adopt this correctional model we need to know more about its effects on both the participating offenders and on the correctional jurisdictions. More studies like the Multi-Site Study of Shock Incarceration are needed before we will have sufficient information about these programs. Until then, we would be well advised to proceed cautiously.

REFERENCES

Andrews, D.A., Zinger, I., Hoge, R.D., Bonta, J., Gendreau, P., and Cullen, F.T. (1990). "Does Correctional Treatment Work? A Clinically Relevant and Psychologically Informed Meta-Analysis." *Criminology,* 28(3):369–404.

Austin, J., Jones, M., and Bolyard, M. (1993). *Assessing the Impact of a County Operated Boot Camp.* Research in Brief, National Institute of Justice, U.S. Department of Justice.

Finkenauer, J.O. (1982). *Scared Straight and the Panacea Phenomenon.* Englewood Cliffs, NJ: Prentice-Hall.

Gendreau, P. and Ross, R.R. (1987). "Revivication of Rehabilitation: Evidence from the 1980s." *Justice Quarterly,* 4:349–408.

MacKenzie, D.L. (1994). "Shock Incarceration as an Alternative for Drug Offenders." In D.L. MacKenzie and C.D. Uchida (eds.), *Drugs and Crime: Evaluating Public Policy Initiatives.* Thousand Oaks, CA: Sage:215–230.

MacKenzie, D.L. (1993). "Boot Camp Prisons 1993." *National Institute of Justice Journal, United States Department of Justice,* 227:21–28.

MacKenzie, D.L. (1991). "Boot Camps: National Institute of Justice, Searching for Answers." *Annual Report of the National Institute of Justice.*

MacKenzie, D.L. and Piquero, A. (1994). "The Impact of Shock Incarceration Programs on Prison Crowding." *Crime and Delinquency,* 40(2):222–249.

MacKenzie, D.L. and Souryal, C. (1994). *Multi-Site Evaluation of Shock Incarceration: Executive Summary.* Report to the National Institute of Justice. Washington, D.C.: National Institute of Justice.

MacKenzie, D.L. and Souryal, C. (1991). "Boot Camp Survey: Rehabilitation, Recidivism Reduction Outrank as Main Goals." *Corrections Today,* 53:90–96.

Morash, M. and Rucker, L. (1990). "A Critical Look at the Ideal of Boot Camp as a Correctional Reform." *Crime and Delinquency,* 36:204–222.

Morris, N. and Tonry, M. (1990). *Between Prison and Probation: Intermediate Punishments in a Rational Sentencing System.* New York: Oxford University Press.

Osler, M.W. (1991). "Shock Incarceration: Hard Realities and Real Possibilities. *Federal Probation,* 55(1):34–42.

Souryal, C. and MacKenzie, D.L. (1994). "Shock Therapy: Can Boot Camps Provide Effective Drug Treatment?" *Corrections Today,* 56(1):48–54.

Toby, J. and Pearson, F.S. (1992). "Juvenile Boot Camps, 1992." In *Boot Camps for Juvenile Offenders: Constructive Intervention and Early Support-Implementation Evaluation.* Final Report to the National Institute of Justice, U.S. Department of Justice.

U.S. General Accounting Office. (1993). "Prison Boot Camps: Short-Term Prison Costs Reduced, but Long Term Impact Uncertain." Washington, D.C.: U.S. Government Printing Office.

Zamble, E.F. and Porporino, F. (1990). "Coping, Imprisonment, and Rehabilitation: Some Data on Their Implications." *Criminal Justice and Behavior,* 17(10):53–70.

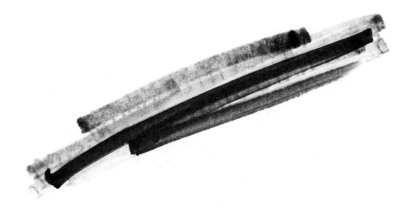